# THE AMERICAN NATION

## A HISTORY

---

### LIST OF AUTHORS AND TITLES

#### GROUP I

##### FOUNDATIONS OF THE NATION

#### GROUP II

##### TRANSFORMATION INTO A NATION

## GROUP V

### NATIONAL EXPANSION

# THE AMERICAN NATION
# A HISTORY

FROM ORIGINAL SOURCES BY ASSOCIATED SCHOLARS

EDITED BY

## ALBERT BUSHNELL HART, LL.D.
PROFESSOR OF HISTORY IN HARVARD UNIVERSITY

ADVISED BY
VARIOUS HISTORICAL SOCIETIES

HENRY CLAY

[From the original life mask by John Henri Isaac Browere]

THE AMERICAN NATION: A HISTORY

VOLUME 14

# RISE OF THE NEW WEST

1819–1829

BY

FREDERICK JACKSON TURNER, Ph.D.

PROFESSOR OF AMERICAN HISTORY IN THE UNIVERSITY
OF WISCONSIN

WITH MAPS

NEW YORK AND LONDON
HARPER & BROTHERS PUBLISHERS

TO

THE MEMORY OF

ANDREW JACKSON TURNER

MY FATHER

TO
THE MEMORY OF
ANDREW JACKSON TURNER
MY FATHER

# CONTENTS

# MAPS

# EDITOR'S INTRODUCTION

IN many previous volumes of the series, the region beyond the Alleghanies has been recognized as an influence and a potentiality in American history. Thwaites, in his *France in America*, shows how the French opened up the country and prepared the way; the Tennessee and Kentucky settlements are described in Howard's *Preliminaries of the Revolution*; Van Tyne's *American Revolution* goes into the earliest western governments; McLaughlin's *Confederation and Constitution* deals with the organization of the new communities by Congress; Bassett's *Federalist System* and Channing's *Jeffersonian System* show how the diplomacy and politics of the country were affected by the appearance of a new group of equal states; while Babcock's *Rise of American Nationality* carries the influence of those states into a broader national life. Professor Turner takes up the west as an integral part of the Union, with a self-consciousness as lively as that of the east or south, with its own aims and prejudices, but a partner in the councils and the benefits of the national government which, as a whole, it is the aim of this volume to describe.

In a way the west is simply a broader east, for up to the end of the period covered by this volume most of the grown men and women in the west came across the mountains to found new homes— the New-Englander in western New York; the Pennsylvanian diverging westward and southwestward; the Virginian in Kentucky; the North-Carolinian in Tennessee and Missouri and, along with the South-Carolinian and Georgian, in the new southwestern states; while north of the Ohio River the principal element up to 1830 was southern.

To describe such a movement and its effects, Professor Turner has the advantage to be a descendant of New-Yorkers, of New England stock, but native to the west, and living alongside the most complete collection of materials upon the west which has ever been brought together—the Library of the Wisconsin State Historical Society. His point of view is that the west and east were always interdependent, and that the rising power of the western states in national affairs was a wholesome and natural outcome of forces at work for half a century. The transformation of the west from a rude and boisterous frontier to a group of states, soon rivalling their parent communities in population and wealth, was not unlike the process through which Massachusetts and Pennsylvania and Virginia passed as colonies, except that the inland people accepted ideals and standards originally English, but worked out and put into shape by their colonist fathers.

As the volume treats of the nation, and not simply of any section, it contains three chapters (i., ii., iii.) on the social and political life in New England, the middle region, and the south. The next four chapters are a systematic account of the west as the settler and the traveller saw it between 1820 and 1830. In chapter v., on Colonization, the settlers are traced from their old homes to their new ones by road and river. Chapter vi., on Social and Economic Development, is a picture of frontier life in the forest and on the farm; chapter vii. brings into relief the need of a market and the difficulty of reaching tide-water with western products—a subject taken up again in the two later chapters on internal improvements; chapter viii., on The Far West, goes with the trapper into the mountains and then across the continent to California and to Oregon, which were included in the ambitions of the buoyant westerner.

Chapters ix. to xi. are a narrative of a succession of national questions involving all sections — the commercial crisis of 1819; the Missouri Compromise, which was in good part a western question; and the slow recrystallization of political parties after 1820. Chapter xii. is on the Monroe Doctrine, which included eastern questions of commerce, southern questions of nearness to Cuba, and western questions of Latin-American neighbors. Chapters xiii. and xvii. describe the efforts by internal improvements to help all the states, and especially

to bind the eastern and western groups together
by the Cumberland Road and by canals. Chapters xiv. to xvi. take up the tariff of 1824, the
presidential election of that year, and its political
results. Chapter xviii. brings into clear light the
causes for the reaction from the ardent nationalism
described in Babcock's *American Nationality*. With
chapter xix., on the tariff of 1828 and the South
Carolina protest, the narrative part of the volume
closes. The Critical Essay on Authorities and a
wealth of foot - notes carry the reader back to
materials little studied hitherto, and prepare the
way for many detailed investigations.

The aim of the volume is not to show the *Rise
of the New West* as though it were a separate story,
but to show how the nation found itself in the
midst of questions involving the west, and how all
parts of the Union were enriched and stimulated by
the appearance of a new section. It opens up new
vistas of historical study.

xviii          AUTHOR'S PREFACE

# AUTHOR'S PREFACE

IN the present volume I have kept before myself the importance of regarding American development as the outcome of economic and social as well as political forces.  To make plain the attitude and influence of New England, the middle region, the south, and the west, and of the public men who reflected the changing conditions of those sections in the period under consideration, has been my principal purpose.

The limits of the volume have prevented the elaboration of some points well worthy of fuller treatment; and, by the plan of the series, certain aspects of the period have been reserved for other writers.

I desire to express my cordial appreciation of the friendly criticism and assistance I have received from the editor, Professor Hart.  To Professor Carl R. Fish, Professor A. A. Young, and Dr. U. B. Phillips, my colleagues, I am indebted for a critical reading of several chapters.  I have drawn on the manuscript sources possessed by Dr. Phillips for information on many points of southern history.

Several of the topics dealt with in the volume have been investigated by graduate students in my seminary; particularly I have profited by the papers of Professor Homer C. Hockett on the Missouri Compromise and the rise of Jacksonian democracy; of Mr. Royal B. Way, now instructor in history in Northwestern University, on internal improvements; and of Dr. W. V. Pooley and Mr. A. C. Boggess on the settlement of Illinois. Mr. S. J. Buck, my assistant in American history, prepared under my direction some of the maps, particularly those of congressional votes.

The map of western fur-trading posts in Captain Chittenden's excellent *History of the American Fur Trade* furnished the basis for the map of western posts and trails. In the construction of the map of highways and waterways, I have used the map of H. S. Tanner, 1825, and Hewett's *American Traveller* (Washington, 1825). From the maps in the Eighteenth Annual Report of the Bureau of Ethnology have been drawn the data for the map of Indian cessions. The editor kindly supplied the map of Russian settlements and claims.

For the portrait of Henry Clay, which forms the frontispiece, thanks are due to Mr. Charles Henry Hart, of Philadelphia, the owner of the life-mask made by J. H. Browere.

FREDERICK J. TURNER.

RISE OF THE NEW WEST

# RISE OF THE NEW WEST

## CHAPTER I

### NATIONALISM AND SECTIONALISM

#### (1815–1830)

THE history of the United States is the history of a growing nation. Every period of its life is a transitional period, but that from the close of the War of 1812 to the election of Andrew Jackson was peculiarly one of readjustment. It was during this time that the new republic gave clear evidence that it was throwing off the last remnants of colonial dependence. The Revolution had not fully severed the United States from the European state system; but now the United States attained complete independence and asserted its predominance in the western continent. It was in this period that the nation strengthened its hold on the Gulf of Mexico by the acquisition of Florida, recognized the independence of the revolting Spanish-American colonies, and took the leadership of the free sisterhood of the New World under the terms of the Monroe Doctrine.

The joyous outburst of nationalism which at first succeeded the dissensions of the period of war revealed itself in measures passed in Congress, under the leadership of Calhoun and Clay; it spoke clearly in the decisions of Judge Marshall; and in the lofty tone of condemnation with which the country as a whole reproached New England for the sectionalism exhibited in the Hartford Convention.[1]

It was not only in the field of foreign relations, in an aroused national sentiment, and in a realization that the future of the country lay in the development of its own resources that America gave evidence of fundamental change. In the industrial field transportation was revolutionized by the introduction of the steamboat and by the development of canals and turnpikes. The factory system, nourished by the restrictions of the embargo and the war, rapidly developed until American manufactures became an interest which, in political importance, outweighed the old industries of shipping and foreign commerce. The expansion of cotton-planting transformed the energies of the south, extended her activity into the newer regions of the Gulf, and gave a new life to the decaying institution of slavery.

From all the older sections, but especially from the south and its colonies in Kentucky and Tennessee, a flood of colonists was spreading along the

[1] Babcock, *Am. Nationality* (*Am. Nation*, XIII.), chaps. ix., xviii.; Gallatin, *Writings*, I., 700.

waters of the west. In the Mississippi Valley the
forests were falling before the blows of the pioneers,
cities were developing where clearings had just let
in the light of day, and new commonwealths were
seeking outlets for their surplus and rising to industrial and political power. It is this vast development of the internal resources of the United States,
the "Rise of the New West," that gives the tone to
the period. "The peace," wrote Webster in later
years, "brought about an entirely new and a most
interesting state of things; it opened to us other
prospects and suggested other duties. We ourselves were changed, and the whole world was
changed. . . . Other nations would produce for themselves, and carry for themselves, and manufacture
for themselves, to the full extent of their abilities.
The crops of our plains would no longer sustain
European armies, nor our ships longer supply those
whom war had rendered unable to supply themselves. It was obvious, that, under these circumstances, the country would begin to survey itself,
and to estimate its own capacity of improvement."[1]

These very forces of economic transformation
were soon followed by a distinct reaction against
the spirit of nationalism and consolidation which
had flamed out at the close of the War of 1812.
This was shown, not only in protests against the
loose-construction tendencies of Congress, and in
denunciations of the decisions of the great chief-

[1] Webster, *Writings* (National ed.), VI., 28.

justice, but more significantly in the tendency of the separate geographical divisions of the country to follow their own interests and to make combinations with one another on this basis.

From one point of view the United States, even in this day of its youth, was more like an empire than a nation. Sectionalism had been fundamental in American history before the period which we have reached. The vast physiographic provinces of the country formed the basis for the development of natural economic and social areas, comparable in their size, industrial resources, and spirit, to nations of the Old World. In our period these sections underwent striking transformations, and engaged, under new conditions, in the old struggle for power. Their leaders, changing their attitude towards public questions as the economic conditions of their sections changed, were obliged not only to adjust themselves to the interests of the sections which they represented, but also, if they would achieve a national career, to make effective combinations with other sections.[1]

This gives the clew to the decade. Underneath the superficial calm of the "Era of Good Feeling," and in contradiction to the apparent absorption of all parties into one, there were arising new issues, new party formations, and some of the most profound changes in the history of American evolution.

[1] Turner, "Problems of American History," in *Congress of Arts and Sciences, St. Louis*, II.

125°     120°     115°     110°     105°     100°

B R I T I S

P A C I F I C

OCCUPIED

JOINTLY

WITH

O R E G O N

Columbia

1818

1846

GREAT

BRITAIN

Snake R.

LINE    OF    1819

ROCKY

NATURAL

BOUNDARY

OF    MISSOURI

M O U N T A I N S

UNORGANIZED TE

MADE    FREE    BY    THE    MISSOURI    COMPROMISE

45°

40°

Great Salt Lake

S P A N I S H

LINE    OF

1818

Arkansas

35°

Santa Fe

36° 30'

LINE

Colorado R.

Gila    R.

P O S S E S S I O N

Pecos R.

30°

O C E A N

Rio    Grande

25°

## UNITED STATES
## 1821

### SCALE OF MILES

0   50  100    200    300    400    500

### LEGEND:

Rio

States absolutely free

States undergoing gradual abolition

Free by the Ordinance of 1787 (held by the courts not to free
pre-existent slaves) and by the constitutions of states

Territory free by Missouri Compromise, 1820

Slave States and Territories

20°

115°     110°     105°     100°    Long

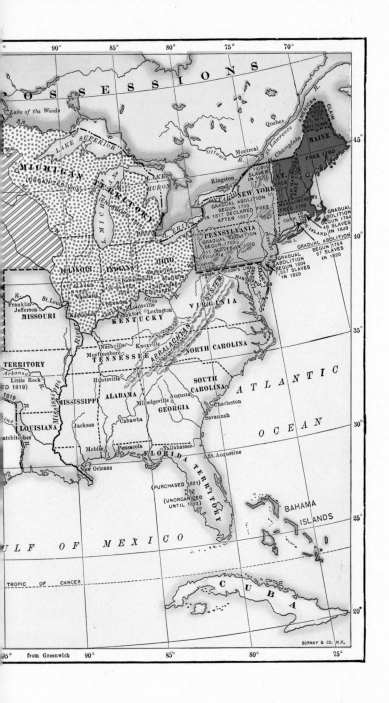

The men of the time were not unaware of these
tendencies. Writing in 1823, Henry Clay declared
that it was a just principle to inquire what great
interests belong to each section of our country,
and to promote those interests, as far as practicable, consistently with the Constitution, having
always an eye to the welfare of the whole. " Assuming this principle," said he, "does any one
doubt that if New York, New Jersey, Pennsylvania,
Delaware, Maryland, and the Western States constituted an independent nation, it would immediately protect the important interests in question?
And is it not to be feared that, if protection is
not to be found for vital interests, from the existing systems, in great parts of the confeder-
acy, those parts will ultimately seek to establish
a system that will afford the requisite protection?"[1]

While the most prominent western statesman
thus expressed his conviction that national affairs
were to be conducted through combinations between sections on the basis of peculiar interests,
Calhoun, at first a nationalist, later the leader of
the south, changed his policy to a similar system
of adjustments between the rival sections. John
Quincy Adams, in 1819, said of Calhoun: "he is
above all sectional and factious prejudices more
than any other statesman of this union with whom

[1] Clay, *Works*, IV., 81, 82; *Annals of Cong.*, 18 Cong., 1 Sess.,
II., 1997, 2423.

I have ever acted." [1]  But Calhoun, by the close of the decade, was not only complaining that the protective policy of certain sections set a dangerous example "of separate representation, and association of great Geographical interests to promote their prosperity at the expense of other interests," but he was also convinced that a great defect in our system was that the separate geographical interests were not sufficiently guarded. [2]  Speaking, in 1831, of the three great interests of the nation— the north, the south, and the west — he declared that they had been struggling in a fierce war with one another, and that the period was approaching which was to determine whether they could be reconciled or not so as to perpetuate the Union. [3]

We see, therefore, that, in the minds of some of the most enlightened statesmen of this decade, American politics were essentially a struggle for power between rival sections.  Even those of most enlarged national sympathies and purposes accepted the fact of sectional rivalries and combinations as fundamental in their policies.  To understand the period, we must begin with a survey of the separate sections in the decade from 1820 to 1830, and determine what were the main interests shown in each and impressed upon the leaders who repre-

[1] Adams, *Memoirs*, V., 361, VI., 75.

[2] Am. Hist. Assoc., *Report* 1899, II., 250.

[3] *Am. Hist. Rev.*, VI., 742; cf. J. Q. Adams, in Richardson, *Messages and Papers*, II., 297; J. Taylor, *New Views*, 261; [Turnbull], *The Crisis*, No. 2.

sented them. For the purposes of such a survey, the conventional division into New England, middle region, south, and west may be adopted. It is true that within each of these sections there were areas which were so different as to constitute almost independent divisions, and which had close affiliations with other sections. Nevertheless, the conventional grouping will reveal fundamental and contrasted interests and types of life between the various sections. In the rivalries of their leaders these sectional differences found political expression. By first presenting a narrative of forces in the separate sections, the narrative of events in the nation will be better understood.

A sectional survey, however, cannot fully exhibit one profound change, not easy to depict except by its results. This was the formation of the self-conscious American democracy, strongest in the west and middle region, but running across all sections and tending to divide the people on the lines of social classes. This democracy came to its own when Andrew Jackson triumphed over the old order of things and rudely threw open the sanctuary of federal government to the populace.

## CHAPTER II

## NEW ENGLAND

### (1820–1830)

BY geographical position, the land of the Puritans was devoted to provincialism. While other sections merged into one another and even had a west in their own midst, New England was obliged to cross populous states in order to reach the regions into which national life was expanding; and her sons who migrated found themselves under conditions that weakened their old affiliations and linked their fortunes with the section which they entered. The ocean had dominated New England's interests and connected her with the Old World; the fisheries and carrying-trade had engrossed her attention until the embargo and the War of 1812 gave importance to her manufactures. In spirit, also, New England was a section apart. The impress of Puritanism was still strong upon her, and the unity of her moral life was exceptional. Moreover, up to the beginning of the decade with which we have to deal, New England had a population of almost unmixed English origin, contrasting sharply, in this respect, with the other sections.[1]

With these peculiarities, New England often played an important sectional rôle, not the least effective instance of which had been her independent attitude in the War of 1812.[2] By 1820, not only were profound economic and social changes affecting the section, but its relative importance as a factor in our political life was declining.[3] The trans‑Alleghany states, which in 1790 reported only a little over one hundred thousand souls, at a time when New England's population was over one million, had in 1820 reached a population of nearly two millions and a quarter, while New England had not much over a million and a half. Ten years later, the latter section had less than two millions, while the western states beyond the Alleghanies had over three millions and a half, and the people northwest of the Ohio River alone numbered nearly a million and a half. In 1820 the total population of New England was about equal to the combined population of New York and New Jersey; but its increase between 1820 and 1830 was hardly three hundred thousand, not much over

---

[1] For the characteristics of New England in colonial times, see Tyler, *England in America*, chaps. xviii., xix.; Andrews, *Colonial Self‑Government*, chaps. xviii., xix.; Greene, *Provincial America*, chaps. xii., xiii., xvi.–xviii.; Bassett, *Federalist System*, chaps. xi., xiii. (*Am. Nation*, IV., V., VI., XI.).

[2] Babcock, *Am. Nationality* (*Am. Nation*, XIII.), chap. ix.

[3] Adams, *United States*, IX., chaps. iv., vii.

half that of New York, and less than the gain of
Ohio. If Maine, the growing state of the group,
be excluded, the increase of the whole section was
less than that of the frontier state of Indiana.
"Our New England prosperity and importance are
passing away," wrote Webster at the beginning of
the period.[1]

Were it not that New England was passing
through a series of revolutionary economic changes,
not fully appreciated at that time, doubtless the
percentage of her growth would have been even
more unfavorable. As it was, the rise of new
manufactures helped to save her from becoming an
entirely stationary section. In the course of the
preceding two decades, New England's shipping
industry had reached an extraordinary height, by
reason of her control of the neutral trade during
the European wars. The close of that period saw
an apparent decline in her relative maritime power
in the Union, but the shipping and commercial interests were still strong. New England possessed
half the vessels owned in the United States and
over half the seamen. Massachusetts alone had a
quarter of the ships of the nation and over a third
of the sailors.[2] Of the exports of the United
States in 1820, the statistics gave to New England
about twenty per cent., nine-tenths of which were

[1] McMaster, *Webster*, 90.
[2] Pitkin, *Statistical View* (ed. of 1835), 350.

from Massachusetts.[1] This is rather an under-estimate of the share of New England, because a portion of the commerce fitted out by her capital and her ships sought the harbor of New York.

Great as was New England's interest in the commercial policy of the United States, the manufactures of the section rose to such importance in the course of this decade that the policy of the section was divided. The statistics of the manufactures of the United States at the beginning and at the end of the period were so defective that little dependence can be placed upon them for details. But the figures for New England were more complete than for the other regions; the product of her cotton mills increased in value from two and one-half million dollars in 1820 to over fifteen and one-half millions in 1831; and her woollen products rose from less than a million dollars to over eleven million dollars. In Massachusetts alone, in the same years, the increase in cottons was from about seven hundred thousand dollars to over seven million seven hundred thousand dollars; and in woollens, from less than three hundred thousand dollars to over seven million three hundred thousand dollars.[2]

In brief, the period witnessed the transfer of the

[1] Shaler, *United States*, I., chap. x.; MacGregor, *Commercial Statistics of America*, 41, 58, 63, 72, 126, 133.

[2] See Secretary of Treasury, *Report, 1854–1855*, pp., 87–92; "Treasury Report," in *House Exec. Docs.*, 22 Cong., 1 Sess., I., No. 308.

industrial centre of gravity from the harbors to the water-falls, from commerce and navigation to manufactures. Besides the textile mills of Rhode Island and Connecticut, the Merrimac mills grew rapidly around Lowell, Massachusetts; the water-powers of New Hampshire became the sites of factory towns, and the industrial revolution which, in the time of the embargo, began to transfer industries from the household to the factory, was rapidly carried on. A labor class began to develop, farmers moved into towns, the daughters worked in the mills. It was not long before Irish immigrants found their way to the section and replaced the natives in the mills. The old social and racial unity began to break down.[1]

Agriculture still occupied the larger number of New England people, but it was relatively a declining interest. As early as 1794, Tench Coxe had characterized New England as a completely settled region, with the exception of Maine and Vermont. The generation that followed saw an expansion of agricultural population until the best valley lands were taken and the hill - sides were occupied by struggling farmers. By 1830 New England was importing corn and flour in large quantities from the other sections. The raising of cattle and sheep

[1] Woollen, "Labor Troubles between 1834 and 1837," in *Yale Review*, I., 87; Martineau, *Society in America*, II., 227, 243, 246; Chevalier, *Society, Manners, and Politics*, 137; Addison, *Lucy Larcom*, 6; Clay, *Works*, V., 467.

increased as grain cultivation declined. The back-country of Maine particularly was being occupied for cattle farms, and in Vermont and the Berk-shires there was, towards the close of the decade, a marked tendency to combine the small farms into sheep pastures. Thus, in the tariff agitation of the latter part of the decade, these two areas of western New England showed a decided sympathy with the interests of the wool - growers of the country at large. This tendency also fostered emigration from New England, since it diminished the number of small farms. By the sale of their lands to their wealthier neighbors, the New England farmers were able to go west with money to invest.[1]

In the outlying parts, like the back-country of Vermont, farmers still lived under primitive in-dustrial conditions, supporting the family largely from the products of the farm, weaving and spin-ning under the conditions of household industry that had characterized the colonial period, slaugh-tering their cattle and hogs, and packing their cheese. When the cold weather set in, caravans of Vermont farmers passed, by sledges, to the commercial centres of New England.[2] But the conditions of life were hard for the back-country farmer, and the time was rapidly approaching when

[1] *Niles' Register*, XLIX., 68; Smith and Rann, *Rutland County* [Vt.], 166; Goodhue, *Hist. of Shoreham* [Vt.], 59; Nat. Assoc. of Wool Manufacturers, *Bulletin*, XXX., 47, 242, 261.

[2] Heaton, *Story of Vermont*, chap. vi.

the attractions of the western prairies would cause a great exodus from these regions.

While New England underwent the economic changes that have been mentioned, a political revolution was also in progress. The old Federalist party and Federalist ideas gradually gave way. Federalism found its most complete expression in Connecticut, "the land of steady habits," where "Innovation" had always been frowned upon by a governing class in which the Congregational clergy were powerful. Permanence in office and the influence of the clergy were prominent characteristics of the Connecticut government.[1] The ceremonies of the counting of votes for governor indicated the position of the dominant classes in this society. This solemnity was performed in the church. "After the Representatives," wrote Dwight, the president of Yale College, "walk the Preacher of the Day, and the Preacher of the succeeding year: and a numerous body of the Clergy, usually more than one hundred, close the procession." He notes that there were several thousand spectators from all over the state, who were perfectly decorous, not even engaging in noisy conversation, and that a public dinner was regularly given by the state to the clergy who were present at the election.[2]

After the War of 1812, this dominance of the

[1] Dwight, *Travels*, I., 262, 263, 291; Welling, "Conn. Federalism," in N. Y. Hist. Soc., *Address*, 1890, pp. 39–41.

[2] Dwight, *Travels*, I., 267.

Congregational clergy throughout the section was attacked by a combination of religious and political forces.[1] There had been a steady growth of denominations like the Baptists and Methodists in New England. As a rule, these were located in the remoter and newer communities, and, where they were strongest, there was certain to be a considerable democratic influence. Not only did these denominations tend to unite against the Federalists and the Congregationalists, but they found useful allies in the members of the old and influential Episcopal church, who had with them a common grievance because of the relations between the state and Congregationalism. Although the original support of the Congregational clergy by public taxation had been modified by successive acts of legislation in most of these states, so that persons not of that church might make their legal contributions for the support of their own clergy,[2] yet this had been achieved only recently and but incompletely.

We find, therefore, that the alliance of Episcopalians and Dissenters against the dominant clergy and the Federalists was the key to internal politics at the opening of our period. "The old political distinctions," wrote the editor of the *Vermont Journal*, "seem to have given place to religious

---

[1] Schouler, *United States*, II., 282, 511, III., 52; Adams, *United States*, IX., 133.

[2] Fearon, *Sketches of America*, 114.

ones." But the religious contentions were so closely interwoven with the struggle of New England's democracy to throw off the control of the established classes, that the contest was in reality rather more political and social than religious. By her constitutional convention of 1818, Connecticut practically disestablished the Congregational church and did away with the old manner of choosing assistants.[1] In the election of 1820 the Republican candidate for governor was elected by a decisive vote, and all of Connecticut's representation in the lower house of Congress was Republican,[2] although, in 1816, the Federalist candidate had been chosen by a small majority.[3] New Hampshire's toleration act was passed in 1819, but she had achieved her revolution as early as 1816, when a union of the anti - Congregational denominations with the Republicans destroyed the ascendency of the Federalists and tried to break that party's control of the educational centre at Dartmouth College.[4]

The contest was not so clearly marked in Massachusetts as in the other states, for the old centres of Congregational power, notably Harvard College, had already begun to feel the liberalizing influence of the Unitarian movement. Congregationalism in

[1] Baldwin, "The Three Constitutions of Conn.," in New Haven Colony Hist. Soc., *Papers*, V., 210–214.

[2] *Niles' Register*, XVIII., 128.

[3] Adams, *United States*, IX., 133.

[4] F. B. Sanborn, *New Hampshire*, 251 et seq.; Barstow, *New Hampshire*, chaps. xi., xii.; Plumer, *William Plumer*, 437–460.

Massachusetts divided into warring camps[1] and was not in a position to exercise the political power it had shown in other states of New England. The discussion in that state between the Unitarian and orthodox wings of the Congregational churches tended, on the whole, to moderate the extreme views of each, as well as to prevent their united domination. In her constitutional convention of 1820, Massachusetts refused to do away with the advantage which the Congregational church had in the matter of public support, and it was not until 1833 that the other denominations secured the complete separation of church and state. The moderate attitude of the Federalists of the state lengthened their tenure of power. Governor Brooks, elected by the Federalists in 1817, was a friend of Monroe, and a moderate who often took Republicans for his counsellors, a genuine representative of what has been aptly termed the "Indian summer of Federalism in Massachusetts."

The Republican party controlled the other states of the section, but there was in New England, as a whole, a gradual decline and absorption, rather than a destruction, of the Federalist party, while, at the same time, marked internal political differences constituted a basis for subsequent political conflicts. Just before he took his seat in Congress in 1823, Webster lamented to Judge Story that New England did not get out of the "dirty squabble of

[1] Walker, Cong. Churches in the U. S., 303–308.

local politics, and assert her proper character and consequence." "We are disgraced," he said, "beyond help or hope by these things. There is a Federal interest, a Democratic interest, a bankrupt interest, an orthodox interest, and a middling interest; but I see no national interest, nor any national feeling in the whole matter."[1]

In general, northern New England—Maine, New Hampshire, and Vermont—showed a distinct tendency towards Democracy; in southern New England the fortifications of Federalism and Congregational power lay in a wide belt along the Connecticut River, while along the sea-coast and in the Berkshire region the Democratic forces showed strength.

From the outlying rural forces, where Democracy was strong, the settlement of New-Englanders in the middle west was to come. To Timothy Dwight, the president of Yale, who voiced the extreme conservatism of Federal New England, the pioneers seemed unable to live in regular society. "They are impatient of the restraints of law, religion, and morality; grumble about the taxes, by which Rulers, Ministers, and School-masters, are supported; and complain incessantly, as well as bitterly, of the extortions of mechanics, farmers, merchants, and physicians; to whom they are always indebted. At the same time, they are usually possessed, in their own view, of uncommon wisdom; understand medical science, politics, and religion, better than those,

[1] McMaster, *Webster*, 99.

who have studied them through life." These rest-
less men, with nothing to lose, who were delighted
with innovation, were, in his judgment, of the type
that had ruined Greece and Rome. "In mercy,
therefore," exclaimed Dwight, "to the sober, in-
dustrious, and well-disposed inhabitants, Providence has opened in the vast western wilderness
a retreat, sufficiently alluring to draw them away
from the land of their nativity. We have many
troubles even now; but we should have many more,
if this body of foresters had remained at home." [1]

Perhaps the most striking feature of New England life was its organization into communities.
What impressed the traveller from other sections
or from the Old World was partly the small farms,
divided into petty fields by stone fences, but, above
all, "the clustering of habitations in villages instead
of dispersing them at intervals of a mile over the
country." The spires of the white churches of
separate hamlets dotted the landscape. Simple
comfort and thrift were characteristic of the region.
"Here," wrote a Virginia planter, travelling in New
England in the early thirties, "is not apparent a
hundredth part of the abject squalid poverty that
our State presents." [2]

The morale of New England was distinctive.
Puritanism had founded the section, and two cen-
turies of Calvinistic discipline had moulded the New

[1] Dwight, *Travels*, II., 458–463.
[2] "Minor's Journal," in *Atlantic Monthly*, XXVI., 333.

England conscience. That serious self-consciousness, that self-scrutiny, almost morbid at times, by
which the Puritan tried to solve the problem of his
personal salvation, to determine whether he was
of the elect,[1] was accompanied by an almost equal
anxiety concerning the conduct of his neighbors.
The community life of New England emphasized
this trait.

Tudor, who was not friendly to the ideals of the
"land of steady habits," criticised "the narrowing
influence of local policy," and lamented the "sort
of habitual, pervading police, made up of Calvinistic
inquisition and village scrutiny" in Connecticut.[2]
Not to be one's brother's keeper and not to assent
to the dictates of community sentiment were indications of moral laxity. This long training in
theological inquiry, this continued emphasis upon
conduct, and this use of community sentiment as
a means of enforcing certain moral and political
ideals, led the New-Englander to war with opposing
conceptions wherever he went.

A test of the ideals of New England is found in
the attitude of those who spread into new regions.
The migrating Yankee was a reformer. A considerable proportion of the New-Englanders who
left the section were "come-outers" in religion as
in politics; many of the Vermonters and the pioneers
who went west were radicals. But the majority of

[1] Wendell, *Cotton Mather*, 6.
[2] Tudor, *Letters on the Eastern States* (ed. of 1821), 60.

these dissenters from the established order carried with them a body of ideas regarding conduct and a way of looking at the world that were deeply influenced by their old Puritan training. If, indeed, they revolted from the older type of Calvinism in the freer air of a new country, they were, by this sudden release from restraint, likely to develop "isms" of their own, which revealed the strong underlying forces of religious thinking. Lacking the restraining influence of the old Congregational system, some of them contented themselves with placing greater emphasis upon emotional religion and eagerly embraced membership in churches like the Baptist or Methodist, or accepted fellowship with Presbyterians and welcomed the revival spirit of the western churches.

Others used their freedom to proclaim a new order of things in the religious world. Most noteworthy was Mormonism, which was founded by a migrating New England family and was announced and reached its first success among the New-Englanders of New York and Ohio. Antimasonry and spiritualism flourished in the Greater New England in which these emancipated Puritans settled. Wherever the New-Englander went he was a leader in reform, in temperance crusades, in abolition of slavery, in Bible societies, in home missions, in the evangelization of the west, in the promotion of schools, and in the establishment of sectarian colleges.

Perhaps the most significant elements in the dis-

integration of the old Congregationalism in New
England itself, however, were furnished by the Uni-
tarians and the Universalists. For nearly a generation the liberal movement in religion had been pro-
gressing. The Unitarian revolt, of which Channing
was the most important leader, laid its emphasis
upon conduct rather than upon a plan of salvation
by atonement. In place of original sin and total
depravity, it came more and more to put stress upon
the fatherhood of God and the dignity of man. The
new optimism of this faith was carried in still another direction by the Universalist movement, with
its gospel of universal salvation.[1]

The strength of the Unitarian movement was
confined to a limited area about Boston, but within
its own sphere of influence it contested successfully
with the old Congregational power, captured Harvard College, and caught the imaginations of large
numbers of the best educated and prosperous classes
of the community. Attempting to adjust themselves between the old order of things on the one
side, and the new forces of evangelism and lib-
eralism on the other, another great body of Congregationalists found a middle ground in a movement of modified Calvinism, which sustained the
life of Congregationalism in large areas of New
England. By these movements of conflict and readjustment, whatever of unity the older Congregational faith had possessed was gradually broken

[1] Cf. Babcock, *Am. Nationality* (*Am. Nation*, XIII.), chap. xi.

down and a renaissance of religious and moral ideas
was ushered in.

This change was soon to find expression in a new
literary movement in New England, a movement
in which poetry and prose were to take on a cheer-
ful optimism, a joy in life, and an idealism. This
new literature reflected the influence of the Unitarian movement, the influence of European romantic
literature, and the influence of German philosophy.
Before long the Transcendentalists proclaimed the
new idealism that was showing itself about Boston.[1] Bryant, Longfellow, Whittier, Hawthorne,
and Emerson were all prophesied in the forces of
intellectual change that now spread over the section.

Even New England's statesmen were deeply influenced by the literary spirit. Daniel Webster,
although the son of a New Hampshire pioneer
whose log cabin was on the edge of the vast forest
that stretched north to Canada, had won an education at the "little college" at Dartmouth; and, after
his removal to Boston, he captivated New England
by his noble commemorative orations and enriched
his arguments before the courts by the splendor of
his style. He united the strong, passionate nature
of his backwoods father with a mind brought under
the influences of the cultured society of Boston.
John Quincy Adams, also, had been professor of
rhetoric and oratory at Harvard, and he found in

[1] Wendell, *Literary Hist. of America*, book V., chaps. iv., v.

the classics a solace when the political world grew dark around him. Edward Everett represented even more clearly the union of the man of letters with the political leader. If we except the brilliant but erratic John Randolph, of Roanoke, no statesman from other sections showed this impress of literature.

While these forces were developing, a liberalizing of the colleges, and particularly of Harvard, by the introduction of new courses in literature and science, was in progress. Reform movements, designed to give fuller expression to common-school public education, began, and already in 1821 Boston had established the first English high-school, precursor of a movement of profound importance in the uplifting of the masses. Lyceums and special schools for the laborers flourished in the new centres of manufacturing. The smaller educational centres, like Dartmouth, Bowdoin, Amherst, and Williams, where the farmer boys of New England worked their way through college, sent out each year men to other sections to become leaders at the bar, in the pulpit, in the press, and in the newer colleges. The careers of Amos Kendall, Prentiss, and others illustrate these tendencies. In short, New England was training herself to be the school-mistress of the nation. Her abiding power was to lie in the influence which she exerted in letters, in education, and in reform. She was to find a new life and a larger sphere of activity in the wide-spread

western communities which were already invaded
by her sons.   In furnishing men of talent in these
fields she was to have an influence out of all relation
to her population.[1]

[1] *Century Mag.*, XLVII., 43.

# CHAPTER III

## THE MIDDLE REGION

### (1820–1830)

THE middle states formed a zone of transition
between the east and the west, the north and
the south.[1] Geographically, they lay on the line of
the natural routes between the Atlantic on the one
side, and the Ohio and the Great Lakes on the
other.[2] The waters of the Susquehanna, rising near
the lake region of central New York, flowed to
Chesapeake Bay, which opened into the Atlantic far
down Virginia's coast-line. The Great Valley ran
through eastern Pennsylvania, across Maryland,
and, in the form of the Shenandoah Valley, made
a natural highway to the interior of North Carolina.
New York City and Philadelphia saw in an intimate
connection with the rising west the pledge of their
prosperity; and Baltimore, which was both a metropolis of the south and of the middle region, ex-

---

[1] For earlier discussions of the middle colonies and states, see
Tyler, *England in America*, chap. xvii.; Andrews, *Colonial Self-
Government*, chaps. v., vii., xviii., xix.; Greene, *Provincial
America*, chaps. xvi.–xviii. (*Am. Nation*, IV., V., VI.)

[2] Gallatin, *Writings*, III., 49; Clinton, in *Laws of the State of
N. Y. in Relation to Erie and Champlain Canals*, I., 140.

tended her trade north to central New York, west
to the Ohio, and south into Virginia, and, like her
rivals, sent her fleets to garner the commercial harvest of the sea.

In the composition of its population, also, the
middle region was a land of transitions between
sections, and a prototype of the modern United
States, composite in its nationality.  In New York
an influential Dutch element still remained; the
New England settlers had colonized the western
half of the state and about equalled the native
population.  In Pennsylvania, Germans and Scotch-
Irishmen had settled in such numbers in the course
of the eighteenth century that, by the time of the
Revolution, her population was almost evenly divided between these stocks and the English.[1]  There
was also a larger proportion of recent immigrants
than in any other state, for by 1830 Pennsylvania
had one unnaturalized alien to every fifty inhabitants.

Following the Great Valley in the middle of the
same century, the Scotch-Irish and German settlers
had poured into the up-country of the south, so
that these interior counties of Virginia and the
Carolinas were like a peninsula thrust down from
Pennsylvania into the south, with economic, racial,
social, and religious connections which made an
intimate bond between the two sections.  A multi-

[1] See Lincoln, *Revolutionary Movement in Pa.*, in University
of Pa., *Publications*, I., 24, 35.

tude of religious sects flourished in tolerant Pennsylvania, and even the system of local government was a combination of the New England town and the southern county.

This region, therefore, was essentially a mediating, transitional zone, including in its midst an outlying New England and a west, and lacking the essential traits of a separate section. It was fundamentally national in its physiography, its composition, and its ideals—a fighting-ground for political issues which found their leaders in the other sections.

Compared with New England, the middle region was a rapidly growing section. The population of New York, Pennsylvania, New Jersey, and Delaware combined was about two and three-quarter millions in 1820, and three and two-third millions in 1830. By that date New York alone balanced all New England in the number of its people. But it was its western half that permitted this growth of the middle section. During the decade 1820–1830, New York west of Oneida Lake increased in population by a percentage more than twice as great, and by an amount almost as great, as that of the populous eastern half of the state. By the end of the decade, about one-third of Pennsylvania's population was found west of her central counties. At that time New York and Pennsylvania became the most populous states in the Union. Virginia and Massachusetts, which in 1790 held the lead, had now fallen to third and eighth place respectively.

New Jersey, meanwhile, lagged far behind, and Delaware's rate of increase was only five and one-half per cent.

In 1829 a member of the Virginia constitutional convention asked: "Do gentlemen really believe, that it is owing to any diversity in the principles of the State Governments of the two states, that New York has advanced to be the first state in the Union, and that Virginia, from being the first, is now the third, in wealth and population? Virginia ceded away her Kentucky, to form a new state; and New York has retained her Genessee—there lies the whole secret."[1]

In the closing years of the eighteenth century and the first decade of the nineteenth the New York lands beyond the sources of the Mohawk had been taken up by a colonization characteristically western. New England farmers swarmed into the region, hard on the heels of the retreating Indians. Scarcely more than a decade before 1820 western New York presented typically frontier conditions. The settlers felled and burned the forest, built little towns, and erected mills, and now, with a surplus of agricultural products, they were suffering from the lack of a market and were demanding transportation facilities. Some of their lumber and flour found its way by the lakes and the St. Lawrence to Montreal, a portion went by rafts down the Allegheny to the waters of the Ohio, and some descend-

[1] Va. Constitutional Convention, *Debates* (1829–1830), 405.

ed the upper tributaries of the Susquehanna and found an outlet in Baltimore or Philadelphia; but these routes were unreliable and expensive, and by one of them trade was diverted from the United States to Canada. There was a growing demand for canals that should give economic unity to New York and turn the tide of her interior commerce along the Mohawk and Lake Champlain into the waters of the Hudson and so to the harbor of New York City. The Erie and the Champlain canals were the outcome of this demand.

It is the glory of De Witt Clinton that he saw the economic revolution which the Erie Canal would work, and that he was able to present clearly and effectively the reasons which made the undertaking practicable and the financial plan which made it possible. He persuaded the legislature by the vision of a greater Hudson River, not only reaching to the western confines of the state, but even, by its connection with Lake Erie, stretching through two thousand miles of navigable lakes and rivers to the very heart of the interior of the United States. To him the Erie Canal was a political as well as an economic undertaking. "As a bond of union between the Atlantic and western states," he declared, "it may prevent the dismemberment of the American empire. As an organ of communication between the Hudson, the Mississippi, the St. Lawrence, the great lakes of the north and west, and their tributary rivers, it will create the greatest inland trade ever witnessed. The most fertile and extensive regions of America will avail themselves of its facilities for a market. All their surplus productions, whether of the soil, the forest, the mines, or the water, their fabrics of art and their supplies of foreign commodities, will concentrate in the city of New-York, for transportation abroad or consumption at home. Agriculture, manufactures, commerce, trade, navigation, and the arts, will receive a correspondent encouragement. That city will, in the course of time become the granary of the world, the emporium of commerce, the seat of manufactures, the focus of great moneyed operations, and the concentrating point of vast, disposable, and accumulating capitals, which will stimulate, enliven, extend, and reward the exertions of human labor and ingenuity, in all their processes and exhibitions. And before the revolution of a century, the whole island of Manhattan, covered with habitations and replenished with a dense population, will constitute one vast city."[1]

Sanguine as were Clinton's expectations, the event more than justified his confidence. By 1825 the great canal system, reaching by way of Lake Champlain to the St. Lawrence, and by way of the Mohawk and the lakes of central New York to Lake Erie, was opened for traffic throughout its whole length. The decrease in transportation charges brought prosperity and a tide of population into western New York; villages sprang up along the

[1] *View of the Grand Canal* (N. Y., 1825), 20.

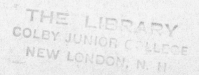

whole line of the canal; the water-power was utilized for manufactures; land values in the western part of the state doubled and in many cases quadrupled; farm produce more than doubled in value. Buffalo and Rochester became cities.[1] The raw products of the disappearing forests of western New York—lumber, staves, pot and pearl ashes, etc., and the growing surplus of agricultural products, began to flow in increasing volume down this greater Hudson River to New York City. The farther west was also turning its streams of commerce into this channel. The tolls of the canal system were over half a million dollars immediately upon its completion; for 1830 they were over a million dollars.[2] By 1833 the annual value of the products sent by way of the Erie and Champlain canals was estimated at thirteen million dollars.[3] At the close of this decade the Ohio system of canals, inspired by the success of the Erie Canal, had rendered a large area of that state tributary to New York. The Great Lake navigation grew steadily, the Western Reserve increased its population, and the harbor of Cleveland became a centre of trade.

The effect of all this upon New York City was

[1] J. Winden, *Influence of the Erie Canal* (MS. Thesis, University of Wisconsin); U. S. Census of 1900, *Population*, I., 430, 432; Callender, in *Quarterly Journal of Economics*, XVII., 22; Hulbert, *Historic Highways*, XIV., chap. v.

[2] McMaster, *United States*, V., 135; Canal Commissioners of N. Y., *Report* (January 17, 1833), App. A.

[3] Pitkin, *Statistical View* (ed. of 1835), 577.

revolutionary. Its population increased from 123,-
000 in 1820 to 202,000 in 1830. Its real and personal estate rose in value from about seventy million
dollars in 1820 to about one hundred and twenty-
five million dollars in 1830.[1] The most significant
result of the canal was the development of the commerce of New York City, which rose from a market
town for the Hudson River to be the metropolis of
the north. The value of the imports of New York
state in 1821 was twenty-four million dollars; in
1825, the year of the completion of the canal, it was
fifty million dollars. This was an exceptional year,
however, and in 1830 the value of the imports was
thirty-six million dollars. In 1821 New York had
thirty-eight per cent. of the total value of imports
into the United States; in 1825, over fifty per cent.;
and this proportion she maintained during our
period. In the exports of domestic origin, New
York was surpassed in 1819 by Louisiana, and in
1820 by South Carolina, but thereafter the state
took and held the lead.[2] In 1823 the amount of
flour sent from the western portion of New York by
the Erie Canal equalled the whole amount which
reached New Orleans from the Mississippi Valley
in that year.[3] The state of New York had by a

[1] U. S. Census of 1900, *Population*, I., 432; MacGregor, *Commercial Statistics of America*, 145.

[2] Compiled from Pitkin, *Statistical View*.

[3] Based on statistics in *Report on Internal Commerce*, 1887, p.
196; Canal Commissioners of N. Y., *Annual Report* (February
20, 1824), 33.

stroke achieved economic unity, and its metropolis at once became the leading city of the country.

Philadelphia lost power as New York City gained it. Though the counties tributary to Philadelphia constituted the old centre of population and political power, the significant fact of growth in Pennsylvania was the increasing importance of Pittsburg at the gateway to the Ohio Valley. In the Great Valley beyond the Blue Ridge lived the descendants of those early Germans and Scotch-Irishmen who early occupied the broad and level fields of this fertile zone, the granary of Pennsylvania. Beyond this rock-walled valley lay the mountains in the west and north of the state, their little valleys occupied by farmers, but already giving promise of the rich yield of iron and coal on which the future greatness of the state was to rest. The anthracite mines of the northeastern corner of the state, which have given to their later possessors such influence over the industries of the country, were just coming into use. The iron ores of the middle mountain counties found their way to the forges at Pittsburg. Already the bituminous coals of the western counties were serving to generate steam-power for the mills upon the upper waters of the Ohio, but, as yet, the iron manufacturers of the state depended on the abundant forests for the production of coke for smelting.

The problem of transportation pressed hard upon

Pennsylvania from the beginning. While Philadelphia was obliged to contest with Baltimore the
possession of the eastern half of the state, she saw
the productions of the western counties descending
the Ohio and Mississippi to New Orleans. Even the
trade in manufactured goods which she had formerly
sent to the western rivers was now menaced from
two quarters: the development of steam navigation
on the Mississippi enabled New Orleans to compete
for this trade; and the construction of the Erie
Canal, with the projected system of tributary canals
in Ohio, made it plain to Pennsylvania that New
York was about to wrest from her the markets of
the west. It had taken thirty days and cost five
dollars a hundred pounds to transport goods from
Philadelphia to Columbus, Ohio; the same articles could be brought in twenty days from New
York, by the Erie Canal, at a cost of two dollars
and a half a hundred.[1] To Pennsylvania the control of the western market, always an important
interest, had led in 1800 to the construction of a
system of turnpikes to connect Philadelphia with
Pittsburg over the mountains, which developed a
great wagon trade. But the days of this wagon
trade were now numbered, for the National Road,
joining the Ohio and the Potomac and passing south
of Pittsburg, diverted a large share of this overland
trade to Baltimore. The superior safety, rapidity, and cheapness of canal communication showed

[1] McMaster, *United States*, V., 136.

Pennsylvania that she must adjust her transportation to the new conditions.

The way was prepared by the experience of corporations attempting to reach the coal - fields of northeastern Pennsylvania. In 1820 practically the whole output from the anthracite fields came from the Lehigh Valley and amounted to three hundred and sixty-five tons—an equivalent of one for each day of the year. By the end of the decade the output of the anthracite fields was about one hundred and seventy-five thousand tons, and the retail price was reduced to six dollars and a half a ton. Navigation had been secured by the coal companies between the mines and Philadelphia by the Schuylkill; the Union Canal connected the Schuylkill and Susquehanna, and New York City was supplied by the Delaware Canal.[1]

This activity in Pennsylvania in the improvement of navigation so far had been the work of corporations; but now, with the growth of population in the west and the completion of the Erie Canal, a popular demand arose for state construction of inland waterways. In 1825 the legislature passed an act under which an extensive system of canals was begun, to connect Philadelphia with Pittsburg, the Allegheny River with Lake Erie, and Philadelphia with the central counties of New York at the

[1] M'Culloch, *Commercial Dictionary* (ed. of 1852), I., 366; U. S. Census of 1880, IV.; Worthington, *Finances of Pa.*

head of the Susquehanna.[1]   Obstacles speedily developed in the jealousies of the various sections of
the state.   The farmers of the Great Valley, whose
interests lay in the development of a communication with Baltimore, were not enthusiastic; the
southern counties of the state, along the line of the
turnpikes, found their interests threatened; and the
citizens of the northwestern counties were unwilling
to postpone their demands for an outlet while the
trunk-line was building.   These jealousies furnish
issues for the politics of the state during the rest of
the decade.[2]

Nevertheless, Pennsylvania was growing rich
through the development of her agriculture and her
manufactures.   The iron industry of the state was
the largest in the Union.   Although the industry
was only in its infancy, Pittsburg was already producing or receiving a large part of the pig-iron that
was produced in Pennsylvania.   The figures of the
census of 1820 give to the middle states over forty
per cent. of the product of pig-iron and castings and
wrought iron in the United States, the value of the
latter article for Pennsylvania being one million
one hundred and fifty-six thousand dollars as against
four hundred and seventy-two thousand dollars for
New York.[3]   The influence of this industry upon

[1] See chap. xvii., below.
[2] McCarthy, *Antimasonic Party*, in Am. Hist. Assoc., *Report*
1902, I., 427.
[3] Secretary of Treasury, *Report*, 1854–1855, p. 90.

Pennsylvania politics became apparent in the discussions over the protective tariff during the decade.

Together, New York and Pennsylvania constituted a region dominated by interest in the production of grain and the manufacture of iron. Vast as was the commerce that entered the port of New York, the capital and shipping for the port were furnished in part by New England, and the real interest of the section was bound up with the developing resources of the interior of the nation.

It must not be forgotten that, in these years of entrance upon its industrial career, the middle region was also the scene of intellectual movements of importance. These were the days when the Knickerbocker school in New York brought independence and reputation to American literature, when Irving, although abroad, worked the rich mine of Hudson River traditions, and Cooper utilized his early experience in the frontier around Lake Otsego to write his "Leatherstocking Tales." Movements for social amelioration abounded. The lighting of New York City and Philadelphia by gas diminished crime. Reform movements with regard to imprisonment for debt and the improvement of the condition of prisons, temperance movements, improvements in the administration of the public schools, and the increase in the number of high-schools were all indicative of the fact that this new democracy was not unresponsive to ideals. Among the New England element of western New York, as has already been

pointed out, there arose some of the most interesting
religious and political movements of the period,
such as Mormonism, Spiritualism, and Antimasonry.
The Presbyterians and Baptists found a sympathetic constituency in the new regions.  It is easy
to see that the traits of these western counties of
the middle states were such that idealistic political movements, as antislavery, would find in them
effective support.

Obviously, the political traits of this section
would have a significance proportionate to the
power of its population and resources.  On the
whole, the middle region was the most democratic
section of the seaboard, but it was managed by the
politicians under a system of political bargaining
for the spoils of office.  The old ascendency which
the great families exercised over New York politics [1]
was on the wane.  The rise of the western half of
the state diminished the influence of the successors
to the patroons; but, nevertheless, family power
continued to make itself felt, and a group of new
men arose, around whom factions formed and dissolved in a kaleidoscope of political change.

During the colonial period, executive patronage
and land grants had been used to promote the interests of the men in power, and the reaction against
executive corruption resulted in a provision in
New York's constitution of 1777 whereby the ex-

[1] Becker, "Nominations in Colonial New York" (*Am. Hist.
Rev.*, VI., 261).

ecutive was limited by the Council of Appointment. The state was divided into four districts, and one senator from each was selected by the House of Representatives to serve in this council.[1] By 1821 the council appointed 8287 military officers and 6663 civil officers. Nearly all the state officers, all the mayors, militia officers, and justices of the peace fell under its control.[2] This concentration of the appointive power in the hands of the dominant faction brought the system of rotation in office, and the doctrine that to the victors belong the spoils of war, to a climax. It led to the building up of political machines by the use of offices, from the lowest to the highest, as the currency for political trading. The governor was checked, but the leaders of the party in power held despotic control over the offices of the state.

This bargaining was facilitated by the extension of the system of nominating conventions. From the local units of town and county upwards, the custom of sending delegates to conventions had early developed in the state. It had become a settled practice for the representatives of one local unit to agree with those of another regarding the order in which their favorite sons should receive office. Town bargained with town, county with county, district with district. In place of the system of control by the established classes, New York's democracy was learn-

---

[1] Fish, *Civil Service*, 87.
[2] Hammond, *Political Parties in N. Y.*, II., 65.

ing to elaborate the machinery of nomination by
the people; but in the process there was developed a race of managing politicians, and the campaigns tended to become struggles between personal
elements for power rather than contests on political
issues.

The finished product of New York politics is
shown in Van Buren, the devotee of "regularity"
in party and the adroit manager of its machinery.
Shrewdness, tact, and self-reliant judgment, urbane
good-humor, mingled with a suspicious and half-
cynical expression, were written on his face. "Little Van" was an affable, firm, and crafty politician.
Although he was not a creative statesman, neither
was he a mere schemer. He had definite ideas, if
not convictions, of the proper lines of policy, and
was able to state them with incisive and forcible
argument when occasion demanded. To him, perhaps, more than to any other of the politicians, fell
the task of organizing the campaign of Crawford,
and afterwards of making the political combinations
that brought in the reign of Andrew Jackson. He
was the leader of that element of New York politics
known as the Bucktails, from the emblem worn by
the Tammany Society. Clinton, his opponent, exercised an influence somewhat akin to the Living-
stons, the Schuylers, the Van Rensselaers, and the
other great family leaders in the baronial days of
New York politics. Brusque, arrogant, and ambitious, he combined the petty enmities of a domineer-

ing politician with flashes of statesman-like insight,
and he crushed his way to success by an extermi-
nating warfare against his enemies. Around him
gathered a personal following embracing one wing
of the Republicans, aided by a large fraction of the
old Federal party. For the most part, his strength
lay along the line of the Erie Canal and in the regions where the New England element was strong.

About these New York rivals were grouped many
lesser lights, for the political organization tended to
create a multitude of able political leaders, many of
them capable of holding high position, but few of
them swayed by compelling ideas or policies.

In Pennsylvania, where the spoils system and the
nominating convention developed contemporaneously with the movement in New York, there were
even fewer men of the highest political rank. Gallatin's effective career belongs to an earlier period, and
he had no successor, as a national figure, among the
Pennsylvania party chieftains.

# CHAPTER IV

## THE SOUTH

### (1820–1830)

IN the decade which forms the subject of this volume, no section underwent more far-reaching changes than did the group of South Atlantic states made up of Maryland, Virginia, the Carolinas, and Georgia, with which this chapter will deal under the name of the south. Then it was that the south came to appreciate the effect of the westward spread of the cotton-plant upon slavery and politics.

The invention of the cotton-gin by Eli Whitney,[1] in 1793, made possible the profitable cultivation of the short-staple variety of cotton. Before this, the labor of taking the seeds by hand from this variety, the only one suited to production in the uplands, had prevented its use; thereafter, it was only a question of time when the cotton area, no longer limited to the tidewater region, would extend to the interior, carrying slavery with it. This invention came at an opportune time. Already the inventions of Arkwright, Hargreaves, and Cartwright had worked a revolution in the textile industries of England, by

[1] *Am. Hist. Review*, III., 99.

means of the spinning-jenny, the power-loom, and the factory system, furnishing machinery for the manufacture of cotton beyond the world's supply.[1]

Under the stimulus of this demand for cotton, year by year the area of slavery extended towards the west. In the twenties, some of the southern counties of Virginia were attempting its cultivation;[2] interior counties of North Carolina were combining cotton-raising with their old industries; in South Carolina the area of cotton and slavery had extended up the rivers well beyond the middle of the state;[3] while in Georgia the cotton planters, so long restrained by the Indian line, broke through the barriers and spread over the newly ceded lands.[4] The accompanying table shows the progress of this crop: It is evident from the figures that tidewater South Carolina and Georgia produced practically all of the cotton crop in 1791, when the total was but two million pounds. By 1821 the old south produced one hundred and seventeen million pounds, and, five years later, one hundred and eighty millions. But how rapidly in these five years the recently settled southwest was overtaking the older section

---

[1] M. B. Hammond, *Cotton Industry*, chaps. i., ii.; Von Halle, " Baumwollproduktion," in Schmoller, *Staats und Social-wissenschaftliche Forschungen*, XV.

[2] Va. Const. Conv., *Debates* (1829 – 1830), 333, 336; Martin, *Gazetteer of Va. and D. C.* (1836), 99.

[3] Schaper, " Sectionalism and Representation in S. C.," in Am. Hist. Assoc. *Report*, 1900, I., 387–393.

[4] Phillips, " Georgia and State Rights," in *Ibid.*, 1901, II., 140 (map).

## COTTON CROP (in million pounds)[1]

|                   | 1791 | 1801 | 1811 | 1821 | 1826  | 1834  |
|-------------------|------|------|------|------|-------|-------|
| South Carolina    | 1.5  | 20.0 | 40.0 | 50.0 | 70.0  | 65.5  |
| Georgia........   | .5   | 10.0 | 20.0 | 45.0 | 75.0  | 75.0  |
| Virginia......    |      | 5.0  | 8.0  | 12.0 | 25.0  | 10.0  |
| North Carolina    |      | 4.0  | 7.0  | 10.0 | 10.0  | 9.5   |
| Total......       | 2.0  | 39.0 | 75.0 | 117.0| 180.0 | 160.0 |
| Tennessee....     |      | 1.0  | 3.0  | 20.0 | 45.0  | 45.0  |
| Louisiana.....    |      |      | 2.0  | 10.0 | 38.0  | 62.0  |
| Mississippi ...   |      |      |      | 10.0 | 20.0  | 85.0  |
| Alabama.....      |      |      |      | 20.0 | 45.0  | 85.0  |
| Florida ......    |      |      |      |      | 2.0   | 20.0  |
| Arkansas.....     |      |      |      |      | .5    | .5    |
| Total......       |      | 1.0  | 5.0  | 60.0 | 150.5 | 297.5 |
| Grand Total.      | 2.0  | 40.0 | 80.0 | 177.0| 330.5 | 457.5 |

is shown by its total of over one hundred and fifty millions. By 1834 the southwest had distanced the older section. What had occurred was a repeated westward movement: the cotton-plant first spread from the sea - coast to the uplands, and then, by the beginning of our period, advanced to the Gulf plains, until that region achieved supremacy in its production.

How deeply the section was interested in this crop, and how influential it was in the commerce of the United States, appears from the fact that, in 1820, the domestic exports of South Carolina and Georgia

[1] Based on MacGregor, *Commercial Statistics*, 462; cf. *De Bow's Review*, XVII., 428; Von Halle, *Baumwollproduktion*, 169; Secretary of Treasury, *Report*, 1855–1856, p. 116. There are discrepancies; the figures are to be taken as illustrative rather than exact; *e. g.*, De Bow gives seventy million pounds for Mississippi in 1826.

amounted to $15,215,000, while the value of the
whole domestic exports for all the rest of the United
States was $36,468,000.[1]  This, however, inadequate-
ly represents the value of the exports from these two
cotton states, because a large fraction of the cotton
was carried by the coastwise trade to northern ports
and appeared in their shipments.  Senator William
Smith, of South Carolina, estimated that in 1818 the
real exports of South Carolina and Georgia amounted
to "more than half as much as that of the other
states of the Union, including the vast and fertile
valley of the Mississippi."  The average annual
amount of the exports of cotton, tobacco, and rice
from the United States between 1821 and 1830 was
about thirty-three million dollars, while all other
domestic exports made a sum of but twenty million
dollars.[2]  Even greater than New England's interest
in the carrying-trade was the interest of the south
in the exchange of her great staples in the markets
of Europe.

Never in history, perhaps, was an economic force
more influential upon the life of a people.  As the
production of cotton increased, the price fell, and
the seaboard south, feeling the competition of the
virgin soils of the southwest, saw in the protective
tariff for the development of northern manufactures the real source of her distress.  The
price of cotton was in these years a barometer

---

[1] Pitkin, *Statistical View* (ed. of 1835), p. 57.
[2] *Ibid.*, 518.

of southern prosperity and of southern discontent.[1]

Even more important than the effect of cotton production upon the prosperity of the south was its effect upon her social system. This economic transformation resuscitated slavery from a moribund condition to a vigorous and aggressive life. Slowly Virginia and North Carolina came to realize that the burden and expense of slavery as the labor system for their outworn tobacco and corn fields was partly counteracted by the demand for their surplus negroes in the cotton-fields of their more southern neighbors. When the lower south accepted the system as the basis of its prosperity and its society, the tendency in the states of the upper south, except in the pine barrens and the hill country, to look upon the institution as a heritage to be reluctantly and apologetically accepted grew fainter. The efforts to find some mode of removing the negro from their midst gradually came to an end, and they adjusted themselves to slavery as a permanent system. Meanwhile, South Carolina and Georgia found in the institution the source of their economic well-being and hotly challenged the right of other sections to speak ill of it or meddle with it in any way, lest their domestic security be endangered.[2]

---

[1] See chap. xix., below; M. B. Hammond, *Cotton Industry*, part i., App. i.; Donnell, *Hist. of Cotton;* Watkins, *Production and Prices of Cotton*.

[2] See Hart, *Slavery and Abolition* (*Am. Nation,* XVI.).

When the south became fully conscious that slavery set the section apart from the rest of the nation, when it saw in nationalizing legislation, such as
protection to manufactures and the construction of
a system of internal improvements, the efforts of
other sections to deprive the cotton states of their
profits for the benefit of an industrial development
in which they did not share, deep discontent prevailed.   With but slight intermission from the days
of Washington to those of Monroe, the tobacco
planters under the Virginia dynasty had ruled the
nation.   But now, when the centre of power within
the section passed from the weakening hands of
Virginia to those of South Carolina, the aggressive
leader of the Cotton Kingdom, the south found
itself a minority section in the Union.   When it
realized this, it denied the right of the majority to
rule, and proceeded to elaborate a system of minority
rights as a protection against the forces of national
development, believing that these forces threatened
the foundations of the prosperity and even the social
safety of the south.

From the middle of the eighteenth century the
seaboard planters had been learning the lesson of
control by a fraction of the population.   The south
was by no means a unified region in its physiography.
The Blue Ridge cut off the low country of Virginia
from the Shenandoah Valley, and beyond this valley the Alleghanies separated the rest of the state
from those counties which we now know as West

Virginia. By the time of the Revolution, in the
Carolinas and Georgia, a belt of pine barrens, skirt-
ing the "fall line" from fifty to one hundred miles
from the coast, divided the region of tidewater
planters of these states from the small farmers of
the up-country. This population of the interior had
entered the region in the course of the second half of
the eighteenth century. Scotch-Irishmen and Germans passed down the Great Valley from Pennsylvania into Virginia, and through the gaps in the
Blue Ridge out to the Piedmont region of the
Carolinas, while contemporaneously other streams
from Charleston advanced to meet them.[1] Thus,
at the close of the eighteenth century, the south was
divided into two areas presenting contrasted types
of civilization. On the one side were the planters,
raising their staple crops of tobacco, rice, and indigo, together with some cultivation of the cereals.
To this region belonged the slaves. On the other
side was this area of small farmers, raising live-
stock, wheat, and corn under the same conditions
of pioneer farming as characterized the interior of
Pennsylvania.

From the second half of the eighteenth century
down to the time with which this volume deals,
there was a persistent struggle between the planters
of the coast, who controlled the wealth of the region,
and the free farmers of the interior of Maryland,

[1] Bassett, in Am. Hist. Assoc., *Report* 1894, p. 141; **Schaper**,
*ibid.*, 1900, I., 317; Phillips, *ibid.*, 1901, II., 88.

Virginia, the Carolinas, and Georgia. The tidewater counties retained the political power which they already possessed before this tide of settlement flowed into the back-country. Refusing in most of these states to reapportion on the basis of numbers, they protected their slaves and their wealth against the dangers of a democracy interested in internal improvements and capable of imposing a tax upon slave property in order to promote their ends. In Virginia, in 1825, for example, the western men complained that twenty counties in the upper country, with over two hundred and twenty thousand free white inhabitants, had no more weight in the government than twenty counties on tidewater, containing only about fifty thousand; that the six smallest counties in the state, compared with the six largest, enjoyed nearly ten times as much political power.[1] To the gentlemen planters of the seaboard, the idea of falling under the control of the farmers of the interior of the south seemed intolerable.

It was only as slavery spread into the uplands, with the cultivation of cotton, that the lowlands began to concede and to permit an increased power in the legislatures to the sections most nearly assimilated to the seaboard type. South Carolina achieved this end in 1808 by the plan of giving to the seaboard the control of one house, while the interior held the other; but it is to be noted that this concession was not made until slavery had pushed so

[1] *Alexandria Herald*, June 13, 1825.

far up the river-courses that the reapportionment
preserved the control in the hands of slave-holding
counties.[1]  A similar course was followed by Virginia in the convention of 1829–1830, when, after a
long struggle, a compromise was adopted, by which
the balance of power in the state legislature was
transferred to the counties of the Piedmont and the
Valley.[2]  Here slave-holding had progressed so far
that the interest of those counties was affiliated
rather with the coast than with the trans-Alleghany
country.  West Virginia remained a discontented
area until her independent statehood in the days
of the Civil War.  These transmontane counties of
Virginia were, in their political activity during our
period, rather to be reckoned with the west than
with the south.

Thus the southern seaboard experienced the need
of protecting the interests of its slave-holding planters against the free democracy of the interior of
the south itself, and learned how to safeguard the
minority.  This experience was now to serve the
south, when, having attained unity by the spread
of slavery into the interior, it found itself as a section in the same relation to the Union which the
slave-holding tidewater area had held towards the
more populous up-country of the south.

[1] Calhoun, *Works*, I., 401; Schaper, *Sectionalism and Representation in S.C.*, in Am. Hist. Assoc., *Report* 1900, I., 434–437.
[2] Va. Const. Conv., *Debates* (1829–1830); Chandler, *Representation in Va.*, in *Johns Hopkins Univ. Studies*, XIV., 286–298.

The unification of the section is one of the most important features of the period. Not only had the south been divided into opposing areas, as we have seen, but even its population was far from homogeneous. By the period of this volume, however, English, French-Huguenots, Scotch-Irish, and Germans had become assimilated into one people, and the negroes, who in 1830 in the South Atlantic states numbered over a million and a half in a white population of not much over two millions, were diffusing themselves throughout the area of the section except in West Virginia and the mountains. Contemporaneously the pioneer farming type of the interior of the section was replaced by the planter type.[1]

As cotton-planting and slave-holding advanced into the interior counties of the old southern states, the free farmers were obliged either to change to the plantation economy and buy slaves, or to sell their lands and migrate. Large numbers of them, particularly in the Carolinas, were Quakers or Baptists, whose religious scruples combined with their agricultural habits to make this change obnoxious. This upland country, too distant from the sea-shore to permit a satisfactory market, was a hive from which pioneers earlier passed into Kentucky and Tennessee, until those states had become populous commonwealths. Now the exodus was increased by this later colonization.[2] The Ohio was crossed, the Mis-

---

[1] *Niles' Register*, XXI., 132; cf. p. 55 below.
[2] See chap. v. below.

souri ascended, and the streams that flowed to the
Gulf were followed by movers away from the regions
that were undergoing this social and economic re-
construction.

This industrial revolution was effective in different
degrees in the different states. Comparatively few
of Virginia's slaves, which by 1830 numbered nearly
half a million, were found in her trans-Alleghany
counties, but the Shenandoah Valley was receiving
slaves and changing to the plantation type. In
North Carolina the slave population of nearly two
hundred and fifty thousand, at the same date, had
spread well into the interior, but cotton did not
achieve the position there which it held farther
south. The interior farmers worked small farms of
wheat and corn, laboring side by side with their
negro slaves in the fields.[1] South Carolina had over
three hundred thousand slaves—more than a majority of her population — and the black belt extended to the interior. Georgia's slaves, amounting
to over two hundred thousand, somewhat less than
half her population, steadily advanced from the
coast and the Savannah River towards the cotton-
lands of the interior, pushing before them the less
prosperous farmers, who found new homes to the
north or south of the cotton-belt or migrated to the
southwestern frontier.[2] Here, as in North Carolina,

[1] Bassett, *Slavery in N. C.*, in *Johns Hopkins Univ. Studies*,
XVII., 324, 399.

[2] Phillips, *Georgia and State Rights*, in Am. Hist. Assoc., *Report* 1901, II., 106.

the planters in the interior of the state frequently followed the plough or encouraged their slaves by wielding the hoe.[1]

Thus this process of economic transformation passed from the coast towards the mountain barrier, gradually eliminating the inharmonious elements and steadily tending to produce a solidarity of interests. The south as a whole was becoming, for the first time since colonial days, a staple-producing region; and, as diversified farming declined, the region tended to become dependent for its supplies of meat products, horses, and mules, and even hay and cereals, upon the north and west.

The westward migration of its people checked the growth of the south. It had colonized the new west at the same time that the middle region had been rapidly growing in population, and the result was that the proud states of the southern seaboard were reduced to numerical inferiority. Like New England, it was an almost stationary section. From 1820 to 1830 the states of this group gained little more than half a million souls, hardly more than the increase of the single state of New York. Virginia, with a population of over a million, increased but 13.7 per cent., and the Carolinas only 15.5 per cent. In the next decade these tendencies were even more clearly shown, for Virginia and the Carolinas then gained but little more than 2 per cent.

[1] Phillips, *Georgia and State Rights*, in Am. Hist. Assoc., *Report* 1901, II., 107.

Georgia alone showed rapid increase. At the beginning of the decade the Indians still held all of the territory west of Macon, at the centre of the state, with the exception of two tiers of counties along the southern border; and, when these lands were opened towards the close of the decade, they were occupied by a rush of settlement similar to the occupation of Oklahoma and Indian Territory in our own day. What Maine was to New England, that Georgia was to the southern seaboard, with the difference that it was deeply touched by influences characteristically western. Because of the traits of her leaders, and the rude, aggressive policy of her people, Georgia belonged at least as much to the west as to the south. From colonial times the Georgia settlers had been engaged in an almost incessant struggle against the savages on her border, and had the instincts of a frontier society.[1]

From 1800 to 1830, throughout the tidewater region, there were clear evidences of decline. As the movement of capital and population towards the interior went on, wealth was drained from the coast; and, as time passed, the competition of the fertile and low-priced lands of the Gulf basin proved too strong for the outworn lands even of the interior of the south. Under the wasteful system of tobacco and cotton culture, without replenishment of the

[1] *Ibid.*, II., 88; Longstreet, *Georgia Scenes;* Gilmer, *Sketches;* Miss. Hist. Soc., *Publications*, VIII., 443.

soil, the staple areas would, in any case, have declined in value.  Even the corn and wheat lands
were exhausted by unscientific farming.[1]  Writing in
1814 to Josiah Quincy,[2] John Randolph of Roanoke
lamented the decline of the seaboard planters.  He
declared that the region was now sunk in obscurity:
what enterprise or capital there was in the country
had retired westward; deer and wild turkeys were
not so plentiful anywhere in Kentucky as near the
site of the ancient Virginia capital, Williamsburg.
In the Virginia convention of 1829, Mr. Mercer estimated that in 1817 land values in Virginia aggre-
gated two hundred and six million dollars, and
negroes averaged three hundred dollars, while in
1829 the land values did not surpass ninety millions,
and slaves had fallen in value to one hundred and
fifty dollars.[3]

In a speech in the Virginia House of Delegates,
in 1832, Thomas Marshall[4] asserted that the whole
agricultural product of Virginia did not exceed in
value the exports of eighty or ninety years before,
when it contained not one-sixth of the population.
In his judgment, the greater proportion of the larger
plantations, with from fifty to one hundred slaves,

[1] Gooch, *Prize Essay on Agriculture in Va.*, in *Lynchburg
Virginian*, July 4, 1833; Martin, *Gazetteer of Va.*, 99, 100.
[2] E. Quincy, *Josiah Quincy*, 353.
[3] Va. Const. Conv., *Debates* (1829–1830), 178; Collins, *Domestic Slave Trade*, 26.
[4] Collins, *Domestic Slave Trade*, 24, cited from *Richmond Enquirer*, February, 2, 1832.

brought the proprietors into debt, and rarely did a plantation yield one and a half per cent. profit on the capital. So great had become the depression that Randolph prophesied that the time was coming when the masters would run away from the slaves and be advertised by them in the public papers.[1]

It was in this period that Thomas Jefferson fell into such financial embarrassments that he was obliged to request of the legislature of Virginia permission to dispose of property by lottery to pay his debts, and that a subscription was taken up to relieve his distress.[2] At the same time, Madison, having vainly tried to get a loan from the United States Bank, was forced to dispose of some of his lands and stocks;[3] and Monroe, at the close of his term of office, found himself financially ruined. He gave up Oak Hill and spent his declining years with his son-in-law in New York City. The old-time tide-water mansions, where, in an earlier day, everybody kept open house, gradually fell into decay.

Sad indeed was the spectacle of Virginia's ancient aristocracy. It had never been a luxurious society. The very wealthy planters, with vast cultivated estates and pretentious homes, were in the minority. For the most part, the houses were moderate frame structures, set at intervals of a mile or so apart, often in parklike grounds, with long avenues of trees. The plantation was a little world in itself.

[1] Collins, *Domestic Slave Trade*, 26.
[2] Randall, *Jefferson*, III., 527, 561.    [3] Hunt, *Madison*, 380.

Here was made much of the clothing for the slaves, and the mistress of the plantation supervised the spinning and weaving. Leather was tanned on the place, and blacksmithing, wood-working, and other industries were carried on, often under the direction of white mechanics. The planter and his wife commonly had the care of the black families whom they possessed, looked after them when they were sick, saw to their daily rations, arranged marriages, and determined the daily tasks of the plantation. The abundant hospitality between neighbors gave opportunity for social cultivation, and politics was a favorite subject of conversation.

The leading planters served as justices of the peace, but they were not dependent for their selection upon the popular vote. Appointed by the governor on nomination of the court itself, they constituted a kind of close corporation, exercising local judicial, legislative, and executive functions. The sheriff was appointed by the governor from three justices of the peace recommended by the court, and the court itself appointed the county clerk. Thus the county government of Virginia was distinctly aristocratic. County-court day served as an opportunity for bringing together the freeholders, who included not only the larger planters, but the small farmers and the poor whites — hangers-on of the greater plantations. Almost no large cities were found in Virginia. The court-house was hardly more than a meeting-place for the rural population. Here farmers exchanged their goods, traded horses, often fought, and listened to the stump speeches of the orators.[1]

Such were, in the main, the characteristics of that homespun plantation aristocracy which, through the Virginia dynasty, had ruled the nation in the days of Washington, Jefferson, Madison, and Monroe. As their lands declined in value, they naturally sought for an explanation and a remedy.[2] The explanation was found most commonly in the charge that the protective tariff was destroying the prosperity of the south; and in reaction they turned to demand the old days of Jeffersonian rural simplicity, under the guardianship of state rights and a strict construction of the Constitution. Madison in vain laid the fall in land values in Virginia to the uncertainty and low prices of the crops, to the quantity of land thrown on the market, and the attractions of the cheaper and better lands beyond the mountains.[3]

Others called attention to the fact that the semi-annual migration towards the west and southwest, which swept off enterprising portions of the people and much of the capital and movable property of the state, also kept down the price of land by the great quantities thereby thrown into the market. Instead of applying a system of scientific farming

[1] Johnson, *Robert Lewis Dabney*, 14–24; Smedes, *A Southern Planter*, 34–37. [2] Randall, *Jefferson*, III., 532.
[3] Madison, *Writings* (ed. of 1865), III., 614.

and replenishment of the soil, there was a tendency for the planters who remained to get into debt in order to add to their possessions the farms which were offered for sale by the movers. Thus there was a flow of wealth towards the west to pay for these new purchases. The overgrown plantations soon began to look tattered and almost desolate. "Galled and gullied hill-sides and sedgy, briary fields"[1] showed themselves in every direction. Finally the planter found himself obliged to part with some of his slaves, in response to the demand from the new cotton-fields; or to migrate himself, with his caravan of negroes, to open a new home in the Gulf region. During the period of this survey the price for prime field-hands in Georgia averaged a little over seven hundred dollars.[2] If the estimate of one hundred and fifty dollars for negroes sold in family lots in Virginia is correct, it is clear that economic laws would bring about a condition where Virginia's resources would in part depend upon her supply of slaves to the cotton-belt.[3] It is clear, also, that the Old Dominion had passed the apogee of her political power.

It was not only the planters of Virginia that suffered in this period of change. As the more extensive and fertile cotton-fields of the new states of the southwest opened, North Carolina and even

---

[1] *Lynchburg Virginian*, July 4, 1833.
[2] Phillips, in *Pol. Sci. Quart.*, XX., 267.
[3] Collins, *Domestic Slave Trade*, 42–46.

South Carolina found themselves embarrassed.
With the fall in cotton prices, already mentioned, it
became increasingly necessary to possess the advantages of large estates and unexhausted soils, in order to extract a profit from this cultivation. From
South Carolina there came a protest more vehement and aggressive than that of the discontented
classes of Virginia. Already the indigo plantation
had ceased to be profitable and the rice planters no
longer held their old prosperity.

Charleston was peculiarly suited to lead in a
movement of revolt. It was the one important
centre of real city life of the seaboard south of
Baltimore. Here every February the planters gathered from their plantations, thirty to one hundred
and fifty miles away, for a month in their town
houses. At this season, races, social gayeties, and political conferences vied with one another in engaging
the attention of the planters. Returning to their
plantations in the early spring, they remained until
June, when considerations of health compelled them
either again to return to the city, to visit the mountains, or to go to such watering-places as Saratoga
in New York. Here again they talked politics and
mingled with political leaders of the north. It was
not until the fall that they were able to return again
to their estates.[1] Thus South Carolina, affording a
combination of plantation life with the social inter-
course of the city, gave peculiar opportunities for

[1] Hodgson, *Letters from North America*, I., 50.

exchanging ideas and consolidating the sentiment of her leaders.

The condition of South Carolina was doubtless exaggerated by Hayne, in his speech in the Senate in 1832, when he characterized it as "not merely one of unexampled depression, but of great and all-pervading distress," with "the mournful evidence of premature decay," "merchants bankrupt or driven away—their capital sunk or transferred to other pursuits—our shipyards broken up—our ships all sold!" "If," said he, "we fly from the city to the country, what do we there behold? Fields abandoned; the hospitable mansions of our fathers deserted; agriculture drooping; our slaves, like their masters, working harder, and faring worse; the planter striving with unavailing efforts to avert the ruin which is before him." He drew a sad picture of the once thriving planter, reduced to despair, gathering up the small remnants of his broken fortune, and, with his wife and little ones, tearing himself from the scenes of his childhood and the bones of his ancestors to seek in the wilderness the reward for his industry of which the policy of Congress had deprived him.[1]

The genius of the south expressed itself most clearly in the field of politics. If the democratic middle region could show a multitude of clever politicians, the aristocratic south possessed an

[1] *Register of Debates*, VIII., pt. i., 80; cf. Houston, *Nullification in S. C.*, 46; McDuffie, in *Register of Debates*, 18th Cong., 2 Sess., 253.

abundance of leaders bold in political initiative and
masterful in their ability to use the talents of their
northern allies.  When the Missouri question was
debated, John Quincy Adams remarked "that if
institutions are to be judged by their results in the
composition of the councils of this Union, the slave-
holders are much more ably represented than the
simple freemen." [1]

The southern statesmen fall into two classes.  On
the one side was the Virginia group, now for the most
part old men, rich in the honors of the nation, still
influential, but, except for Monroe, no longer directing party policy.  Jefferson and Madison were in
retirement in their old age; Marshall, as chief-justice,
was continuing his career as the expounder of the
Constitution in accordance with Federalist ideals;
John Randolph, his old eccentricities increased by
disease and intemperance, remained to proclaim the
extreme doctrines of southern dissent and to impale
his adversaries with javelins of flashing wit.  A
maker of phrases which stung and festered, he was
still capable of influencing public opinion somewhat
in the same way as are the cartoonists of modern
times.  But "his course through life had been like
that of the arrow which Alcestes shot to heaven,
which effected nothing useful, though it left a long
stream of light behind it." [2]  In North Carolina, the
venerable Macon remained to protest like a later

[1] Adams, *Memoirs*, IV., 506.
[2] *Lynchburg Virginian*, May 9, 1833.

Cato against the tendencies of the times and to raise a warning voice to his fellow slave-holders against national consolidation.

In the course of this decade, the effective leadership of the south fell to Calhoun and Crawford.[1] About these statesmen were grouped energetic and able men like Hayne, McDuffie, and Hamilton of South Carolina, and Cobb and Forsyth of Georgia —men who sometimes pushed their leaders on in a sectional path which the latter's caution or personal ambitions made them reluctant to tread. Nor must it be forgotten that early in the decade the south lost two of her greatest statesmen, the wise and moderate Lowndes, of South Carolina, and Pinkney, the brilliant Maryland orator. In the course of the ten years which we are to sketch, the influence of economic change within this section transformed the South Carolinians from warm supporters of a liberal national policy into the straitest of the sect of state - sovereignty advocates, intent upon raising barriers against the flood of nationalism that threatened to overwhelm the south. In relating the changing policy of the southern political leaders, we shall again observe the progress and the effects of the economic transformations which it has been the purpose of this chapter to portray.

[1] See chap. xi. below.

# CHAPTER V

## COLONIZATION OF THE WEST

### (1820–1830)

THE rise of the new west was the most significant
fact in American history in the years immediately following the War of 1812.  Ever since the
beginnings of colonization on the Atlantic coast a
frontier of settlement had advanced, cutting into
the forest, pushing back the Indian, and steadily
widening the area of civilization in its rear.[1]   There
had been a west even in early colonial days; but
then it lay close to the coast.  By the middle of
the eighteenth century the west was to be found
beyond tide-water, advancing towards the Alleghany
Mountains.   When this barrier was crossed and the
lands on the other side of the mountains were won, in
the days of the Revolution, a new and greater west,
more influential on the nation's destiny, was created.[2]

[1] Three articles by F. J. Turner, viz.: "Significance of the
Frontier in American History," in Am. Hist. Assoc., *Report*
1893, 199–227; "Problem of the West," in "*Atlantic Monthly*,
LXXVIII., 289; "Contributions of the West to American Democracy," *ibid.*, XCI., 83.

[2] Howard, *Preliminaries of Revolution*, chap. xiii.; Van Tyne,
*Am. Revolution*, chap. xv.; McLaughlin, *Confederation and Constitution*, chap. viii. (*Am. Nation*, VIII., IX., X.).

The men of the "Western Waters" or the "Western World," as they loved to call themselves, developed under conditions of separation from the older settlements and from Europe. The lands, practically free, in this vast area not only attracted the settler, but furnished opportunity for all men to hew out their own careers. The wilderness ever opened a gate of escape to the poor, the discontented, and the oppressed. If social conditions tended to crystallize in the east, beyond the Alleghanies there was freedom. Grappling with new problems, under these conditions, the society that spread into this region developed inventiveness and resourcefulness; the restraints of custom were broken, and new activities, new lines of growth, new institutions were produced. Mr. Bryce has well declared that "the West is the most American part of America. . . . What Europe is to Asia, what England is to the rest of Europe, what America is to England, that the Western States and Territories are to the Atlantic States." [1] The American spirit — the traits that have come to be recognized as the most characteristic—was developed in the new commonwealths that sprang into life beyond the seaboard. In these new western lands Americans achieved a boldness of conception of the country's destiny and democracy. The ideal of the west was its emphasis upon the worth and possibilities of the common man, its belief in the right of every man to rise to the full

[1] Bryce, *American Commonwealth* (ed. of 1895), II., 830.

measure of his own nature, under conditions of social mobility. Western democracy was no theorist's dream. It came, stark and strong and full of life, from the American forest.[1]

The time had now come when this section was to make itself felt as a dominant force in American life. Already it had shown its influence upon the older sections. By its competition, by its attractions for settlers, it reacted on the east and gave added impulse to the democratic movement in New England and New York. The struggle of Baltimore, New York City, and Philadelphia for the rising commerce of the interior was a potent factor in the development of the middle region. In the south the spread of the cotton-plant and the new form which slavery took were phases of the westward movement of the plantation. The discontent of the old south is partly explained by the migration of her citizens to the west and by the competition of her colonists in the lands beyond the Alleghanies. The future of the south lay in its affiliation to the Cotton Kingdom of the lower states which were rising on the plains of the Gulf of Mexico.

Rightly to understand the power which the new west was to exert upon the economic and political life of the nation in the years between 1820 and 1830, it is necessary to consider somewhat fully the

[1] F. J. Turner, "Contributions of the West to American Democracy," in *Atlantic Monthly*, XCI., 83, and "The Middle West," in *International Monthly*, IV., 794.

statistics of growth in western population and industry.

The western states ranked with the middle region and the south in respect to population. Between 1812 and 1821 six new western commonwealths were added to the Union: Louisiana (1812), Indiana (1816), Mississippi (1817), Illinois (1818), Alabama (1819), and Missouri (1821). In the decade from 1820 to 1830, these states, with their older sisters, Kentucky, Tennessee, and Ohio, increased their population from 2,217,000 to nearly 3,700,000, a gain of about a million and a half in the decade. The percentages of increase in these new communities tell a striking story. Even the older states of the group grew steadily. Kentucky, with 22 per cent., Louisiana, with 41, and Tennessee and Ohio, each with 61, were increasing much faster than New England and the south, outside of Maine and Georgia. But for the newer communities the percentages of gain are still more significant: Mississippi, 81 per cent.; Alabama, 142; Indiana, 133; and Illinois, 185. The population of Ohio, which hardly more than a generation before was "fresh, untouched, unbounded, magnificent wilderness," [1] was now nearly a million, surpassing the combined population of Massachusetts and Connecticut.

A new section had arisen and was growing at such a rate that a description of it in any single year would be falsified before it could be published. Nor

[1] Webster, *Writings* (National ed.), V., 252.

DISTRIBUTION
OF
POPULATION
1830

Unoccupied areas
2 to 18 inhabitants
to the square mile
18 to over 90 inhabit-
ants to the square mile

BURMAY & CO., N.Y.

DISTRIBUTION
OF
POPULATION
1820

Unoccupied areas
2 to 18 inhabitants
to the square mile
18 to over 90 inhabit-
ants to the square mile

is the whole strength of the western element revealed by these figures. In order to estimate the weight of the western population in 1830, we must add six hundred thousand souls in the western half of New York, three hundred thousand in the interior counties of Pennsylvania, and over two hundred thousand in the trans-Alleghany counties of Virginia, making an aggregate of four million six hundred thousand. Fully to reckon the forces of backwoods democracy, moreover, we should include a large fraction of the interior population of Maine, New Hampshire, and Vermont, North Carolina, and Georgia, and northern New York. All of these regions were to be influenced by the ideals of democratic rule which were springing up in the Mississippi Valley.

In voting-power the western states alone—to say nothing of the interior districts of the older states— were even more important than the figures for population indicate. The west itself had, under the apportionment of 1822, forty-seven out of the two hundred and thirteen members of the House of Representatives, while in the Senate its representation was eighteen out of forty-eight—more than that of any other section. Clearly, here was a region to be reckoned with; its economic interests, its ideals, and its political leaders were certain to have a powerful, if not a controlling, voice in the councils of the nation.

At the close of the War of 1812 the west had much

homogeneity. Parts of Kentucky, Tennessee, and Ohio had been settled so many years that they no longer presented typical western conditions; but in most of its area the west then was occupied by pioneer farmers and stock-raisers, eking out their larder and getting peltries by hunting, and raising only a small surplus for market. By 1830, however, industrial differentiation between the northern and southern portions of the Mississippi Valley was clearly marked. The northwest was changing to a land of farmers and town-builders, anxious for a market for their grain and cattle; while the southwest was becoming increasingly a cotton-raising section, swayed by the same impulses in respect to staple exports as those which governed the southern seaboard. Economically, the northern portion of the valley tended to connect itself with the middle states, while the southern portion came into increasingly intimate connection with the south. Nevertheless, it would be a radical mistake not to deal with the west as a separate region, for, with all these differences within itself, it possessed a fundamental unity in its social structure and its democratic ideals, and at times, in no uncertain way, it showed a consciousness of its separate existence.

In occupying the Mississippi Valley the American people colonized a region far surpassing in area the territory of the old thirteen states. The movement was, indeed, but the continuation of the advance of the frontier which had begun in the earliest days of

American colonization. The existence of a great body of land, offered at so low a price as to be practically free, inevitably drew population towards the west. When wild lands sold for two dollars an acre, and, indeed, could be occupied by squatters almost without molestation, it was certain that settlers would seek them instead of paying twenty to fifty dollars an acre for farms that lay not much farther to the east—particularly when the western lands were more fertile. The introduction of the steamboat on the western waters in 1811, moreover, soon revolutionized transportation conditions in the West.[1] At the beginning of the period of which we are treating, steamers were ascending the Mississippi and the Missouri, as well as the Ohio and its tributaries. Between the close of the War of 1812 and 1830, moreover, the Indian title was extinguished to vast regions in the west. Half of Michigan was opened to settlement; the northwestern quarter of Ohio was freed; in Indiana and Illinois (more than half of which had been Indian country prior to 1816) all but a comparatively small region of undesired prairie lands south of Lake Michigan was ceded; almost the whole state of Missouri was freed from its Indian title; and, in the Gulf region, at the close of the decade, the Indians held but two isolated

[1] Flint, *Letters*, 260; Monette, in Miss. Hist. Soc., *Publications*, VII., 503; Hall, *Statistics of the West*, 236, 247; Lloyd, *Steamboat Disasters* (1853), 32, 40–45; Preble, *Steam Navigation*, 64; McMaster, *United States*, IV., 402; Chittenden, *Early Steamboat Navigation on the Missouri*, chap. ix.

islands of territory, one in western Georgia and eastern Alabama, and the other in northern and central Mississippi. These ceded regions were the fruit of the victories of William Henry Harrison in the northwest, and of Andrew Jackson in the Gulf region. They were, in effect, conquered provinces, just opened to colonization.

The maps of the United States census, giving the distribution of population in 1810, 1820, and 1830,[1] exhibit clearly the effects of the defeat of the Indians, and show the areas that were occupied in these years. In 1810 settlement beyond the mountains was almost limited to a zone along the Ohio River and its tributaries, the Cumberland and the Tennessee. In the southwest, the vicinity of Mobile showed sparse settlement, chiefly survivals of the Spanish and English occupation; and, along the fluvial lands of the eastern bank of the lower Mississippi, in the Natchez region, as well as in the old province of Louisiana, there was a considerable area occupied by planters.

By 1820 the effects of the War of 1812 and the rising tide of westward migration became manifest. Pioneers spread along the river-courses of the northwest well up to the Indian boundary. The zone of settlement along the Ohio ascended the Missouri, in the rush to the Boone's Lick country, towards the centre of the present state. From the settlements of middle Tennessee a pioneer farming area

[1] See maps of population; compare U. S. Census of 1900, *Statistical Atlas*, plates 4, 5, 6.

reached southward to connect with the settlements
of Mobile, and the latter became conterminous with
those of the lower Mississippi.

By 1830 large portions of these Indian lands,
which were ceded between 1817 and 1829, received
the same type of colonization. The unoccupied
lands in Indiana and Illinois were prairie country,
then deemed unsuited for settlement because of the
lack of wood and drinking-water. It was the hardwoods that had been taken up in the northwest,
and, for the most part, the tracts a little back from
the unhealthful bottom-lands, but in close proxim-
ity to the rivers, which were the only means of
transportation before the building of good roads.
A new island of settlement appeared in the northwestern portion of Illinois and the adjacent regions
of Wisconsin and Iowa, due to the opening of the
lead-mines. Along the Missouri Valley and in the
Gulf region the areas possessed in 1820 increased in
density of population. Georgia spread her settlers
into the Indian lands, which she had so recently
secured by threatening a rupture with the United
States.[1]

Translated into terms of human activity, these
shaded areas, encroaching on the blank spaces of the
map, meant much for the history of the United
States. Even in the northwest, which we shall first
describe, they represent, in the main, the migration

[1] MacDonald, *Jacksonian Democracy* (*Am. Nation*, XV.),
chap. x.

of southern people.   New England, after the distress
following the War of 1812 and the hard winter of
1816–1817, had sent many settlers into western
New York and Ohio; the Western Reserve had increased in population by the immigration of Connecticut people; Pennsylvania and New Jersey had
sent colonists to southern and central Ohio, with
Cincinnati as the commercial centre.   In Ohio the
settlers of middle-state origin were decidedly more
numerous than those from the south, and New
England's share was distinctly smaller than that
of the south.   In the Ohio legislature in 1822 there
were thirty-eight members of middle-state birth,
thirty-three of southern (including Kentucky), and
twenty-five of New England.   But Kentucky and
Tennessee (now sufficiently settled to need larger and
cheaper farms for the rising generation), together
with the up-country of the south, contributed the
mass of the pioneer colonists to most of the Mississippi Valley prior to 1830.[1]   Of course, a large fraction of these came from the Scotch-Irish and German stock that in the first half of the eighteenth
century passed from Pennsylvania along the Great
Valley to the up-country of the south.   Indiana, so
late as 1850, showed but ten thousand natives of

[1] See, for Ohio, *Niles' Register*, XXI., 368 (leg. session of 1822),
and *Nat. Republican*, January 2, 1824; for Illinois in 1833,
*Western Monthly Magazine*, I., 199; for Missouri convention of
1820, *Niles' Register*, XVIII., 400; for Alabama in 1820, *ibid.*,
XX., 64.   Local histories, travels, newspapers, and the census
of 1850 support the text.

New England, and twice as many persons of
southern as of middle states origin.  In the history of Indiana, North Carolina contributed a large
fraction of the population, giving to it its "Hoo-
sier" as well as much of its Quaker stock.  Illinois in this period had but a sprinkling of New-
Englanders, engaged in business in the little towns.
The southern stock, including settlers from Kentucky and Tennessee, was the preponderant class.
The Illinois legislature for 1833 contained fifty-eight
from the south (including Kentucky and Tennessee),
nineteen from the middle states, and only four from
New England.  Missouri's population was chiefly
Kentuckians and Tennesseeans.

The leaders of this southern element came, in
considerable measure, from well-to-do classes, who
migrated to improve their conditions in the freer
opportunities of a new country.  Land speculation, the opportunity of political preferment, and
the advantages which these growing communities
brought to practitioners of the law combined to
attract men of this class.  Many of them, as we shall
see, brought their slaves with them, under the systems of indenture which made this possible.  Missouri, especially, was sought by planters with their
slaves.  But it was the poorer whites, the more
democratic, non-slaveholding element of the south,
which furnished the great bulk of the settlers north
of the Ohio.  Prior to the close of the decade the
same farmer type was in possession of large parts of

the Gulf region, whither, through the whole of our period, the slave-holding planters came in increasing numbers.

Two of the families which left Kentucky for the newer country in these years will illustrate the movement. The Lincoln family [1] had reached that state by migration from the north with the stream of backwoodsmen which bore along with it the Calhouns and the Boones. Abraham Lincoln was born in a hilly, barren portion of Kentucky in 1809. In 1816, when Lincoln was a boy of seven, his father, a poor carpenter, took his family across the Ohio on a raft, with a capital consisting of his kit of tools and several hundred gallons of whiskey. In Indiana he hewed a path into the forest to a new home in the southern part of the state, where for a year the family lived in a "half-faced camp," or open shed of poles, clearing their land. In the hardships of the pioneer life Lincoln's mother died, as did many another frontier woman. In 1830 Lincoln was a tall, strapping youth, six feet four inches in height, able to sink his axe deeper than other men into the opposing forest. At that time his father moved to the Sangamon country of Illinois with the rush of landseekers into that new and popular region. Near the home of Lincoln in Kentucky was born, in 1808, Jefferson Davis,[2] whose father, shortly before the War

---

[1] Tarbell, *Lincoln*, I., chaps. i.–iv.; Herndon, *Lincoln*, I., chaps. i.–iv.; Nicolay and Hay, *Lincoln*, I., chaps. i.–iii.
[2] Mrs. Davis, *Jefferson Davis*, I., 5.

of 1812, went with the stream of southward movers
to Louisiana and then to Mississippi.   Davis's brothers fought under Jackson in the War of 1812, and
the family became typical planters of the Gulf region.

Meanwhile, the roads that led to the Ohio Valley
were followed by an increasing tide of settlers from
the east.   "Old America seems to be breaking up,
and moving westward," wrote Morris Birkbeck in
1817, as he passed on the National Road through
Pennsylvania.   "We are seldom out of sight, as we
travel on this grand track, towards the Ohio, of
family groups, behind and before us. . . . A small
waggon (so light that you might almost carry it,
yet strong enough to bear a good load of bedding,
utensils and provisions, and a swarm of young
citizens,—and to sustain marvellous shocks in its
passage over these rocky heights) with two small
horses; sometimes a cow or two, comprises their
all; excepting a little store of hard-earned cash
for the land office of the district; where they may
obtain a title for as many acres as they possess half-
dollars, being one fourth of the purchase-money.
The waggon has a tilt, or cover, made of a sheet,
or perhaps a blanket.   The family are seen before,
behind, or within the vehicle, according to the road
or the weather, or perhaps the spirits of the party.
. . . A cart and single horse frequently affords the
means of transfer, sometimes a horse and pack-
saddle.   Often the back of the poor pilgrim bears

all his effects, and his wife follows, naked-footed, bending under the hopes of the family." [1]

The southerners who came by land along the many bad roads through Tennessee and Kentucky usually travelled with heavy, long-bodied wagons, drawn by four or six horses. [2]  These family groups, crowding roads and fords, marching towards the sunset, with the canvas-covered wagon, ancestor of the prairie-schooner of the later times, were typical of the overland migration.  The poorer classes travelled on foot, sometimes carrying their entire effects in a cart drawn by themselves. [3]  Those of more means took horses, cattle, and sheep, and sometimes sent their household goods by wagon or by steamboat up the Mississippi. [4]

The routes of travel to the western country were numerous. [5]  Prior to the opening of the Erie Canal the New England element either passed along the Mohawk and the Genesee turnpike to Lake Erie, or crossed the Hudson and followed the line of the Catskill turnpike to the headwaters of the Allegheny, or, by way of Boston, took ship to New York, Philadelphia, or Baltimore, in order to follow a more southerly route.  In Pennsylvania the principal route was the old road which, in a general way,

[1] Birkbeck, *Notes on a Journey from Va. to Ill.*, 25, 26.
[2] *Hist. of Grundy County, Ill.*, 149.
[3] *Niles' Register*, XXI., 320.
[4] Howells, *Life in Ohio, 1813–1840*, 86;  Jones, *Ill. and the West*, 31;  *Hist. of Grundy County, Ill.*, 149.
[5] See map, page 226.

followed the line that Forbes had cut in the French
and Indian War from Philadelphia to Pittsburg by
way of Lancaster and Bedford. By this time the
road had been made a turnpike through a large portion of its course. From Baltimore the traveller
followed a turnpike to Cumberland, on the Potomac,
where began the old National Road across the
mountains to Wheeling, on the Ohio, with branches
leading to Pittsburg. This became one of the great
arteries of western migration and commerce, connecting, as it did at its eastern end, with the Shenandoah Valley, and thus affording access to the
Ohio for large areas of Virginia. Other routes lay
through the passes of the Alleghanies, easily reached
from the divide between the waters of North Carolina and of West Virginia. Saluda Gap, in northwestern South Carolina, led the way to the great
valley of eastern Tennessee. In Tennessee and Kentucky many routes passed to the Ohio in the region of Cincinnati or Louisville.

When the settler arrived at the waters of the
Ohio, he either took a steamboat or placed his
possessions on a flatboat, or ark, and floated down
the river to his destination. From the upper waters
of the Allegheny many emigrants took advantage of
the lumber-rafts, which were constructed from the
pine forests of southwestern New York, to float to
the Ohio with themselves and their belongings.
With the advent of the steamboat these older
modes of navigation were, to a considerable extent,

superseded. But navigation on the Great Lakes had not sufficiently advanced to afford opportunity for any considerable movement of settlement, by this route, beyond Lake Erie.

In the course of the decade the cost of reaching the west varied greatly with the decrease in the transportation rates brought about by the competition of the Erie Canal, the improvement of the turnpikes, and the development of steamboat navigation. The expense of the long overland journey from New England, prior to the opening of the Erie Canal, made it extremely difficult for those without any capital to reach the west. The stage rates on the Pennsylvania turnpike and the old National Road, prior to the opening of the Erie Canal, were about five or six dollars a hundred-weight from Philadelphia or Baltimore to the Ohio River; the individual was regarded as so much freight.[1] To most of the movers, who drove their own teams and camped by the wayside, however, the actual expense was simply that of providing food for themselves and their horses on the road. The cost of moving by land a few years later is illustrated by the case of a Maryland family, consisting of fifteen persons, of whom five were slaves. They travelled about twenty miles a day, with a four-horse wagon, three hundred miles, to Wheeling, at an expense of seventy-five dollars.[2] The expense of travelling by

[1] Evans, *Pedestrious Tour*, 145.
[2] *Niles' Register*, XLVIII., 242.

stage and steamboat from Philadelphia to St. Louis at the close of the decade was about fifty-five dollars for one person; or by steamboat from New Orleans to St. Louis, thirty dollars, including food and lodging. For deck-passage, without food or lodging, the charge was only eight dollars.[1] In 1823 the cost of passage from Cincinnati to New Orleans by steamboat was twenty-five dollars; from New Orleans to Cincinnati, fifty dollars.[2] In the early thirties one could go from New Orleans to Pittsburg, as cabin passenger, for from thirty-five to forty-five dollars.[3]

---

[1] *Ill. Monthly Magazine*, II., 53.
[2] *Niles' Register*, XXV., 95.
[3] *Emigrants' and Travellers' Guide through the Valley of the Mississippi*, 341.

# CHAPTER VI

## SOCIAL AND ECONOMIC DEVELOPMENT OF THE WEST

### (1820–1830)

ARRIVED at the nearest point to his destination on the Ohio, the emigrant either cut out a road to his new home or pushed up some tributary of that river in a keel-boat. If he was one of the poorer classes, he became a squatter on the public lands, trusting to find in the profits of his farming the means of paying for his land. Not uncommonly, after clearing the land, he sold his improvements to the actual purchaser, under the customary usage or by pre-emption laws.[1] With the money thus secured he would purchase new land in a remoter area, and thus establish himself as an independent land-owner. Under the credit system[2] which existed at the opening of the period, the settler purchased his land in quantities of not less than one hundred and sixty acres at two dollars per acre, by a cash payment of fifty cents per acre and the rest in

[1] Hall, *Statistics of the West*, 180; Kingdom, *America*, 56; Peck, *New Guide for Emigrants to the West* (1837), 119–132.
[2] Emerick, *Credit and the Public Domain*.

instalments running over a period of four years; but
by the new law of 1820 the settler was permitted to
buy as small a tract as eighty acres from the government at a minimum price of a dollar and a quarter
per acre, without credit. The price of labor in the
towns along the Ohio, coupled with the low cost of
provisions, made it possible for even a poor day-
laborer from the East to accumulate the necessary
amount to make his land-purchase.[1]

Having in this way settled down either as a
squatter or as a land-owner, the pioneer proceeded
to hew out a clearing in the midst of the forest.[2]
Commonly he had selected his lands with reference
to the value of the soil, as indicated by the character
of the hardwoods, but this meant that the labor of
clearing was the more severe in good soil. Under
the sturdy strokes of his axe the light of day was let
into the little circle of cleared ground.[3] With the
aid of his neighbors, called together under the social
attractions of a "raising," with its inevitable accom-
paniment of whiskey and a "frolic," he erected his
log-cabin. "America," wrote Birkbeck, "was bred
in a cabin."[4]

Having secured a foothold, the settler next proceeded to "girdle" or "deaden" an additional forest

[1] See, for example, Peck, *New Guide for Emigrants to the West*
(1837), 107–134; Bradbury, *Travels*, 286.
[2] Kingdom, *America*, 10, 54, 63; Flint, *Letters*, 206; McMaster,
*United States*, V., 152–155; Howells, *Life in Ohio*, 115.
[3] Hall, *Statistics of the West*, 98, 101, 145.
[4] Birkbeck, *Notes on Journey*, 94.

area, preparatory to his farming operations. This consisted in cutting a ring through the bark around the lower portion of the trunk, to prevent the sap from rising. In a short time the withered branches were ready for burning, and in the midst of the stumps the first crop of corn and vegetables was planted. Often the settler did not even burn the girdled trees, but planted his crop under the dead foliage.

In regions nearer to the east, as in western New York, it was sometimes possible to repay a large portion of the cost of clearing by the sale of pot and pearl ashes extracted from the logs, which were brought together into huge piles for burning.[1] This was accomplished by a "log-rolling," under the united efforts of the neighbors, as in the case of the "raising." More commonly in the west the logs were wasted by burning, except such as were split into rails, which, laid one above another, made the zig-zag "worm-fences" for the protection of the fields of the pioneer.

When a clearing was sold to a later comer, fifty or sixty dollars, in addition to the government price of land, was commonly charged for forty acres, enclosed and partly cleared.[2] It was estimated that the cost of a farm of three hundred and twenty acres at the edge of the prairie in Illinois, at this time, would be divided as follows: for one hundred and sixty acres

[1] *Life of Thurlow Weed* (Autobiography), I., 11.
[2] Kingdom, *America*, 10, 54.

of prairie, two hundred dollars; for fencing it into four forty-acre fields with rail-fences, one hundred and sixty dollars; for breaking it up with a plough, two dollars per acre, or three hundred and twenty dollars; eighty acres of timber land and eighty acres of pasture prairie, two hundred dollars. Thus, with cabins, stables, etc., it cost a little over a thousand dollars to secure an improved farm of three hundred and twenty acres.[1] But the mass of the early settlers were too poor to afford such an outlay, and were either squatters within a little clearing, or owners of eighty acres, which they hoped to increase by subsequent purchase. Since they worked with the labor of their own hands and that of their sons, the cash outlay was practically limited to the original cost of the lands and articles of husbandry. The cost of an Indiana farm of eighty acres of land, with two horses, two or three cows, a few hogs and sheep, and farming utensils, was estimated at about four hundred dollars.

The peculiar skill required of the axeman who entered the hardwood forests, together with readiness to undergo the privations of the life, made the backwoodsman in a sense an expert engaged in a special calling.[2] Frequently he was the descendant

---

[1] J. M. Peck, *Guide for Emigrants* (1831), 183–188; cf. Birkbeck (London, 1818), *Letters*, 45, 46, 69–73; S. H. Collins, *Emigrant's Guide;* Tanner (publisher), *View of the Valley of the Miss.* (1834), 232; J. Woods, *Two Years' Residence*, 146, 172.

[2] J. Hall, *Statistics of the West*, 101; cf. Chastellux, *Travels in North America* (London, 1787), I., 44.

of generations of pioneers, who, on successive frontiers, from the neighborhood of the Atlantic coast towards the interior, had cut and burned the forest, fought the Indians, and pushed forward the line of civilization. He bore the marks of the struggle in his face, made sallow by living in the shade of the forest, "shut from the common air," [1] and in a constitution often racked by malarial fever. Dirt and squalor were too frequently found in the squatter's cabin, and education and the refinements of life were denied to him. Often shiftless and indolent, in the intervals between his tasks of forest-felling he was fonder of hunting than of a settled agricultural life. With his rifle he eked out his sustenance, and the peltries furnished him a little ready cash. His few cattle grazed in the surrounding forest, and his hogs fed on its mast.

The backwoodsman of this type represented the outer edge of the advance of civilization. Where settlement was closer, co-operative activity possible, and little villages, with the mill and retail stores, existed, conditions of life were ameliorated, and a better type of pioneer was found. Into such regions circuit-riders and wandering preachers carried the beginnings of church organization, and schools were started. But the frontiersmen proper constituted a moving class, ever ready to sell out their clearings in

[1] Birkbeck, *Notes on Journey*, 105-114.
[2] Babcock, *Forty Years of Pioneer Life* ("Journals and Correspondence of J. M. Peck"), 101.

order to press on to a new frontier, where game more abounded, soil was reported to be better, and where the forest furnished a welcome retreat from the uncongenial encroachments of civilization. If, however, he was thrifty and forehanded, the backwoodsman remained on his clearing, improving his farm and sharing in the change from wilderness life.

Behind the type of the backwoodsman came the type of the pioneer farmer. Equipped with a little capital, he often, as we have seen, purchased the clearing, and thus avoided some of the initial hardships of pioneer life. In the course of a few years, as saw-mills were erected, frame-houses took the place of the log-cabins; the rough clearing, with its stumps, gave way to well-tilled fields; orchards were planted; live-stock roamed over the enlarged clearing; and an agricultural surplus was ready for export. Soon the adventurous speculator offered corner lots in a new town-site, and the rude beginnings of a city were seen.

Thus western occupation advanced in a series of waves:[1] the Indian was sought by the fur-trader; the fur-trader was followed by the frontiersman, whose live-stock exploited the natural grasses and the acorns of the forest; next came the wave of primitive agriculture, followed by more intensive farming

[1] J. M. Peck, *New Guide to the West* (Cincinnati, 1848), chap. iv.; T. Flint, *Geography and Hist. of the Western States*, 350 et seq.; J. Flint, *Letters from America*, 206; cf. Turner, *Significance of the Frontier in American History*, in Am. Hist. Assoc., *Report* 1893, p. 214; McMaster, *United States*, V., 152–160.

and city life. All the stages of social development went on under the eye of the traveller as he passed from the frontier towards the east. Such were the forces which were steadily pushing their way into the American wilderness, as they had pushed for generations.

While thus the frontier folk spread north of the Ohio and up the Missouri, a different movement was in progress in the Gulf region of the west. In the beginning precisely the same type of occupation was to be seen: the poorer classes of southern emigrants cut out their clearings along rivers that flowed to the Gulf and to the lower Mississippi, and, with the opening of this decade, went in increasing numbers into Texas, where enterprising Americans secured concessions from the Mexican government.[1]

Almost all of the most recently occupied area was but thinly settled. It represented the movement of the backwoodsman, with axe and rifle, advancing to the conquest of the forest. But closer to the old settlements a more highly developed agriculture was to be seen. Hodgson, in 1821, describes plantations in northern Alabama in lands ceded by the Indians in 1818. Though settled less than two years, there were within a few miles five schools and four places of worship. One plantation had one hundred acres

---

[1] Garrison, *Texas*, chaps. xiii., xiv.; Wooten (editor), *Comprehensive Hist. of Texas*, I., chaps. viii., ix.; Texas State Hist. Assoc., *Quarterly*, VII., 29, 289; Bugbee, "Texas Frontier," in Southern Hist. Assoc., *Publications*, IV., 106.

in cotton and one hundred and ten in corn, although a year and a half before it was wilderness.[1]

But while this population of log - cabin pioneers was entering the Gulf plains, caravans of slave-holding planters were advancing from the seaboard to the occupation of the cotton-lands of the same region. As the free farmers of the interior had been replaced in the upland country of the south by the slave-holding planters, so now the frontiersmen of the southwest were pushed back from the more fertile lands into the pine hills and barrens. Not only was the pioneer unable to refuse the higher price which was offered him for his clearing, but, in the competitive bidding of the public land sales,[2] the wealthier planter secured the desirable soils. Social forces worked to the same end. When the pioneer invited his slave-holding neighbor to a "raising," it grated on his sense of the fitness of things to have the guest appear with gloves, directing the gang of slaves which he contributed to the function.[3] Little by little, therefore, the old pioneer life tended to retreat to the less desirable lands, leaving the slave-holder in possession of the rich "buck-shot" soils that spread over central Alabama and Mississippi and

[1] Hodgson, *Letters from North Am.*, I., 269; see Riley (editor), "Autobiography of Lincecum," in Miss. Hist. Soc., *Publications*, VIII., 443, for the wanderings of a southern pioneer in the recently opened Indian lands of Georgia and the southwest in these years.

[2] *Northern Ala.* (published by Smith & De Land), 249; Brown, *Hist. of Ala.*, 129–131; Brown, *Lower South*, 24–26.

[3] Smedes, *A Southern Planter*, 67.

the fat alluvium that lined the eastern bank of the Mississippi. Even to-day the counties of dense negro population reveal the results of this movement of segregation.

By the side of the picture of the advance of the pioneer farmer, bearing his household goods in his canvas-covered wagon to his new home across the Ohio, must therefore be placed the picture of the southern planter crossing through the forests of western Georgia, Alabama, and Mississippi, or passing over the free state of Illinois to the Missouri Valley, in his family carriage, with servants, packs of hunting-dogs, and a train of slaves, their nightly camp-fires lighting up the wilderness where so recently the Indian hunter had held possession.[1]

But this new society had a characteristic western flavor. The old patriarchal type of slavery along the seaboard was modified by the western conditions in the midst of which the slave-holding interest was now lodged. Planters, as well as pioneer farmers, were exploiting the wilderness and building a new society under characteristic western influences. Rude strength, a certain coarseness of life, and aggressiveness characterized this society, as it did the whole of the Mississippi Valley.[2] Slavery furnished a new in-

[1] Hodgson, *Letters from North Am.*, I., 138; *Niles' Register*, XLIV., 222; Smedes, *A Southern Planter*, 52–54; Flint, *Geography and History of the Western States*, II., 350, 379; Bernhard, Duke of Saxe-Weimar, *Travels*, II., chaps. xvi., xvii.

[2] Baldwin, *Flush Times in Ala.*; cf. Gilmer, *Sketches of Georgia, etc.*

gredient for western forces to act upon.   The system took on a more commercial tinge: the plantation had to be cleared and made profitable as a purely business enterprise.

The slaves were purchased in considerable numbers from the older states instead of being inherited in the family.  Slave-dealers passed to the southwest, with their coffles of negroes brought from the outworn lands of the old south.  It was estimated in 1832 that Virginia annually exported six thousand slaves for sale to other states.[1]  An English traveller reported in 1823 that every year from ten to fifteen thousand slaves were sold from the states of Delaware, Maryland, and Virginia, and sent to the south.[2]  At the same time, illicit importation of slaves through New Orleans reached an amount estimated at from ten to fifteen thousand a year.[3]  It was not until the next decade that this incoming tide of slaves reached its height, but by 1830 it was clearly marked and was already transforming the southwest.  Mississippi doubled the number of her slaves in the decade, and Alabama nearly trebled hers.  In the same period the number of slaves of Maryland, Virginia, and North Carolina increased but slightly.

As the discussion of the south has already made clear, the explanation of this transformation of the

[1] Collins, *Domestic Slave Trade*, 50.
[2] Blane, *Excursion through U. S.*, 226; Hodgson, *Letters from North Am.*, I., 194.          [3] Collins, *Domestic Slave Trade*, 44.

southwest into a region of slave-holding planters lies
in the spread of cotton into the Gulf plains.  In 1811
this region raised but five million pounds of cotton;
ten years later its product was sixty million pounds;
and in 1826 its fields were white with a crop of
over one hundred and fifty million pounds.  It soon
outstripped the seaboard south.  Alabama, which
had practically no cotton crop in 1811, and only
ten million pounds in 1821, had in 1834 eighty-five
million pounds,[1] a larger crop than either South
Carolina or Georgia.

Soon after 1830 the differences between the
northern and southern portions of the Mississippi
Valley were still further accentuated.  (1) From New
York and New England came a tide of settlement,
in the thirties, which followed the Erie Canal and
the Great Lakes, and began to occupy the prairie
lands which had been avoided by the southern axe-
men.  This region then became an extension of the
greater New England already to be seen in New
York.  (2) The southern pioneers in the northwest
formed a transitional zone between this northern area
and the slave states south of the Ohio.  (3) In the
Gulf plains a greater south was in process of formation, but by no means completely established.  As
yet it was a mixture of pioneer and planter, slave
and free, profoundly affected by its western traits.[2]

[1] See table of cotton crop, *ante*, p. 47.
[2] Curry, "A Settlement in East Ala.," in *Am. Hist. Magazine*,
II., 203.

The different states of the south were steadily sending in bands of colonists. In Alabama, for example,
the Georgians settled, as a rule, in the east; the
Tennesseeans, moving from the great bend of the
Tennessee River, were attracted to the northern and
middle section; and the Virginians and Carolinians
went to the west and southwest, following the bottom-lands near the rivers.[1]

---

[1] Brown, *Hist. of Ala,,* 129, 130; *Northern Ala.* (published by
Smith & De Land), pt. iv., 243 et seq.

# CHAPTER VII

## WESTERN COMMERCE AND IDEALS

### (1820–1830)

BY 1820 the west had developed the beginnings of many of the cities which have since ruled over the region. Buffalo and Detroit were hardly more than villages until the close of this period. They waited for the rise of steam navigation on the Great Lakes and for the opening of the prairies. Cleveland, also, was but a hamlet during most of the decade; but by 1830 the construction of the canal connecting the Cuyahoga with the Scioto increased its prosperity, and its harbor began to profit by its natural advantages.[1] Chicago and Milwaukee were mere fur - trading stations in the Indian country. Pittsburg, at the head of the Ohio, was losing its old pre-eminence as the gateway to the west, but was finding recompense in the development of its manufactures. By 1830 its population was about twelve thousand.[2] Foundries, rolling - mills, nail - factories, steam-engine shops, and distilleries were busily at

---

[1] Whittlesey, *Early Hist. of Cleveland*, 456; Kennedy, *Hist. of Cleveland*, chap. viii.

[2] Thurston, *Pittsburg and Allegheny in the Centennial Year*, 61.

work, and the city, dingy with the smoke of soft coal, was already dubbed the "young Manchester" or the "Birmingham" of America. By 1830 Wheeling had intercepted much of the overland trade and travel to the Ohio, profiting by the old National Road and the wagon trade from Baltimore.[1]

Cincinnati was rapidly rising to the position of the "Queen City of the West." Situated where the river reached with a great bend towards the interior of the northwest, in the rich farming country between the two Miamis, and opposite the Licking River, it was the commercial centre of a vast and fertile region of Ohio and Kentucky;[2] and by 1830, with a population of nearly twenty-five thousand souls, it was the largest city of the west, with the exception of New Orleans. The centre of steamboat-building, it also received extensive imports of goods from the east and exported the surplus crops of Ohio and adjacent parts of Kentucky. Its principal industry, however, was pork-packing, from which it won the name of "Porkopolis"[3] Louisville, at the falls of the Ohio, was an important place of trans-shipment, and the export centre for large quantities of tobacco. There were considerable manufactures of rope and bagging, products of the Kentucky hemp-fields; and new cotton and woollen factories

---

[1] Martin, *Gazetteer of Va.*, 407.

[2] Melish, *Information to Emigrants*, 108.

[3] Drake and Mansfield, *Cincinnati in 1826*, p. 70; *Winter in the West*, I., 115.

were struggling for existence.[1]   St. Louis occupied a unique position, as the entrepôt of the important fur-trade of the upper Mississippi and the vast water system of the Missouri, as well as the outfitting-point for the Missouri settlements.   It was the capital of the far west, and the commercial centre for Illinois. Its population at the close of the decade was about six thousand.

Only a few villages lay along the Mississippi below St. Louis until the traveller reached New Orleans, the emporium of the whole Mississippi Valley.   As yet the direct effect of the Erie Canal was chiefly limited to the state of New York.   The great bulk of western exports passed down the tributaries of the Mississippi to this city, which was, therefore, the centre of foreign exports for the valley, as well as the port from which the coastwise trade in the products of the whole interior departed.   In 1830 its population was nearly fifty thousand.

The rise of an agricultural surplus was transforming the west and preparing a new influence in the nation.   It was this surplus and the demand for markets that developed the cities just mentioned. As they grew, the price of land in their neighborhood increased; roads radiated into the surrounding country; and farmers, whose crops had been almost worthless from the lack of transportation facilities, now found it possible to market their surplus at a

[1] Durrett, *Centenary of Louisville* (Filson Club, *Publications*, No. 8), 50–101; *Louisville Directory, 1832*, p. 131.

small profit.  While the west was thus learning the
advantages of a home market, the extension of cotton and sugar cultivation in the south and southwest gave it a new and valuable market.  More
and more, the planters came to rely upon the northwest for their food supplies and for the mules and
horses for their fields.  Cotton became the engross-
ing interest of the plantation belt, and, while the
full effects of this differentiation of industry did not
appear in the decade of this volume, the beginnings
were already visible.[1]   In 1835, Pitkin[2] reckoned
the value of the domestic and foreign exports of the
interior as far in excess of the whole exports of the
United States in 1790.  Within forty years the development of the interior had brought about the
economic independence of the United States.

During most of the decade the merchandise to
supply the interior was brought laboriously across
the mountains by the Pennsylvania turnpikes and
the old National Road; or, in the case of especially
heavy freight, was carried along the Atlantic coast
into the gulf and up the Mississippi and Ohio by
steamboats.  The cost of transportation in the
wagon trade from Philadelphia to Pittsburg and
Baltimore to Wheeling placed a heavy tax upon the
consumer.[3]  In 1817 the freight charge from Philadelphia to Pittsburg was sometimes as high as seven

---

[1] Callender, " Early Transportation and Banking Enterprises
of the States," in *Quarterly Journal of Econ.*, XVII., 3–54.

[2] Pitkin, *Statistical View* (1835), 534.

[3] *Niles' Register*, XX., 180.

to ten dollars a hundredweight; a few years later
it became from four to six dollars; and in 1823 it
had fallen to three dollars. It took a month to
wagon merchandise from Baltimore to central Ohio.
Transportation companies, running four-horse freight
wagons, conducted a regular business on these turnpikes between the eastern and western states. In
1820 over three thousand wagons ran between Philadelphia and Pittsburg, transporting merchandise
valued at about eighteen million dollars annually.[1]

The construction of the National Road reduced
freight rates to nearly one-half what they were at
the close of the War of 1812; and the introduction of
steam navigation from New Orleans up the Mississippi cut water-rates by that route to one-third of
the former charge.[2]   Nevertheless, there was a crying
need for internal improvements, and particularly for
canals, to provide an outlet for the increasing products of the west. "Even in the country where I
reside, not eighty miles from tidewater," said
Tucker,[3] of Virginia, in 1818, "it takes the farmer
one bushel of wheat to pay the expense of carrying
two to a seaport town."

[1] Birkbeck, *Journey from Va.*, 128; Ogden, *Letters from the
West*, 8; Cobbett, *Year's Residence*, 337; Evans, *Pedestrious
Tour*, 145; *Philadelphia in 1824*, 45; Searight, *Old Pike*, 107,
112; Mills, *Treatise on Inland Navigation* (1820), 89, 90, 93,
95–97; *Journal of Polit. Econ.*, VIII., 36.
[2] *Annals of Cong.*, 18 Cong., 1 Sess., I., 991; cf. Fearon, *Sketches*,
260; *Niles' Register*, XXV., 95; *Cincinnati Christian Journal*, July
27, 1830.        [3] *Annals of Cong.*, 15 Cong., 1 Sess., I., 1126.

The bulk of the crop, as compared with its value, practically prevented transportation by land farther than a hundred miles.[1] It is this that helps to explain the attention which the interior first gave to making whiskey and raising live-stock; the former carried the crop in a small bulk with high value, while the live-stock could walk to a market. Until after the War of 1812, the cattle of the Ohio Valley were driven to the seaboard, chiefly to Philadelphia or Baltimore. Travellers were astonished to see on the highway droves of four or five thousand hogs, going to an eastern market. It was estimated that over a hundred thousand hogs were driven east annually from Kentucky alone. Kentucky hog-drivers also passed into Tennessee, Virginia, and the Carolinas with their droves.[2] The swine lived on the nuts and acorns of the forest; thus they were peculiarly suited to pioneer conditions. At first the cattle were taken to the plantations of the Potomac to fatten for Baltimore and Philadelphia, much in the same way that, in recent times, the cattle of the Great Plains are brought to the feeding-grounds in the corn belt of Kansas, Nebraska, and Iowa.[3] Towards the close of the decade, however, the feeding-grounds shifted into Ohio, and the pork-packing industry, as we have seen, found its centre at Cin-

[1] McMaster, *United States*, III., 464.
[2] *Life of Ephraim Cutler*, 89; Birkbeck, *Journey*, 24; Blane, *Excursion through U. S.* (London, 1824), 90; *Atlantic Monthly*, XXVI., 170.
[3] Michaux, *Travels*, 191: Palmer, *Journal of Travels*, 36.

cinnati,[1] the most important source of supply for
the hams and bacon and salt pork which passed
down the Mississippi to furnish a large share of the
plantation food.  From Kentucky and the rest of
the Ohio Valley droves of mules and horses passed
through the Tennessee Valley to the south to supply
the plantations.  Statistics at Cumberland Gap for
1828 gave the value of live-stock passing the turnpike gate there at $1,167,000.[2]  Senator Hayne, of
South Carolina, declared that in 1824 the south was
supplied from the west, through Saluda Gap, with
live-stock, horses, cattle, and hogs to the amount of
over a million dollars a year.[3]

But the outlet from the west over the roads to
the east and south was but a subordinate element
in the internal commerce.  Down the Mississippi
floated a multitude of heavily freighted craft: lumber rafts from the Allegheny, the old-time arks, with
cattle, flour, and bacon, hay-boats, keel-boats, and
skiffs, all mingled with the steamboats which plied
the western waters.[4]  Flatboatmen, raftsmen, and
deck-hands constituted a turbulent and reckless
population, living on the country through which
they passed, fighting and drinking in true "half-

[1] Hall, *Statistics of the West* (1836), 145–147.
[2] *Emigrants' and Travellers' Guide to the West* (1834), 194.
[3] Speech in Senate in 1832, *Register of Debates in Cong.*, VIII.,
pt. i., 80; cf. *Annals of Cong.*, 18 Cong., 1 Sess., I., 1411.
[4] Flint, *Recollections of the Last Ten Years*, 101–110; E. S.
Thomas, *Reminiscences*, I., 290–293; Hall, *Statistics of the West*
(1836), 236; Howells, *Life in Ohio*, 85; Schultz, *Travels*, 129;
Hulbert, *Historic Highways*, IX., chaps. iii., iv., v.

horse, half-alligator" style.   Prior to the steamboat,
all of the commerce from New Orleans to the upper
country was carried on in about twenty barges,
averaging a hundred tons each, and making one trip
a year.   Although the steamboat did not drive out
the other craft, it revolutionized the commerce of
the river.   Whereas it had taken the keel-boats
thirty to forty days to descend from Louisville to
New Orleans, and about ninety days to ascend the
fifteen hundred miles of navigation by poling and
warping up-stream, the steamboat had shortened
the time, by 1822, to seven days down and sixteen
days up.[1]   As the steamboats ascended the various
tributaries of the Mississippi to gather the products
of the growing west, the pioneers came more and
more to realize the importance of the invention.
They resented the idea of the monopoly which Ful-
ton and Livingston wished to enforce prior to the
decision of Chief-Justice Marshall, in the case of
Gibbons *vs*. Ogden—a decision of vital interest to
the whole interior.[2]

They saw in the steamboat a symbol of their own
development.   A writer in the *Western Monthly Review*,[3] unconsciously expressed the very spirit of the

[1] *Annals of Cong.*, 17 Cong., 2 Sess., 407; McMaster, *United
States*, V., 166; *National Gazette*, September 26, 1823 (list of
steamboats, rates of passage, estimate of products); Blane,
*Excursion through the U. S.*, 119; *Niles' Register*, XXV., 95.

[2] Thomas, *Travels through the Western Country*, 62; *Alexandria
Herald*, June 23, 1817.

[3] Timothy Flint's *Western Monthly Review* (May, 1827), I.,
25; William Bullock, *Sketch of a Journey*, 132.

self-contented, hustling, materialistic west in these words: "An Atlantic cit, who talks of us under the name of backwoodsmen, would not believe, that such fairy structures of oriental gorgeousness and splendor, as the Washington, the Florida, the Walk in the Water, the Lady of the Lake, etc. etc., had ever existed in the imaginative brain of a romancer, much less, that they were actually in existence, rushing down the Mississippi, as on the wings of the wind, or plowing up between the forests, and walking against the mighty current 'as things of life,' bearing speculators, merchants, dandies, fine ladies, every thing real, and every thing affected, in the form of humanity, with pianos, and stocks of novels, and cards, and dice, and flirting, and love-making, and drinking, and champaigne, and on the deck, perhaps, three hundred fellows, who have seen alligators, and neither fear whiskey, nor gun-powder. A steamboat, coming from New Orleans, brings to the remotest villages of our streams, and the very doors of the cabins, a little Paris, a section of Broadway, or a slice of Philadelphia, to ferment in the minds of our young people, the innate propensity for fashions and finery. Within a day's journey of us, three distinct canals are in respectable progress towards completion. . . . . Cincinnati will soon be the centre of the 'celestial empire,' as the Chinese say; and instead of encountering the storms, the sea sickness, and dangers of a passage from the gulf of Mexico to the Atlantic, whenever the Erie canal shall be com-

pleted, the opulent southern planters will take their
families, their dogs and parrots, through a world of
forests, from New Orleans to New York, giving us
a call by the way. When they are more acquainted
with us, their voyage will often terminate here."

By 1830 the produce which reached New Orleans
from the Mississippi Valley amounted to about
twenty-six million dollars.[1] In 1822 three million
dollars' worth of goods was estimated to have passed
the Falls of the Ohio on the way to market, repre-
senting much of the surplus of the Ohio Valley. Of
this, pork amounted to $1,000,000 in value; flour
to $900,000; tobacco to $600,000; and whiskey to
$500,000.[2] The inventory of products reveals the
Mississippi Valley as a vast colonial society, producing the raw materials of a simple and primitive
agriculture. The beginnings of manufacture in the
cities, however, promised to bring about a movement for industrial independence in the west. In
spite of evidences of growing wealth, there was such
a decline in agricultural prices that, for the farmer
who did not live on the highways of commerce, it
was almost unprofitable to raise wheat for the market.

An Ohio pioneer of this time relates that at the
beginning of the decade fifty cents a bushel was a

---

[1] *Quarterly Journal of Economics*, XVII., 20; Pitkin, *Statistical
View* (ed. of 1835), 534–536.

[2] *National Republican*, March 7, 1823; cf. *National Gazette*,
September 26, 1823; Blane, *Excursion through the U. S.*, 119.

great price for wheat at the river; and as two horses and a man were required for four days to make the journey of thirty-five miles to the Ohio, in good weather, with thirty-five or forty bushels of wheat, and a great deal longer if the roads were bad, it was not to be expected that the farmer could realize more than twenty-five cents in cash for it. But there was no sale for it in cash. The nominal price for it in trade was usually thirty cents.[1] When wheat brought twenty-five cents a bushel in Illinois in 1825, it sold at over eighty cents in Petersburg, Virginia, and flour was six dollars a barrel at Charleston, South Carolina.[2]

These are the economic conditions that assist in understanding the political attitude of western leaders like Henry Clay and Andrew Jackson. The cry of the east for protection to infant industries was swelled by the little cities of the west, and the demand for a home market found its strongest support beyond the Alleghanies. Internal improvements and lower rates of transportation were essential to the prosperity of the westerners. Largely a debtor class, in need of capital, credit, and an expansion of the currency, they resented attempts to restrain the reckless state banking which their optimism fostered.

But the political ideals and actions of the west

---

[1] Howells, *Life in Ohio*, 138; see M'Culloch, *Commercial Dictionary*, I., 683, 684; Hazard, *U.S. Commercial and Statistical Register*, I., 251; O'Reilly, *Sketches of Rochester*, 362.

[2] *Niles' Register*, XXIX, 165.

are explained by social quite as much as by economic forces. It was certain that this society, where equality and individualism flourished, where assertive democracy was supreme, where impatience with the old order of things was a ruling passion, would demand control of the government, would resent the rule of the trained statesmen and official classes, and would fight nominations by congressional caucus and the continuance of presidential dynasties. Besides its susceptibility to change, the west had generated, from its Indian fighting, forest-felling, and expansion, a belligerency and a largeness of outlook with regard to the nation's territorial destiny. As the pioneer, widening the ring-wall of his clearing in the midst of the stumps and marshes of the wilderness, had a vision of the lofty buildings and crowded streets of a future city, so the west as a whole developed ideals of the future of the common man, and of the grandeur and expansion of the nation.

The west was too new a section to have developed educational facilities to any large extent. The pioneers' poverty, as well as the traditions of the southern interior from which they so largely came, discouraged extensive expenditures for public schools.[1] In Kentucky and Tennessee the more prosperous planters had private tutors, often New England collegians, for their children. For example, Amos Kendall, later postmaster-general, was tutor

[1] McMaster, *United States*, V., 370–372.

in Henry Clay's family. So-called colleges were numerous, some of them fairly good. In 1830 a writer made a survey of higher education in the whole western country and reported twenty-eight institutions, with seven hundred and sixty-six graduates and fourteen hundred and thirty undergraduates. Less than forty thousand volumes were recorded in the college and "social" libraries of the entire Mississippi Valley.[1] Very few students went from the west to eastern colleges; but the foundations of public education had been laid in the land grants for common schools and universities. For the present this fund was generally misappropriated and wasted, or worse. Nevertheless, the ideal of a democratic education was held up in the first constitution of Indiana, making it the duty of the legislature to provide for "a general system of education, ascending in a regular graduation from township schools to a State university, wherein tuition shall be gratis, and equally open to all." [2]

Literature did not flourish in the west, although the newspaper press [3] followed closely after the retreating savage; many short-lived periodicals were founded,[4] and writers like Timothy Flint and James

---

[1] Am. Quarterly Register (November, 1830), III., 127–131.

[2] Poore, Charters and Constitutions, pt. i., 508 (art. ix., sec. 2 of Constitution of Ind., 1816).

[3] W. H. Perrin, Pioneer Press of Ky. (Filson Club Publications).

[4] Venable, Beginnings of Literary Culture in the Ohio Valley, chap. iii.; W. B. Cairns, Development of American Literature from 1815 to 1833, in University of Wis., Bulletin (Phil. and Lit. Series), I., 60–63.

Hall were not devoid of literary ability.   Lexington, in Kentucky, and Cincinnati made rival claims to be the "Athens of the West."   In religion, the west was partial to those denominations which prevailed in the democratic portions of the older sections. Baptists, Methodists, and Presbyterians took the lead.[1]

The religious life of the west frequently expressed itself in the form of emotional gatherings, in the camp-meetings and the revivals, where the rude, unlettered, but deeply religious backwoods preachers moved their large audiences with warnings of the wrath of God.   Muscular Christianity was personified in the circuit-rider, who, with his saddle-bags and Bible, threaded the dreary trails through the forest from settlement to settlement.   From the responsiveness of the west to religious excitement, it was easy to perceive that here was a region capable of being swayed in large masses by enthusiasm. These traits of the camp-meeting were manifested later in political campaigns.

Thus this society beyond the mountains, recruited from all the older states and bound together by the Mississippi, constituted a region swayed for the most part by common impulses.   By the march of the westerners away from their native states to the

---

[1] *Am. Quarterly Register*, III., 135 (November, 1830);  Schermerhorn and Mills, *View of U.S. West of the Alleghany Mountains* (Hartford, 1814);  *Home Missionary*, 1829, pp. 78, 79;  1830, p. 172;  McMaster, *United States*, IV., 550–555.

public domain of the nation, and by their organization as territories of the United States, they lost that state particularism which distinguished many of the old commonwealths of the coast. The section was nationalistic and democratic to the core. The west admired the self-made man and was ready to follow its hero with the enthusiasm of a section more responsive to personality than to the programmes of trained statesmen. It was a self-confident section, believing in its right to share in government, and troubled by no doubts of its capacity to rule.

# CHAPTER VIII

## THE FAR WEST

### (1820–1830)

IN the decade of which we write, more than two-thirds of the present area of the United States was Indian country—a vast wilderness stretching from the Great Lakes to the Pacific Ocean. East of the Mississippi, the pioneers had taken possession of the hardwoods of the Ohio, but over the prairies between them and the Great Lakes the wild flowers and grasses grew rank and undisturbed. To the north, across Michigan and Wisconsin, spread the sombre, white-pine wilderness, interlaced with hardwoods, which swept in ample zone along the Great Lakes, and, in turn, faded into the treeless expanse of the prairies beyond the Mississippi. To the south, in the Gulf plains, Florida was, for the most part, a wilderness; and, as we have seen, great areas of Mississippi, Alabama, and Georgia were still unoccupied by civilization.

West of the Mississippi lay a huge new world—an ocean of grassy prairie that rolled far to the west, till it reached the zone where insufficient rainfall transformed it into the arid plains, which stretched

away to the foot-hills of the Rocky Mountains.
Over this vast waste, equal in area to France, Ger-
many, Spain, Portugal, Austria-Hungary, Italy, Den-
mark, and Belgium combined, a land where now
wheat and corn fields and grazing herds produce
much of the food supply for the larger part of
America and for great areas of Europe, roamed the
bison and the Indian hunter. Beyond this, the
Rocky Mountains and the Sierra Nevadas, enclos-
ing high plateaus, heaved up their vast bulk through
nearly a thousand miles from east to west, concealing
untouched treasures of silver and gold. The great
valleys of the Pacific coast in Oregon and California
held but a sparse population of Indian traders, a
few Spanish missions, and scattered herdsmen.

At the beginning of Monroe's presidency, the
Pacific coast was still in dispute between England,
Spain, Russia, and the United States. Holding to
all of Texas, Spain also raised her flag over her
colonists who spread from Mexico along the valley
of the Rio Grande to Santa Fé, and she claimed the
great unoccupied wilderness of mountain and desert
comprising the larger portion of Colorado, Arizona,
Utah, and Nevada, as well as California. In the
decade of 1820–1830, fur-traders threaded the dark
and forbidding defiles of the mountains, unfolded
the secrets of the Great Basin, and found their way
across the Rockies to California and Oregon; the
government undertook diplomatic negotiations to
safeguard American rights on the Pacific, and ex-

tended a line of forts well into the Indian country; while far-seeing statesmen on the floor of Congress challenged the nation to fulfil its destiny by
planting its settlements boldly beyond the Rocky
Mountains on the shores of the Pacific. It was a
call to the lodgment of American power on that
ocean, the mastery of which is to determine the
future relations of Asiatic and European civiliza-
tions.[1]

A survey of the characteristics of the life of the
far west shows that, over Wisconsin and the larger
part of Michigan, the Indian trade was still carried
on by methods introduced by the French.[2] Astor's
American Fur Company practically controlled the
trade of Wisconsin and Michigan. It shipped its
guns and ammunition, blankets, gewgaws, and
whiskey from Mackinac to some one of the principal
posts, where they were placed in the light birch
canoes, manned by French boatmen, and sent
throughout the forests to the minor trading-posts.
Practically all of the Indian villages of the tributaries of the Great Lakes and of the upper Mississippi were regularly visited by the trader. The
trading-posts became the nuclei of later settlements;
the traders' trails grew into the early roads, and
their portages marked out the location for canals.

[1] Cf. Babcock, *Am. Nationality* (*Am. Nation*, XIII.), chap.
xv.

[2] Masson, *Le Bourgeois de Nordwest;* Parkman, *Old Ré-
gime.*

Little by little the fur-trade was undermining the Indian society and paving the way for the entrance of civilization.[1]

In the War of 1812, all along the frontier of Indiana, Illinois, and Missouri, as well as in the southwest, the settlers had drawn back into forts, much as in the early days of the occupation of Kentucky and Tennessee, and the traders and the Indians had been entirely under the influence of Great Britain. In the negotiations at Ghent, that power, having captured the American forts at Mackinac, Prairie du Chien, and Chicago, tried to incorporate in the treaty a provision for a neutral belt, or buffer state, of Indian territory in the northwest, to separate Canada from the United States.[2] Taught by this experience, the United States, at the close of the war, passed laws excluding aliens from conducting the Indian trade, and erected forts at Green Bay, Prairie du Chien, Chicago, and Fort Snelling. By order of Secretary of War Calhoun, Governor Cass, of Michigan, made an expedition in 1820 along the south shore of Lake Superior into Minnesota, to compel the removal of English flags and to replace British by American influence.[3] At the same time, an expedition under Major Long visited

[1] Turner, *Character and Influence of the Fur Trade in Wis.*, in Wis. Hist. Soc., *Transactions*, 1889.

[2] Cf. Babcock, *Am. Nationality* (*Am. Nation*, XIII.), chap. x.

[3] Schoolcraft, *Hist. of Indian Tribes*, VI., 422; *ibid.*, *Narrative Journal;* "Doty's Journal," in Wis. Hist. Soc., *Collections*, XIII., 163.

125°    120°    115°    110°

B R I T
LINE

ROCKY

Columbia R.

Flatheads
1829

Ft. Nisqually
Cayuse
Coeur d'Alene
J.S.SMITH

Ft. Chatsop
(Astoria)
Ft. Vancouver
Columbia
Nez Percés
Ft. Walla Walla
U N O

U. S. SMITH

Pierre's Hole
Jackson Hole
Wind R.

Umpqua
OREGON
Ft. Boise
J. S. SMITH 1829
Ft. Hall
Ft. Bonneville
Sublette's

ASTORIA R.
Mt. Shasta
S N A K E S
(Shoshoni)
OREGON TRAIL

PACIFIC

Bear

Cache Valley
Ogden's Hole
Utah

Great Salt Lake
Browns Hole
Ft. Uintah
New

LATER
CALIFORNIA
TRAIL
PA ROUTE
Humboldt R.
(MAY AND JUNE)

Utah Lake
Ashley's Post
Old

L. Tahoe
Sacramento R.
SMITH 1826
Green R.

J. S. SMITH 1827
Sevier Lake
Grand R.

San Francisco
San Jose
Monterey
SMITH 1827

AND
SMITH 1826
Colorado R.
Navaho
San

Santa Barbara
SPANISH TRAIL
J. S. SMITH 1826

Mohave
Los Angeles SMITH
SMITH 1826
Apache
Colorado R.
Gila R.

San Diego SMITH

M E X I C A N

**WESTERN INDIANS**
**TRADING POSTS**
**AND**
**ROUTES OF TRAVEL**
**1820-1835**
**Based on Chittenden's American Fur Trade**

SCALE OF MILES

0   50   100    200    300    400

120°    115°    110°   Longitude

45°
40°
35°
30°

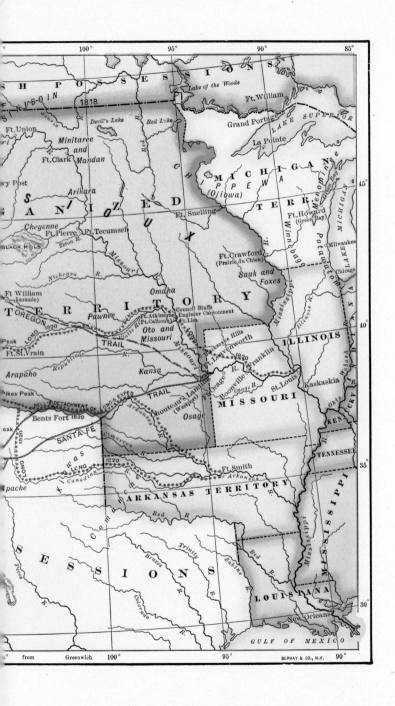

the upper waters of the Minnesota River on a similar errand.[1] An agent who was sent by the government to investigate the Indian conditions of this region in 1820, recommended that the country now included in Wisconsin, northern Michigan, and part of Minnesota should be an Indian reservation, from which white settlements should be excluded, with the idea that ultimately the Indian population should be organized as a state of the Union.[2]

The Creeks and Cherokees, Choctaws, and Chickasaws of the Gulf region were more advanced towards civilization than the Indians of the northwest. While the latter lived chiefly by hunting and trapping, the southwestern Indians had developed a considerable agriculture and a sedentary life. For that very reason, however, they were the more obnoxious to the pioneers who pressed upon their territory from all sides; and, as we shall see, strenuous efforts were made to remove them beyond the Mississippi.

Throughout the decade the problem of the future of the Indians east of this river was a pressing one, and the secretaries of war, to whose department the management of the tribes belonged, made many plans and recommendations for their civilization, improvement, and assimilation. But the advance of the frontier broke down the efforts to preserve

[1] Keating, *Long's Expedition.*
[2] Morse, *Report on Indian Affairs in 1820.*

and incorporate these primitive people in the dominant American society.[1]

Across the Mississippi, settlement of the whites had, in the course of this decade, pushed up the Missouri well towards the western boundary of the state, and, as the map of the settlement shows, had made advances towards the interior in parts of Arkansas as well. But these were only narrow wedges of civilization thrust into the Indian country, the field of operations of the fur-traders. Successors to the French traders who had followed the rivers and lakes of Canada far towards the interior, the Hudson's Bay Company, and the Northwest Company under British charters had carried their operations from the Great Lakes to the Pacific long before Americans entered the west. As early as 1793, Alexander Mackenzie reached the Pacific from the Great Lakes by way of Canada.[2] The year before, an English ship under Vancouver explored the northwestern coast in the hope of finding a passage by sea to the north and east. He missed the mouth of the Columbia, which in the following month was entered by an American, Captain Gray, who ascended the river twenty miles. The expedition of Lewis and Clark, 1804–1806, made the first crossing of the continent from territory of the United States,

---

[1] *Am. State Paps., Indian*, II., 275, 542, et passim; J. Q. Adams, *Memoirs*, VII., 89, 90, 92; Richardson, *Messages and Papers*, II., 234, et seq.

[2] Mackenzie, *Travels*.

and strengthened the claims of that country to the region of the Columbia.[1]

John Jacob Astor's attempt to plant a trading-post at Astoria[2] had been defeated by the treachery of his men, who, at the opening of the War of 1812, turned the post over to the British Northwest fur-traders. The two great branches of the Columbia, the one reaching up into Canada, and the other pushing far into the Rocky Mountains, on the American side, constituted lines of advance for the rival forces of England and the United States in the struggle for the Oregon country. The British traders rapidly made themselves masters of the region.[3] By 1825 the Hudson's Bay Company monopolized the English fur-trade and was established at Fort George (as Astoria was rechristened), Fort Walla-Walla, and Fort Vancouver, near the mouth of the Willamette. Here, for twenty-two years, its agent, Dr. John McLoughlin, one of the many Scotchmen who have built up England's dominion in the new countries of the globe, ruled like a benevolent monarch over the realms of the British traders.[4] From these Oregon posts as centres they passed as far south as the region of Great Salt Lake, in what was then Mexican territory.

While the British traders occupied the northwest coast the Spaniards held California. Although they

[1] Cf. Channing, *Jeffersonian System* (*Am. Nation*, XII.), chap. vii.    [2] Irving, *Astoria*.    [3] Coues (editor), *Greater Northwest*.
[4] Schafer, *Pacific Northwest*, chap. viii.

established the settlement of San Francisco in the
year of the declaration of American independence,
settlement grew but slowly.   The presidios, the missions, with their Indian neophytes, and the cattle
ranches feebly occupied this imperial domain.   Yankee trading-ships gathered hides and tallow at San
Diego, Monterey, and San Francisco; Yankee whalers,
seal-hunters, and fur-traders sought the northwest
coast and passed on to China to bring back to Boston
and Salem the products of the far east.[1]   But Spain's
possession was not secure.   The genius for expansion which had already brought the Russians to
Alaska drew them down the coast even to California,
and in 1812 they established Fort Ross at Bodega
Bay, a few miles below the mouth of Russian River,
north of San Francisco.   This settlement, as well as
the lesser one in the Farallone Islands, endured for
nearly a generation, a menace to Spain's ascendency
in California in the chaotic period when her colonies
were in revolt.[2]

In the mean time, from St. Louis as a centre,
American fur-traders, the advance-guard of settlement, were penetrating into the heart of the vast
wilderness between the Mississippi and the Pacific
coast.[3]   This was a more absolute Indian domain
than was the region between the Alleghanies and
the Mississippi at the end of the seventeenth cen-

[1] R. H. Dana, *Two Years before the Mast.*
[2] H. H. Bancroft, *Hist. of California,* II., 628; Hittel, *Hist. of
California.*      [3] Chittenden, *Am. Fur Trade of the Far West.*

tury—an empire of mountains and prairies, where
the men of the Stone Age watched with alarm the
first crawling waves of that tide of civilization that
was to sweep them away. The savage population
of the far west has already been described in an
earlier volume of this series.[1]

With the development of the Rocky Mountain
Fur Company, the most flourishing period of the St.
Louis trade in the far west began. The founder of
this company was William H. Ashley, a Virginian.
Between the autumn of 1823 and the spring of the
next year, one of his agents erected a post at the
mouth of the Bighorn, and sent out his trappers
through the Green River valley, possibly even to
Great Salt Lake. A detachment of this party found
the gateway of the Rocky Mountains, through the
famous South Pass by way of the Sweetwater branch
of the north fork of the Platte. This pass commanded the routes to the great interior basin and
to the Pacific Ocean. What Cumberland Gap was
in the advance of settlement across the Alleghanies, South Pass was in the movement across
the Rocky Mountains; through it passed the
later Oregon and California trails to the Pacific
coast.

On the lower Missouri and at various places in the

[1] Farrand, *Basis of Am. Hist.* (*Am. Nation,* II.), chaps. viii.,
ix., xii.; see also chap. iv. On the location of the Indians, see
map, p. 309; Chittenden, *Am. Fur Trade,* II., pt. v., chaps. viii.,
ix., x.; Bureau of Ethnology, *Seventh Annual Report.*

interior,[1] stockaded trading-posts were erected by
the Rocky Mountain Fur Company and its rival, the
American Fur Company. In these posts the old
fur-trade life of the past went on, with French half-
breed packmen and boatmen, commanded by the
bourgeois. But in some of the best trading-grounds
the savages declined to permit the erection of posts,
and so, under Ashley's leadership, bands of mounted
American trappers, chiefly Kentuckians, Tennesseeans, and Missourians, were sent out to hunt and
trade in the rich beaver valleys of the mountains.
The Rocky Mountain trappers were the successors
to the Alleghany frontiersmen, carrying on in this
new region, where nature wrought on a vaster plan,
the old trapping life which their ancestors had carried on through Cumberland Gap in the "dark and
bloody ground" of Kentucky.

Yearly, in June and July, a rendezvous was held
in the mountains, to which the brigades of trappers
returned with the products of their hunt, to receive
the supplies for the coming year. Here, also, came
Indian tribes to trade, and bands of free trappers,
lone wanderers in the mountains, to sell their furs
and secure supplies.[2] The rendezvous was usually
some verdure-clad valley or park set in the midst
of snow-capped mountains, a paradise of game.
Such places were Jackson's Hole, at the foot of the
lofty Tetons, Pierre's Hole, not far away, and

[1] See map, p. 114; Chittenden, *Am. Fur Trade*, I., 44–51 (describes posts, etc.).    [2] Irving, *Bonneville*, chap. i.

Ogden's Hole, near the present site of Ogden, in Utah. Great Salt Lake was probably first visited by Bridger in 1824, and the next year a party of Hudson Bay trappers were expelled by Americans who took possession of their furs. In 1826, Ashley carried a six-pounder cannon on wheels to Utah Lake for the defence of his post.

A new advance of the American fur-trader was made when Jedediah Smith succeeded Ashley as the leader in Rocky Mountain trade and exploration. In 1826 he left the Salt Lake rendezvous with a party of trappers to learn the secrets of the lands between the Rocky Mountains and the Pacific Ocean. Proceeding to the southwest along the Virgin River, Smith descended it to the Colorado, and crossed the desert to San Diego, California. Here, by the intercession of a Yankee captain then in that port, he obtained supplies from the Spaniards, and turned to the northwest, travelling parallel to the coast for some three hundred miles to wintering grounds on the headwaters of the San Joaquin and the Merced. Leaving most of his party behind, he crossed the mountains, by a route south of the Humboldt, and returned to Great Salt Lake.

Almost immediately he set out again for California by the previous route, and in 1827 reached the San José mission. Here he was arrested by the Spanish authorities and sent under guard to Monterey, where another Yankee skipper secured his release. Wintering once more in California, this time on the American Fork, he reached the coast in the spring of 1828, and followed the Umpquah River towards the Oregon country. While he was absent, his camp was attacked by the Indians and fifteen of his men killed. Absolutely alone, Smith worked his way through the forest to Fort Vancouver, where he enjoyed the hospitality of Dr. McLoughlin through the winter. In the following spring he ascended the Columbia to the Hudson Bay posts among the Flatheads, and made his way in the summer of 1829 to the rendezvous of his company at the Tetons. In three years this daring trader, braving the horrors of the desert and passing unscathed from Indian attacks which carried off most of his companions, opened to knowledge much of the vast country between Great Salt Lake and the Pacific.[1] In 1831, while on the Santa Fé trail, Smith and his companions lost their way. Perishing with thirst, he finally reached the Cimaron, where, as he was digging for water in its sandy bed, he was shot by an Indian.

Thus the active men of the Rocky Mountain Fur Company, in the decade between 1820 and 1830, revealed the sources of the Platte, the Green, the Yellowstone, and the Snake rivers, and the characteristics of the Great Salt Lake region; they pioneered the way to South Pass, descended Green River by boat, carried cannon into the interior basin; showed the practicability of a wagon route

[1] H. H. Bancroft, *California*, III., 152–160, citing the sources.

through the Rockies, reached California from Salt Lake, crossed the Sierras and the deserts of Utah and Nevada, and became intimately acquainted with the activity of the British traders of the northwest coast.[1]

Already an interest in Oregon and the Rocky Mountain region was arising on the eastern seaboard. In 1832, Captain Bonneville, an officer in the United States army, on leave of absence, passed with a wagon-train into the Rocky Mountains, where for nearly three years he trapped and traded and explored.[2] Walker, one of his men, in 1833, reached California by the Humboldt River (a route afterwards followed by the emigrants to California), and made known much new country. A New England enthusiast, Hall Kelley, had for some years been lecturing on the riches of the Oregon country and the need of planting an agricultural colony there. It was natural that Boston should be interested in the Oregon country, which was visited by so many vessels from that port. In 1820, New England missionaries settled in the Hawaiian Islands, closely connected by trade with the coast. In 1832, Nathaniel Wyeth, of Cambridge, Massachusetts, led a party of New - Englanders west, with the plan of establishing a trading and fishing post on the waters of the Columbia.[3]

---

[1] Chittenden, *Am. Fur Trade*, I., 306.

[2] Irving, *Bonneville*.

[3] Chittenden, *Am. Fur Trade*, I., 435; Wyeth's "Journals" are published by the Oregon Hist. Soc.; cf. Irving, *Bonneville*, chap. vi.

With Wyeth, on a second expedition in 1834, went the Reverend Jason Lee and four Methodist missionaries. Two years later came Dr. Marcus Whitman and another company of missionaries with their wives; they brought a wagon through South Pass and over the mountains to the Snake River, and began an agricultural colony. Thus the old story of the sequence of fur-trader, missionary, and settler was repeated. The possession of Oregon by the British fur-trader was challenged by the American farmer.

Contemporaneously with the development of the fur-trade in the Rocky Mountains, a trade was opened between St. Louis and the old Spanish settlements at Santa Fé. Although even in the days of Washington adventurous frontiersmen like George Rogers Clark had set their eyes on Santa Fé and the silver-mines of the southwest, it was not until the Mexican revolution (1821), when Spain's control was weakened throughout her whole domain, that systematic trade was possible. In 1822, Becknell, of Missouri, took a wagon-train to Santa Fé, to trade for horses and mules and to trap en route. Year after year thereafter, caravans of Missouri traders found their way across the desert, by the Santa Fé trail, with cottons and other dry-goods furnished from St. Louis, and brought back horses, mules, furs, and silver. The trade averaged about one hundred and thirty thousand dollars a year, and was an important source of supply of specie for the

west; and it stimulated the interest of St. Louis in
the Mexican provinces. The mode of handling the
wagon - trains that passed between Missouri and
Santa Fé furnished the model for the caravans that
later were to cross the plains in the rush to the gold-
fields of California.[1]

By 1833 the important western routes were
clearly made known.[2] The Oregon trail, the Santa
Fé trail, the Spanish trail, and the Gila route[3] had
been followed by frontiersmen into the promised
land of the Pacific coast and the southwest. In
the course of ten years, not only had the principal
secrets of the topography of the Rocky Mountains,
the Great Basin, the passes across the Sierra Nevadas been revealed, but also the characteristics of
the Spanish-American settlements of California and
the Rio Grande region. Already pioneers sought
Texas, and American colonization was preparing for another and greater conquest of the wilderness.

The interest of the United States government in
the far west in this period was shown in exploration and diplomacy. Calhoun projected an extension of the forts of the United States well up the
Missouri into the Indian country, partly as protection to the traders and partly as a defence against

[1] Gregg, *Commerce of the Prairies;* Chittenden, *Am. Fur Trade*,
II., chap. xxix.

[2] Semple, *Am. Hist. and its Geographic Conditions*, chap. x.

[3] *Personal Narrative of James O. Pattie;* H. H. Bancroft, *Hist.
of California*, III., 162.

English aggressions. Two Yellowstone expeditions [1] were designed to promote these ends. The first of these, 1819–1820, was a joint military and scientific undertaking; but the military expedition, attempting to ascend the Missouri in steamboats, got no farther than Council Bluffs. Mismanagement, extravagance, and scandal attended the undertaking, and the enterprise was made an occasion for a political onslaught on Calhoun's management of the war department.

The scientific expedition, under Major Long, of the United States Engineering Corps, ascended the Missouri in the *Western Engineer*, the first steamboat which navigated those waters above St. Louis —a stern-wheeler, with serpent-mouthed figure-head, through which the steam escaped, bringing terror to the savages along the banks. The expedition advanced far up the South Platte, discovered Long's Peak, and camped near the site of Denver. Thence the party passed to La Junta, Colorado, whence it broke into two divisions, one of which descended the Arkansas; the other reached the Canadian River (which it mistook for the Red) and descended to its junction with the Arkansas. The effort to push the military power of the government to the mouth of the Yellowstone failed, and the net result, on the military side, was a temporary post near the present site of Omaha.

[1] Chittenden, *Am. Fur Trade*, II., 562; *Long's Expedition* (*Early Western Travels*, XIV.–XVII.).

The most important effect of the expedition was to give currency to Long's description of the country through which he passed as the "Great American Desert," unfit for cultivation and uninhabitable by agricultural settlers. The whole of the region between the Missouri River and the Rocky Mountains seemed to him adapted as a range for buffalo, "calculated to serve as a barrier to prevent too great an extension of our population westward," and to secure us against the incursions of enemies in that quarter.[1] A second expedition, in 1825, under General Atkinson and Major O'Fallon, reached the mouth of the Yellowstone, having made treaties with various Indian tribes on the way.

In the mean time, Congress and the president were busy with the question of Oregon. By the convention of 1818, with Great Britain, the northern boundary of the United States was carried from the Lake of the Woods to the Rocky Mountains, along the forty-ninth parallel. Beyond the mountains, the Oregon country was left open, for a period of ten years, to joint occupation of both powers, without prejudice to the claims of either. Having thus postponed the Oregon question, the secretary of state, John Quincy Adams, turned to his Spanish relations. Obliged by Monroe to relinquish our claim to Texas in the treaty of 1819, by which we obtained Florida, he insisted on so drawing our boundary-line

[1] *Long's Expedition* (*Early Western Travels*, XVII.), 147, 148.

in the southwest as to acquire Spain's title to the
Pacific north of the forty-second parallel, and to the
lands that lay north and east of the irregular line
from the intersection of this parallel with the Rocky
Mountains to the Sabine.   Adams was proud of securing this line to the Pacific Ocean, for it was the
first recognition by an outside power of our rights
in the Oregon country.[1]

Although Russia put forward large and exclusive
claims north of the fifty-first parallel, which we challenged, the contest for Oregon lay between England
and the United States.   At the close of 1820, Floyd,
of Virginia, moved in the House of Representatives
to inquire into the feasibility of the occupation of
the Columbia River; and early the next year[2] a
committee report was brought in, discussing the
American rights.   Floyd's bill provided for the military occupation of the Columbia River, donation of
lands to actual settlers, and control of the Indians.
No vote was reached, however, and it was not until
the close of 1822 that the matter secured the attention of Congress.

Whatever may have been his motives, Floyd
stated with vividness the significance of western
advance in relation to the Pacific coast.   He showed
that, while in 1755, nearly a hundred and fifty years

---

[1] *Treaties and Conventions* (ed. of 1889), 416, 1017; Babcock,
*Am. Nationality* (*Am. Nation*, XIII.), chap. xvi.; J. Q. Adams,
*Memoirs*, IV., 275.

[2] *Annals of Cong.*, 16 Cong., 2 Sess., 945; J. Q. Adams, *Memoirs*, V., 238, 243–260.

after the foundation of Jamestown, the population of Virginia had spread but three hundred miles into the interior of the country, during the last forty-three years population had spread westward more than a thousand miles. He recalled the days when more than a month was required to furnish Kentucky with eastern goods, by way of Pittsburg, and when it required a voyage of over a month to pass from Louisville to New Orleans and nearly three months for the upward voyage. This had now been shortened by steamboat to seven days down and sixteen days up. From these considerations and the time from St. Louis to the mouth of the Columbia by steamboat and wagon, he argued that Oregon was no more distant from St. Louis in 1822 than St. Louis was twenty years before from Philadelphia. The fur-trade, the whale and seal fisheries, the trade with China, and the opportunity for agricultural occupation afforded by Oregon were all set forth.[1]

Against the proposal, his opponents argued inexpediency rather than our treaties with Great Britain. Tracy, of New York, doubted the value of the Oregon country, and, influenced perhaps by Long's report, declared that "nature has fixed limits for our nation; she has kindly introduced as our Western barrier, mountains almost inaccessible, whose base she has skirted with irreclaimable deserts of sand."[2] In a later debate, Smyth, of

[1] *Annals of Cong.*, 17 Cong., 2 Sess., 397.     [2] *Ibid.*, 590.

Virginia, amplified this idea by a proposal to limit
the boundaries of the United States, so that it
should include but one or two tiers of states beyond the Mississippi. He would remove the Indians beyond this limit, and, if American settlements
should cross it, they might be in alliance with, or
under the protection of, the United States, but outside of its bounds.[1]

Baylies, of Massachusetts, declared that there were
living witnesses "who have seen a population of
scarcely six hundred thousand swelled into ten millions; a population which, in their youth, extended
scarcely an hundred miles from the ocean, spreading
beyond the mountains of the West, and sweeping
down those mighty waters which open into regions
of such matchless fertility and beauty." "Some
now within these walls may, before they die, witness
scenes more wonderful than these; and in aftertimes
may cherish delightful recollections of this day,
when America, almost shrinking from the 'shadows
of coming events,' first placed her feet upon un-
trodden ground, scarcely daring to anticipate the
grandeur which awaited her." Tucker, of Virginia,
agreed that settlement "marches on, with the increasing rapidity of a fire, and nothing will stop it
until it reaches the shores of the Pacific," which he
estimated would be by 1872. But he was loath
to see it accelerated, believing that the people
on the east and the west side of the Rocky Moun-

[1] *Register of Debates*, 18 Cong., 2 Sess., I., 37.

tains would have a permanent separation of interests.[1]

Nor were even western men sanguine that the nation could retain the Pacific coast as an integral part of its vast empire. Senator Benton, of Missouri, was the congressional champion of the far west. Born in interior North Carolina, he had followed the frontier to Tennessee, and then, after killing his man in a duel and exchanging pistol-shots in a free fight with Jackson, he removed to the new frontier at St. Louis. Pedantic and ponderous, deeply read in curious historical lore, in many ways he was not characteristic of the far west, but in the coarse vigor with which he bore down opposition by abuse, and in the far horizon line of the policies he advocated, he thoroughly represented its traits.

Familiar as he was with frontier needs and aspirations, he urged the United States to block England's control of the northwest, and to assert title to the Oregon territory, with the idea of ultimately founding a new and independent American nation there. It is true that he admitted that along the ridge of the Rocky Mountains "the western limit of this republic should be drawn, and the statue of the fabled god Terminus should be raised upon its highest peak, never to be thrown down." [2]

Nevertheless, in his utterances the ideal of expansion was not to be mistaken. He spoke bravely in

[1] Annals of Cong., 17 Cong., 2 Sess., 422.
[2] Register of Debates, I., 712.

favor of the protection and extension of the fur-
trade,[1] pointing out that inasmuch as England occupied Oregon, she would, under the law of nations,
have the right of possession until the question of
sovereignty were decided.  He warned his countrymen, in 1823, that Great Britain would monopolize
the Pacific Ocean, and by obtaining control of the
Rocky Mountain fur-trade would be able to launch
the Indians of the north and west against the frontiers of Missouri and Arkansas, Illinois and Michigan, upon the first renewal of hostilities between the
United States of America and the king of Great
Britain.[2]

Benton believed that, within a century, a population greater than that of the United States of 1820
would exist on the west side of the Rocky Mountains; and he saw in the occupation of the northwest coast the means of promoting a trade between
the valley of the Mississippi, the Pacific Ocean, and
Asia.  Upon the people of eastern Asia, he thought,
the establishment of a civilized power on the opposite coast of America would produce great benefits.
"Science, liberal principles in government, and the
true religion, might cast their lights across the intervening sea.  The valley of the Columbia might become the granary of China and Japan, and an outlet
to their imprisoned and exuberant population. . . .
Russia and the legitimates menace Turkey, Persia,

---

[1] *Annals of Cong.*, 17 Cong., 1 Sess., I., 416; cf. *ibid.*, 18 Cong.,
1 Sess., I., 456.          [2] *Ibid.*, 17 Cong., 2 Sess., 246–251.

China, and Japan; they menace them for their riches and dominions; the same Powers menace the two Americas for the popular forms of their Governments. To my mind the proposition is clear, that Eastern Asia and the two Americas, as they have become neighbors, should become friends."[1]

With true western passion he denounced the relinquishment of Texas by the treaty of 1819. "The magnificent valley of the Mississippi is ours," he proclaimed, "with all its fountains, springs, and floods and woe to the statesman who shall undertake to surrender one drop of its water, one inch of its soil, to any foreign power." He was ready for a war with Spain, believing that it would give the United States the Floridas and Cuba, "the geographical appurtenance of the valley of the Mississippi"; that it would free the New from the Old World; and that it would create a cordon of republics across the two continents of North and South America. He pointed to the west as the route to the east—the long-sought way to India; and, in imagination, he outlined the states to be laid off "from the center of the valley of the Mississippi to the foot of the shining mountains." "It is time," he wrote, "that Western men had some share in the destinies of this republic."[2]

[1] *Register of Debates*, I., 712.  [2] Meigs, *Benton*, 98, 99, cf. 91.

# CHAPTER IX

## THE CRISIS OF 1819 AND ITS RESULTS

### (1819–1820)

IN 1820 the United States had a population of about nine and one-half millions; in 1830, nearly thirteen millions. It was spread out from east to west like a page in the history of society. On the Atlantic seaboard were the centres of American civilization that had grown up in colonial days in close touch with Europe. From this region of commerce and manufacture, the nation, on its march towards the west, changed through successive types of industrial life until in the Rocky Mountains the frontier fur-trader mingled with the Indians. The successive stages of social evolution which at first were exhibited in narrow belts on the Atlantic coast had now spread nearly across the continent.[1]

Not only was the country vast in extent, it was rapidly growing. In the decade the nation increased its population by over three million and a quarter inhabitants, an addition which nearly equalled the whole population of any one of the three great sec-

[1] Turner, "Significance of the Frontier," in Am. Hist. Assoc., *Report* 1893, pp. 200, 206, 208.

tions, the middle states, the south, and the west. As traveller after traveller passed over the routes of his predecessor in this period, reporting the life by the wayside and in the towns, we can almost see American society unfolding with startling rapidity under our gaze; farms become hamlets, hamlets grow into prosperous cities; the Indian and the forests recede; new stretches of wilderness come into view in the farther west, and we see the irresistible tide of settlement flowing towards the solitudes.

Nevertheless, at the opening of our survey the nation was in the gloom of the panic of 1819. This was brought on by the speculative reaction that immediately followed the war, when the long-pent-up crops of cotton found a market at the extraordinary price of nearly thirty cents a pound, and as high as seventy-eight dollars per acre was bid for government land in the offices of the southwest.[1] The policy of the government fostered reckless purchases of public land. In the critical times of the closing years of the war, the treasury agreed to accept the notes of state banks in payment for lands, on condition that these banks should resume specie payment; and then the banks, while taking only nominal steps towards resumption, loaned their paper freely to the settlers and speculators who wished to invest in the public domain.

Under the credit system already mentioned, the pioneer was tempted to exhaust his funds in making

[1] *Annals of Cong.*, 16 Cong., 1 Sess., 446.

his first partial payment, and to rely upon loans from some "wild cat" bank wherewith to complete the purchase of the hundred and sixty acres, the smallest tract offered under the terms of the law; planters, relying equally on the state banks, bought great tracts of land at absurd prices; speculators, tempted by the rapid rise in land values and by the ease of securing loans, purchased large quantities in the hope of selling before it became necessary to complete their payment. On the seaboard, extravagance abounded as a reaction from the economies of war times, imported manufactures found a ready market, and the domestic factories were in distress.

While state banks greatly multiplied and expanded their circulation freely to meet the demands of borrowers,[1] the United States Bank not only failed to check the movement, but even contributed to it. After a dance of speculation, the bank, in the summer of 1818, was facing ruin, and it took drastic means to save itself. Its measures compelled the state banks to redeem their notes in specie or close their doors.[2]

By the spring of 1819 the country was in the throes of a panic. State-bank issues were reduced from one hundred million dollars in 1817 to forty-five millions in 1819. Few banks in the south and

---

[1] Sumner, *Hist. of Banking*, I., chaps. iv.–vi.

[2] Catterall, *Second Bank*, chap. iii.; Dewey, *Financial Hist. of the U. S.*, chap. vii.; Babcock, *Am. Nationality* (*Am. Nation*, XIII.), chap. xiii.

west were able to redeem their notes in specie before 1822; but they pressed their debtors harshly. Staple productions fell to less than half of their former price; land values declined fifty to seventy per cent.; manufacturers were in distress; laborers were out of work; merchants were ruined.[1]  The conditions are illustrated in the case of Cincinnati. By the foreclosure of mortgages, the national bank came to own a large part of the city—hotels, coffee-houses, warehouses, stables, iron foundries, residences, and vacant lots. "All the flourishing cities of the West," cried Benton, "are mortgaged to this money power. They may be devoured by it at any moment. They are in the jaws of the monster!" Throughout the south and west the bank became familiarly known as The Monster.[2]

Even in the days of its laxity the national bank was obnoxious in many quarters of the country. By the state constitution of 1816 Indiana attempted to prevent the establishment within its limits of any bank not chartered by the state; and Illinois incorporated a similar provision in her constitution of 1818. Between 1817 and 1819 Maryland, Tennessee, Georgia, North Carolina, Kentucky, and Ohio all passed acts taxing the United States Bank.[3] Ohio, defying the decision of the supreme court in

---

[1] J. Q. Adams, *Memoirs*, IV., 375; Jefferson, *Writings*, X., 257; Benton, *View*, I., 5; *Niles' Register*, XVI., 114; Hodgson, *Travels*, II., 128; Sumner, *Hist. of Banking*, I., chaps. vii., viii.

[2] Catterall, *Second Bank*, 67.          [3] *Ibid.*, 64, 65.

the case of McCulloch *vs.* Maryland, which asserted the constitutionality of the bank and denied to the states the right to tax it, forcibly collected the tax and practically outlawed the bank.[1]

From the beginning of our history the frontier had been a debtor region, always favorable to an expansion of the currency and to laws to relieve the debtor class. It was but the continuation of an old practice when the western legislatures in this time of stringency attempted measures of relief for their citizens. Kentucky's "litter" of forty banks chartered in the session of 1818–1819 had been forced to the wall by the measures of the national bank. After the panic, Kentucky repealed the charters of these banks and incorporated the Bank of the Commonwealth of Kentucky, an institution without stockholders and under officers elected by the legislature and paid by the state. Its notes were assigned to the counties in proportion to the taxable property, to be loaned on mortgage securities to those who needed them "for the purpose of paying his, her or their just debts," or to purchase products for exportation. The only real capital of the bank was a legislative appropriation of seven thousand dollars to buy the material and plates for printing notes. In short, the treasury of the state was used as a kind of land bank of the sort favored in colonial days for the relief of the debtors.[2] The legislature

[1] See chap. xv., below.
[2] Cf. Greene, *Provincial America* (*Am. Nation*, VI.), chap. xvii.

then passed a replevin law giving the debtor a delay of two years to satisfy an execution, in case the creditor refused to accept notes of the Bank of the Commonwealth of Kentucky as payment; otherwise the debtor received an extension of but one year. By another law, land could not be sold under execution to pay a debt unless it brought three-fourths of its value as appraised by a board of neighbors, usually themselves debtors and interested in supporting values.

In 1823 the court of appeals of Kentucky declared the replevin and stay laws unconstitutional. In retaliation the legislature, in December, 1824, repealed the law establishing the court of appeals, and a new court was created favorable to the "relief system." This act the old court also declared unconstitutional, and a contest followed between the "old court" and the "new court" parties, which lasted until 1826, when the "old court," "anti-relief" party was victorious. In the mean time, similar relief measures had been passed in Tennessee, Illinois, Missouri, and other western states.[1]

The distress brought about by the panic of 1819, the popular antagonism to banks in general, and especially to the Bank of the United States, as "engines of aristocracy," oppressive to the common people, and the general discontent with the estab-

[1] Sumner, *Hist. of Banking*, I., chap. x.; *ibid.*, 122, 146, 157, 161; Durrett, *Centenary of Louisville;* McMaster, *United States*, V., 160.

lished order, had, as we have seen, produced a movement comparable to the populistic agitation of our own time.

Upon the general government the first effect of this period of distress was a general reduction of the revenue. Imports fell from about $121,000,000 in 1818 to $87,000,000 in 1819. Customs receipts, which in 1816 were over $36,000,000, were but $13,000,000 in 1821. Receipts for public lands, which amounted to $3,274,000 in 1819, were but $1,635,000 in 1820. In December, 1819, Crawford, the secretary of the treasury, was obliged to announce a deficit which required either a reduction in expenditures or an increase in revenue. Congress provided for two loans, one of $3,000,000 in 1820, and another of $5,000,000 in 1821. A policy of retrenchment was vigorously instituted, levelled chiefly at the department of war. Internal improvement schemes which had been urged in Congress in 1818 were now temporarily put to rest. With the year 1822, however, conditions brightened, and the treasury began a long term of prosperity.[1]

One of the most important results of the crisis was the complete reorganization of the system of disposal of the public lands. The public domain was more than a source of revenue to the general government; it was one of the most profoundly influential factors in shaping American social conditions. The settler who entered the wilderness with but a

[1] Dewey, *Financial Hist. of the U. S.*, 168.

small capital, or who became a squatter on the public lands without legal title, was impatient with the
policy which made revenue the primary consideration of the government.  Benton expressed this
view in 1826,[1] when he said: "I speak to statesmen,
and not to compting clerks; to Senators, and not
to *Quæstors* of provinces; to an assembly of legisla-
tors, and not to a keeper of the King's forests.  I
speak to Senators who know this to be a Republic,
not a Monarchy; who know that the public lands
belong to the People and not to the Federal Government."  The effect of the credit system had been,
as we have seen, to stimulate speculation and to
plunge the settlers deeply in debt to the general
government.

By 1820 these payments for the public lands were
over twenty-two million dollars in arrears.  Relief
measures passed by Congress from time to time had
extended the period of payment and made other
concessions.  Now the government had to face the
problem of reconstructing its land laws or of continuing the old credit system and relentlessly expel-
ling the delinquent purchasers from their hard-won
homes on the public domain.  Although the legal
title remained in the government, the latter alternative was so obviously dangerous and inexpedient that Congress passed two new acts.  The first[2]
(April 24, 1820) reduced the price of land from

[1] *Register of Debates*, 19 Cong., 1 Sess., I., 727.
[2] *U. S. Statutes at Large*, III., 566.

two dollars to one dollar and twenty-five cents per acre, abolished the system of credit, and provided that lands might be purchased in multiples of eighty acres. Thus the settler with one hundred dollars could secure full title to a farm. This was followed by a relief act (March 2, 1821), recommended by Secretary Crawford,[1] allowing previous purchasers to relinquish their claims to land for which they had not paid, and apply payments already made to full purchase of a portion of the land to be retained by the buyer, all overdue interest to be remitted.[2] It is significant that this system was not unlike the relief system which had been so popular in the west.

This adjustment of the land question by no means closed the agitation. A few years later Benton repeatedly urged Congress to graduate the price of public lands according to their real value, and to donate to actual settlers lands which remained unsold after they had been offered at fifty cents an acre.[3] The argument rested chiefly on the large number of men unable to secure a farm even under the cheaper price of 1820; the great quantity of public land which remained unsold after it had been offered; the advantage to the revenues from filling the vacant lands with a productive population; and the injustice to the western states, which found them-

---

[1] *Am. State Paps., Finance*, III., 551, 718; *U. S. Statutes at Large*, III., 566.    [2] *Ibid.*, III., 612.
[3] Speech in the Senate, May 16, 1826, Meigs, *Benton*, 163-170

selves unable to obtain revenue by taxing unsold public lands and which were limited in their power of eminent domain and jurisdiction as compared with the eastern states, which owned their public lands. In this agitation lay the germs of the later homestead system, as well as of the propositions to relinquish the federal public lands to the states within which they lay.

With manufacturers in distress, thousands of operatives out of employment, and the crops of parts of the middle states and the west falling in price to a point where it hardly paid to produce them, an appeal to Congress to raise the duties established by the tariff of 1816[1] was inevitable. Hence, in the spring of 1820 a new tariff bill was presented by Baldwin, of Pennsylvania, the member from Pittsburg. He came from a city which felt the full effects of the distress of the manufacturers, especially those of iron and glass, and which was one of the important centres of the great grain-raising area of the middle states and the Ohio Valley.

Baldwin believed that the time had arrived when, "all the great interests of the country being equally prostrate, and one general scene of distress pervading all its parts," there should be a common effort to improve conditions by a new tariff, intended not for the sake of restoring the depleted treasury, but distinctly for protection. Its advocates proposed to meet the failure of the system of revenue, not by

[1] Babcock, *Am. Nationality* (*Am. Nation*, XIII.), chap. xiv.

encouraging importations, but by internal taxes and excises on the manufactured goods protected by the impost. Additional revenue would be secured by higher duties on sugar, molasses, coffee, and salt. The bill increased ad valorem duties by an amount varying from twenty-five to sixty-six per cent. additional. For woollen and cotton manufactures the rate of additional duty was about one-third; on hemp, an important product in Kentucky, about two-thirds. Duty on forged iron bars was increased from seventy-five cents to one dollar and twenty-five cents per hundred-weight. On many other articles the increase of duty amounted to from twenty to one hundred per cent.

Naturally the home-market argument played an important part in the debates. It was relied upon especially by Henry Clay in his closing speech,[1] in which he argued that the rapidity of growth of the United States as compared with Europe made the ratio of the increase of her capacity of consumption to that of our capacity of production as one to four. Already he thought Europe was showing a want of capacity to consume our surplus; in his opinion, cotton, tobacco, and bread-stuffs had already reached the maximum of foreign demand. From this he argued that home manufactures should be encouraged to consume the surplus, and that some portion of American industry should be diverted from agriculture to manufacturing.

[1] *Annals of Cong.*, 16 Cong., 1 Sess., II., 2034.

Industrial independence also required this action. England had recently imposed new duties on wool and cotton, and her corn laws contributed to limit her demand for our flour. "I am, too," he said, "a friend of free trade, but it must be a free trade of perfect reciprocity. If the governing considerations were cheapness; if national independence were to weigh nothing ; if honor nothing; why not subsidize foreign powers to defend us?" He met the argument of the deficiency of labor and of the danger of developing overcrowded and pauperized manufacturing centres by reasoning that machinery would enable the Americans to atone for their lack of laborers; and that while distance and attachment to the native soil would check undue migration of laborers to the west, at the same time the danger of congestion in the east would be avoided by the attraction of the cheap western lands.

Lowndes, of South Carolina, who with Calhoun had been one of the prominent supporters of the tariff in 1816, now made the principal speech in opposition: he denied the validity of the argument in favor of a home market and contended that the supply of domestic grain would in any case exceed the demand; and that, however small the export, the price of the portion sent abroad would determine that of the whole. It is important to observe that the question of constitutionality was hardly raised. The final vote in the House (April 29, 1820) stood 91 to 78. New England gave 18 votes in favor and 17 opposed; the middle region, including Delaware, gave 56 votes for and 1 vote against; the south, including Maryland and her sister states on the southern seaboard, gave 5 votes in favor and 50 opposed. The northwest gave its 8 votes in favor, and the southwest, including Kentucky, gave 4 votes in favor and 10 opposed. The vote of New England was the most divided of that of any section. From the manufacturing states of Connecticut and Rhode Island but one member, a Connecticut man, voted in opposition to the bill. The only 3 negative votes from Massachusetts proper came from the commercial region of Boston and Salem. That portion of Massachusetts soon to become the state of Maine gave 4 votes in opposition and only 2 in favor, the latter coming from the areas least interested in the carrying-trade. New Hampshire and Vermont gave their whole vote in opposition, except for one affirmative from Vermont. Kentucky's vote was 4 in favor to 3 opposed, Speaker Clay not voting.

In general, the distribution of the vote shows that the maritime interests united with the slave-holding planters, engaged in producing tobacco, cotton, and sugar, in opposition. On the other side, the manufacturing areas joined with the grain and wool raising regions of the middle and western states to support the measure. From the states of New York, New Jersey, Pennsylvania, Delaware, Ohio, Indiana, and Illinois, casting altogether 65 votes, but one man voted against the bill, and he was burned in effigy by his constituents and resigned the same year. Of the 53 votes cast by the south and south-west, outside of the border states of Maryland and Kentucky, there were but 5 affirmative votes. It is seen, therefore, that in the House of Representatives, on the tariff issue, the middle states and the Ohio Valley were combined against the south and southwest, while New England's influence was nullified by her division of interests. By a single vote, on a motion to postpone, the measure failed in the Senate; but the struggle was only deferred.

The most important aspect of the panic of 1819 was its relation to the forces of unrest and democratic change that were developing in the United States. Calhoun and John Quincy Adams, conversing in the spring of 1820 upon politics, had the gloomiest apprehensions. There had been, within two years, Calhoun said, "an immense revolution of fortunes in every part of the Union; enormous numbers of persons utterly ruined; multitudes in deep distress; and a general mass of disaffection to the Government not concentrated in any particular direction, but ready to seize upon any event and looking out anywhere for a leader." They agreed that the Missouri question and the debates on the tariff were merely incidental to this state of things, and that this vague but wide-spread discontent, caused by the disordered circumstances of individuals, had resulted in a general impression that there was something radically wrong in the administration of the government.[1]

Although this impression was the result of deeper influences than those to which it was attributed by these statesmen, yet the crisis of 1819, which bore with peculiar heaviness upon the west and south, undoubtedly aggravated all the discontent of those regions. To the historian the movement is profoundly significant, for ultimately it found its leader in Andrew Jackson. More immediately it led to the demand for legislation to prevent imprisonment for debt,[2] to debates over a national bankruptcy law,[3] to the proposal of constitutional amendments leading to the diminution of the powers of the supreme court, to a reassertion of the sovereignty of the states,[4] and to new legislation regarding the public lands and the tariff. The next few years bore clear evidence of the deep influence which this period of distress had on the politics and legislation of the country.

[1] Adams, *Memoirs*, V., 128; cf. IV., 498.
[2] See, for example, *Annals of Cong.*, 16 Cong., 2 Sess., 1224; McMaster, *United States*, IV., 532-535.
[3] *Annals of Cong.*, 16 Cong., 2 Sess., I., 757, 759, 792, 1203 et passim.    [4] See chap. xviii., below.

# CHAPTER X

## THE MISSOURI COMPROMISE

### (1819–1821)

IN the dark period of the commercial crisis of 1819, while Congress was considering the admission of Missouri, the slavery issue flamed out, and revealed with startling distinctness the political significance of the institution, fateful and ominous for the nation, transcending in importance the temporary financial and industrial ills.

The advance of settlement in the United States made the slavery contest a struggle for power between sections, marching in parallel columns into the west, each carrying its own system of labor.[1] By 1819 the various states of the north, under favorable conditions of climate and industrial life, had either completely extinguished slavery or were in the process of emancipation;[2] and by the Ordinance of 1787 the old Congress had excluded the institution in the territory north of the Ohio River. Thus Mason and Dixon's line and the Ohio made a boundary between the slave-holding and the free streams of population

[1] For previous questions of slavery, see Channing, *Jeffersonian System* (*Am. Nation*, XII.), chap. viii.    [2] See map, p. 6.

that flowed into the Mississippi Valley. Not that this line was a complete barrier: the Ordinance of 1787 was not construed to free the slaves already in the old French towns of the territory; and many southern masters brought their slaves into Ohio, Indiana, and Illinois by virtue of laws which provided for them under the fiction of indented servants.[1] Indeed, several efforts were made in the territory of Indiana at the beginning of the nineteenth century to rescind the prohibition of 1787; but to this petition Congress, under the strange leadership of John Randolph, gave a negative;[2] and, after a struggle between the southern slavery and antislavery elements by which the state had been settled, Indiana entered the Union in 1816 as a free state, under an agreement not to violate the Ordinance of 1787.

Illinois, on her admission in 1818, also guaranteed the provisions of the Ordinance of 1787, and, not without a contest, included in her constitution an article preventing the introduction of slavery, but so worded that the system of indenture of negro servants was continued in a modified form. The issue of slavery still continued to influence Illinois elections, and, as the inhabitants saw well-to-do planters pass with their slaves across the state to recruit the property and population of Missouri, a movement (1823–1824) in favor of revising their constitution so as to admit slavery required the most vigorous

[1] Harris, *Negro Servitude in Ill.*, 10; Dunn, *Indiana*, chaps. ix., x.
[2] *Ibid.*, chap. xii.; Hinsdale, *Old Northwest*, chap. xviii.

opposition to hold the state to freedom. The leader of the antislavery forces in Illinois was a Virginian, Governor Coles (once private secretary to President Madison), who had migrated to free his slaves after he became convinced that it was hopeless to make the fight which Jefferson advised him to carry on in favor of gradual emancipation in his native state.[1] In both Indiana and Illinois, the strength of the opposition to slavery and indented servitude came from the poorer whites, particularly from the Quaker and Baptist elements of the southern stock, and from the northern settlers.

In Maryland, Virginia, and North Carolina, ever since the decline of the tobacco culture, a strong opposition to slavery had existed, shown in the votes of those states on the Ordinance of 1787, and in the fact that as late as 1827 the great majority of the abolition societies of the United States were to be found in this region.[2] But the problem of dealing with the free negro weighed upon the south. Even in the north these people were unwelcome. They frequently became a charge upon the community, and they were placed under numerous disabilities.[3]

The idea of deporting freedmen from the United

[1] Harris, *Negro Servitude in Ill.*, chap. iv.; Washburne, *Coles*, chaps. iii., v.

[2] Dunn, *Indiana*, 190; Bassett, in *Johns Hopkins Univ. Studies*, XVI., No. vi.; cf. Hart, *Slavery and Abolition* (*Am. Nation*, XVI.), chap. xi.

[3] McMaster, *United States*, IV., 558; Gordy, *Political Hist. of U. S.*, II., 405.

States found support both among the humanitarians, who saw in it a step towards general emancipation, and among the slave‑holders who viewed the increase of the free negroes with apprehension. To promote this solution of the problem, the Colonization Society [1] was incorporated in 1816, and it found support, not only from antislavery agitators like Lundy, who edited the *Genius of Universal Emancipation* at Baltimore, but also from slave‑holders like Jefferson, Clay, and Randolph. It was the design of this society to found on the coast of Africa a colony of free blacks, brought from the United States. Although, after unsuccessful efforts, Liberia was finally established in the twenties, with the assistance of the general government (but not under its jurisdiction), it never promoted state emancipation. Nevertheless, at first it met with much sympathy in Virginia, where in 1820 the governor proposed to the legislature the use of one‑third of the state revenue as a fund to promote the emancipation and deportation of the negroes.[2]

The unprofitableness of slavery in the border states, where outworn fields, the decline of tobacco culture, and the competition of western lands bore hard on the planter,[3] now became an argument in

[1] McPherson, *Liberia;* McMaster, *United States*, IV., 556 et seq.

[2] Jefferson, *Writings* (Ford's ed.), X., 173, 178; *Niles' Register*, XVII., 363; King, *Life and Corresp. of King*, VI., 342; Adams, *Memoirs*, IV., 293.

[3] See chap. iv. above; Hart, *Slavery and Abolition* (*Am. Nation*, XVI.), chap. iv.

favor of permitting slavery to pass freely into the new country of the west. Any limitation of the area of slavery would diminish the value of the slaves and would leave the old south to support, under increasingly hard conditions, the redundant and unwelcome slave population in its midst. The hard times from 1817 to 1820 rendered slave property a still greater burden to Virginia. Moreover, the increase of the proportion of slaves to whites, if slavery were confined to the region east of the Mississippi, might eventually make possible a servile insurrection, particularly if foreign war should break out. All of these difficulties would be met, in the opinion of the south, by scattering the existing slaves and thus mitigating the evil without increasing the number of those in bondage.

It was seen that the struggle was not simply one of morals and of rival social and industrial institutions, but was a question of political power between the two great and opposing sections, interested, on the one side, in manufacturing and in the raising of food products under a system of free labor; and, on the other, in the production of the great staples, cotton, tobacco, and sugar, by the use of slave labor. Already the southern section had shown its opposition to tariff and internal improvements, which the majority of the northern states vehemently favored. In other words, the slavery issue was seen to be a struggle for sectional domination.

At the beginning of the nation in 1790, the popu-

lation of the north and the south was almost ex-
actly balanced. Steadily, however, the free states
drew ahead, until in 1820 they possessed a population of 5,152,000 against 4,485,000 for the slave-
holding states and territories; and in the House of
Representatives, by the operation of the three-fifths
ratio, the free states could muster 105 votes to but
81 for the slave states. Thus power had passed
definitely to the north in the House of Representatives. The instinct for self-preservation that led the
planters to stand out against an apportionment in
their legislatures which would throw power into the
hands of non-slaveholders now led them to seek for
some means to protect the interests of their minority
section in the nation as a whole. The Senate offered
such an opportunity: by the alternate admission of
free and slave states from 1802 to 1818, out of the
twenty-two states of the nation eleven were slave-
holding and eleven free. If the south retained this
balance, the Senate could block the action of the
majority which controlled the lower House.

Such was the situation when the application of
Missouri for admission as a state in 1819 presented to
Congress the whole question of slavery beyond the
Mississippi, where freedom and slavery had found a
new fighting-ground. East of the Mississippi the Ohio
was a natural dividing-line; farther west there appeared no obvious boundary between slavery and
freedom. By a natural process of selection, the
valleys of the western tributaries of the Mississippi,

as far north as the Arkansas and Missouri, in which
slaves had been allowed while it was a part of French
and Spanish Louisiana (no restraints having been
imposed by Congress), received an increasing proportion of the slave-holding planters. It would, in
the ordinary course of events, become the area of
slave states.

The struggle began in the House of Representatives, when the application of Missouri for statehood was met by an amendment, introduced by
Tallmadge of New York, February 13, 1819,[1] providing that further introduction of slavery be pro-
hibited, and that all children born within the state
after admission should be free at the age of twenty-
five years.[2] Tallmadge had already shown his attitude on this question when in 1818 he opposed the
admission of Illinois under its constitution, which
seemed to him to make insufficient barriers to
slavery. Brief as was the first Missouri debate, the
whole subject was opened up by arguments to which
later discussion added but little. The speaker,
Henry Clay, in spite of the fact that early in his
political career he had favored gradual emancipation
in Kentucky, led the opposition to restriction. His
principal reliance was upon the arguments that the
evils of slavery would be mitigated by diffusion, and
that the proposed restriction was unconstitutional.
Tallmadge and Taylor, of New York, combated these

[1] *Annals of Cong.*, 15 Cong., 2 Sess., I., 1170.
[2] See amended form in *House Journal*, 15 Cong., 2 Sess., 272.

arguments so vigorously and with such bold challenge of the whole system of slavery in new territories, that Cobb, of Georgia, declared, "You have kindled a fire which all the waters of the ocean cannot put out, which seas of blood can only extinguish."[1]

The first clause of Tallmadge's motion was carried (February 16, 1819) by a vote of 87 to 76, and the second by 82 to 78.[2] Taylor was emboldened to offer (February 18) to the bill for the organization of Arkansas territory an amendment by which slavery should be excluded, whereupon McLane, of Delaware, tentatively proposed that a line should be drawn west of the Mississippi, dividing the territories between freedom and slavery. Thus early was the whole question presented to Congress. In the Senate, Tallmadge's amendment was lost (February 27) by a vote of 22 to 16, several northern senators adhering to the south; and Congress adjourned without action.[3]

The issue was then transferred to the people, and in all quarters of the Union vehement discussions took place upon the question of imposing an anti-slavery restriction upon Missouri. Mass-meetings in the northern states took up the agitation, and various state legislatures, including Pennsylvania, New York, New Jersey, Ohio, and even the slave state of Delaware, passed resolutions with substan-

[1] *Annals of Cong.*, 15 Cong., 2 Sess., I., 1204.    [2] *Ibid.*, 1214.
[3] But Arkansas was organized as a territory without restriction.

tial unanimity against the further introduction of slaves into the territories of the United States, and against the admission of new slave states. Pennsylvania, so long the trusted ally of the south, invoked her sister states "to refuse to covenant with crime" by spreading the "cruelties of slavery, from the banks of the Mississippi to the shores of the Pacific." From the south came equally insistent protests against restriction.[1]

No argument in the debate in 1819 was more effective than the speech of Rufus King in the Senate, which was widely circulated as a campaign document expressing the northern view. King's antislavery attitude, shown as early as 1785, when he made an earnest fight to secure the exclusion of slavery from the territories,[2] was clearly stated in his constitutional argument in favor of restriction on Missouri, and his speech may be accepted as typical.[3] But it was also the speech of an old-time Federalist, apprehensive of the growth of western power under southern leadership.

He held that, under the power of making all needful rules and regulations respecting the territory and other property of the United States, Congress had the right to prohibit slavery in the Louisiana pur-

---

[1] *Niles' Register*, XVII., 296, 307, 334, 342–344, 395, 399, 400, 416; Ames, *State Docs. on Federal Relations*, No. 5, p. 4.

[2] McLaughlin, *Confederation and Constitution* (*Am. Nation*, X.), chap. vii.

[3] *Niles' Register*, XVII., 215; King, *Life and Corresp. of King*, VI., 690.

chase, which belonged to the United States in full dominion. Congress was further empowered, but not required, to admit new states into the Union. Since the Constitution contained no express provision respecting slavery in a new state, Congress could make the perpetual prohibition of slavery a condition of admission. In support of this argument, King appealed to the precedent of the Ordinance of 1787, and of the states of Ohio, Indiana, and Illinois, all admitted on the conditions expressed in that ordinance. In admitting the state of Louisiana in 1812, a different group of conditions had been attached, such as the requirement of the use of the English language in judicial and legislative proceedings.

The next question was the effect of the Louisiana treaty, by which the United States had made this promise: "The inhabitants of the ceded territory shall be incorporated in the Union of the United States, and admitted as soon as possible, according to the principles of the Federal constitution, to the enjoyment of all the rights, advantages and immunities of citizens of the United States; and in the mean time they shall be maintained and protected in the free enjoyment of their liberty, property and the religion which they profess." [1] King contended that, by the admission of Missouri to the Union, its inhabitants would obtain all of the "federal" rights which citizens of the United States derived from its

[1] U. S. Treaties and Conventions, 332.

Constitution, though not the rights derived from the constitutions and laws of the various states. In his opinion, the term *property* did not describe slaves, inasmuch as the terms of the treaty should be construed according to diplomatic usage, and not all nations permitted slavery. In any case, property acquired since the territory was occupied by the United States was not included in the treaty, and, therefore, the prohibition of the future introduction of slaves into Missouri would not affect its guarantees.

Could Missouri, after admission, revoke the consent to the exclusion of slavery under its powers as a sovereign state? Such action, King declared, would be contrary to the obligations of good faith, for even sovereigns were bound by their engagements. Moreover, the judicial power of the United States would deliver from bondage any person detained as a slave in a state which had agreed, as a condition of admission, that slavery should be excluded.

Having thus set forth the constitutional principles, King next took up the expediency of the exclusion of slavery from new states. He struck with firm hand the chord of sectional rivalry in his argument against the injustice to the north of creating new slave-holding states, which would have a political representation, under the "federal ratio," not possessed by the north. Under this provision for counting three-fifths of the slaves, five free persons in Virginia (so he argued) had as much power in the choice of representatives to Congress and in the appointment of presidential electors as seven free persons in any of the states in which slavery did not exist.  The disproportionate power and influence allowed to the original slave-holding states was a necessary sacrifice to the establishment of the Constitution; but the arrangement was limited to the old thirteen states, and was not applicable to the states made out of territory since acquired.  This argument had been familiar to New England ever since the purchase of Louisiana.  Finally, he argued that the safety of the Union demanded the exclusion of slavery west of the Mississippi, where the exposed and important frontier needed a barrier of free citizens against the attacks of future assailants.

To the southern mind, King's sectional appeal unblushingly raised the prospect of the rule of a free majority over a slave-holding minority, the downfall of the ascendency so long held by the south, and the creation of a new Union, in which the western states should be admitted on terms of subordination to the will of the majority, whose power would thus become perpetual.[1]

When the next Congress met, in December, 1819, the admission of Alabama was quickly completed; and the House also passed a bill admitting Maine to the Union, Massachusetts having agreed to this division of the ancient commonwealth, on condition

[1] King, *Life and Corresp. of King*, VI., 205, 267, 279, 288, 329, 339–344, 501; Jefferson, *Writings* (Ford's ed.), X., 162, 172, 280; Tyler, *Tylers*, I., 316.

that consent of Congress should be obtained prior to March 4, 1820. The Senate, quick to see the opportunity afforded by the situation, combined the bill for the admission of Maine with that for the unrestricted admission of Missouri, a proposition carried (February 16, 1820) by a vote of 23 to 21. Senator Thomas, who represented Illinois, which, as we have seen, was divided in its interests on the question of slavery, and who, as the vote showed, could produce a tie in the Senate, moved a compromise amendment, providing for the admission of Missouri as a slave state and for the prohibition of slavery north of 36° 30′ in the rest of the Louisiana purchase; and on the next day his amendment passed the Senate by a vote of 34 to 10.

The debate in the Senate was marked by another speech of Rufus King, just re-elected a senator from New York by an almost unanimous vote. With this prestige, and the knowledge that the states of Pennsylvania and New York stood behind him, he reiterated his arguments with such power that John Quincy Adams, who listened to the debate, wrote in his diary that "the great slave-holders in the House gnawed their lips and clenched their fists as they heard him."[1]

The case for the south was best presented by William Pinkney, of Maryland, the leader of the American bar, a man of fashion, but an orator of the first rank. His argument, on lines that the debates

---

[1] Adams, *Memoirs*, IV., 522; see *Cong. Globe*, 30 Cong., 2 Sess., App. 63–67.

had made familiar, was stated with such eloquence, force, and graphic power that it produced the effect of a new presentation. Waiving the question whether Congress might refuse admission to a state, he held that, if it were admitted, it was admitted into a union of equals, and hence could not be subjected to any special restriction.[1] Without denying the danger of the extension of slavery, he argued that it was not for Congress to stay the course of this dark torrent. "If you have power," said he, "to restrict the new states on admission, you may squeeze a new-born sovereign state to the size of a pigmy." There would be nothing to hinder Congress "from plundering power after power at the expense of the new states," until they should be left empty shadows of domestic sovereignty, in a union between giants and dwarfs, between power and feebleness. In vivid oratory he conjured up this vision of an unequal union, into which the new state would enter, "shorn of its beams," a mere servant of the majority. From the point of view of the political theory of a confederation, his contention had force, and the hot-tempered west was not likely to submit to an inferior status in the Union. Nevertheless, the debates and votes in the Constitutional Convention of 1787 seem to show that the fathers of the Constitution intended to leave Congress free to impose limitations on the states at admission.[2]

[1] *Annals of Cong.*, 16 Cong., 1 Sess., I., 389 et seq.
[2] Elliot, *Debates*, V., 492.

In the mean time, the House of Representatives was continuing the discussion on the old lines. Although the arguments brought out little that had not been stated in the first Missouri debate, they were restated day after day with an amplitude and a bitterness of feeling that aggravated the hostility between the rival forces. Even under this provocation, most southern members expressed their opinions on the morality and expediency of slavery in language that affords a strange contrast to their later utterances: in almost every case they lamented its existence and demanded its dispersion throughout the west as a means of alleviating their misfortune. Although most of the men who spoke on the point were from the regions where cotton was least cultivated, yet even Reid, of Georgia, likened the south to an unfortunate man who "wears a cancer in his bosom."[1] Tyler of Virginia, afterwards president of the United States, characterized slavery as a dark cloud, and asked, "Will you permit the lightnings of its wrath to break upon the South when by the interposition of a wise system of legislation you may reduce it to a summer's cloud?"[2] John Randolph, the ultra-southerner, was quoted as saying that all the misfortunes of his life were light in the balance when compared with the single misfortune of having been born a master of slaves.

In addition to the argument of "mitigation by

[1] *Annals of Cong.*, 16 Cong., 1 Sess., I., 1025.
[2] *Ibid.*, II., 1391.

diffusion," the south urged the injustice of excluding its citizens from the territories by making it
impossible for the southern planter to migrate
thither with his property.   On the side of the north,
it was argued with equal energy that the spread of
slaves into the west would inevitably increase their
numbers and strengthen the institution.   Since free
labor was unable to work in the midst of slave labor,
northern men would be effectively excluded from
the territories which might be given over to slavery.
Economic law, it was urged, would make it almost
certain that, in order to supply the vast area which
it was proposed to devote to slavery, the African
slave-trade would be reopened.  As the struggle
waxed hot, as the arguments brought out with increasing clearness the fundamental differences between the sections, threats of disunion were freely
exchanged.[1]   Even Clay predicted the existence of
several new confederacies.[2]   Nor were the extrem-
ists of the north unwilling to accept this alternative.[3]
But the danger of southern secession was diminished because Monroe was ready to veto any bill
which excluded slavery from Missouri.[4]

While still engaged in its own debates, the House
received the compromise proposal from the Senate.
At first the majority remained firm and refused to

[1] Adams, *Memoirs*, V., 13, 53;  Benton, *Abridgment of Debates*,
XIII., 607.                         [2] Adams, *Memoirs*, IV., 526.
[3] King, *Life and Corresp. of King*, VI., 274, 286, 287, 387.
[4] *Cong. Globe*, 30 Cong., 2 Sess., App. 67.

accept it.[1]   March 1, 1820, the House passed its own
bill imposing the restriction on Missouri, by a vote
of 91 to 82.   By the efforts of the compromisers,
however, a committee of conference was arranged,
which on the very next day resulted in the surrender of the House.   The vote on striking out the
restriction on Missouri was 90 to 87.   New England gave 7 ayes to 33 nays; the middle states, 8 to
46; the south cast 58 votes for striking out, and
none against it; the northwest gave all its 8 votes
against striking out the restriction; while the 17
southwestern votes were solidly in favor of admitting
Missouri as a slave state.

Thus, while the southern phalanx in opposition
remained firm, enough members were won over from
the northern ranks to defeat the restrictionists.
Some of these deserters[2] from the northern cause
were influenced by the knowledge that the admission of Maine would fail without this concession;
others, by the constitutional argument; others, by
the fear of disunion; and still others, by the apprehension that the unity of the Democratic party was
menaced by the new sectional alignment, which included among its leaders men who had been prominent in the councils of the Federalists.   By the final
solution, it was agreed (134 to 42) to admit Missouri

---

[1] Woodburn, in Am. Hist. Assoc., *Report* 1893, p. 251–297.
[2] See King, *Life and Corresp. of King*, VI., 291, 329; Benton,
*View*, I., 10; Adams, *Memoirs*, V., 15, 307.   Randolph applied
to them the term "doughfaces."

as a slave state and Maine as a free state; while all
of the rest of the territory possessed by the United
States west of the Mississippi and north of 36° 30′
was pledged to freedom.

Yet the fate of the measure was uncertain, for
some of Monroe's southern friends strongly urged
him still to veto the compromise.[1] The president
submitted to the cabinet the question whether Congress had the right to prohibit slavery in a territory,
and whether the section of the Missouri bill which
interdicted slavery forever in the territory north of
36° 30′ was applicable only to the territorial condition, or also to states made from the territory.
John Quincy Adams notes in his diary that "it was
unanimously agreed that Congress have the power
to prohibit slavery in the Territories"; though he
adds that neither Crawford, Calhoun, nor Wirt could
find any express power to that effect given in the
Constitution.[2] In order to avoid the difficulty arising from the fact that Adams alone believed the
word "forever" to apply to states as well as territories, the president modified the question so that
all would be able to answer that the act was constitutional, leaving each member to construe the
section to suit himself.

Although apparently the Missouri struggle was
thus brought to a conclusion, it is necessary to take
note of two succeeding episodes in the contest,

[1] *Cong. Globe*, 30 Cong., 2 Sess., App. 64.
[2] Adams, *Memoirs*, V., 5.

which immediately revived the whole question, embittered the antagonism, threatened the Union, and were settled by new compromises. In her constitution, Missouri not only incorporated guarantees of a slavery system, but also a provision against the admission of free negroes to the state. Application for admission to the Union under this constitution in the fall of 1820 brought on a contest perhaps more heated and more dangerous to the Union than the previous struggle. Holding that Missouri's clause against free negroes infringed the provision of the federal Constitution guaranteeing the rights of citizens of the respective states, northern leaders reopened the whole question by refusing to vote for the admission of Missouri with the obnoxious clause. Again the north revealed its mastery of the House, and the south its control of the Senate, and a deadlock followed. Under the skilful management of Clay, a new compromise was framed, by which Missouri was required, through her legislature, to promise that the objectionable clause should never be construed to authorize the passage of any laws by which any citizen of either of the states of the Union should be excluded from the enjoyment of any of the privileges and immunities to which such citizen was entitled under the Constitution of the United States. This Missouri accepted, but the legislature somewhat contemptuously added that it was without power to bind the state.[1]

[1] *Niles' Register*, XX., 388, cf. 300.

While this debate was in progress, and the problem of the status of Missouri, which had already established a constitution and claimed to be a state, was under consideration, the question of counting the Missouri vote in the presidential election of 1820 was raised. For this a third compromise was framed by Clay, by which the result of the election was stated as it would be with and without Missouri's vote. Since Monroe had been elected by a vote all but unanimous, the result was in either case the same; this theoretical question, nevertheless, was fraught with dangerous possibilities. Missouri was finally admitted by the proclamation of President Monroe, dated August 10, 1821, more than three years from the first application for statehood.

In a large view of American history, the significance of this great struggle cannot be too highly emphasized. Although the danger passed by and the ocean became placid, yet the storm in many ways changed the coast-line of American politics and broke new channels for the progress of the nation. The future had been revealed to far-sighted statesmen, who realized that this was but the beginning, not the end, of the struggle. "This momentous question," wrote Jefferson, "like a fire bell in the night, awakened and filled me with terror. I considered it at once as the knell of the Union. It is hushed, indeed, for the moment. But this is a reprieve only, not a final sentence. A geographical line, coinciding with a marked principle, moral and political, once conceived and held up to the angry passions of men, will never be obliterated; and every new irritation will mark it deeper and deeper." [1]

John Quincy Adams relates a contemporaneous conversation with Calhoun, in which the latter took the ground that, if a dissolution of the Union should follow, the south would be compelled to form an alliance, offensive and defensive, with Great Britain, though he admitted that it would be returning pretty much to the colonial state. When Adams, with unconscious prophecy of Sherman's march through Georgia, pressed Calhoun with the question whether the north, cut off from its natural outlet upon the ocean, "would fall back upon its rocks bound hand and foot, to starve, or whether it would not retain its powers of locomotion to move southward by land," Calhoun answered that the southern states would find it necessary to make their communities military. [2]

To Adams himself the present question was but a "title page to a great tragic volume." He believed that, if dissolution of the Union should result from the slavery question, it would be followed by universal emancipation of the slaves, and he was ready to contemplate such a dissolution of the Union, upon a point involving slavery and no other, believing that "the Union might then be reorganized on the fundamental principle of emancipation." "This ob-

---

[1] Jefferson, *Writings* (Ford's ed.), X., 157.
[2] Adams, *Memoirs*, IV., 530, 531.

ject," wrote he, "is vast in its compass, awful in its prospects, sublime and beautiful in its issue. A life devoted to it would be nobly spent or sacrificed."[1] Looking forward to civil war, he declared: "So glorious would be its final issue, that as God shall judge me I do not say that it is not to be desired."[2] But as yet he confided these thoughts to his diary.

The south was far from contented with the compromise, and her leading statesmen, Calhoun especially, came bitterly to regret both the concession in the matter of admitting federal control over slavery in the territories, and the division of the Louisiana purchase into spheres of influence which left to the slave-holding section that small apex of the triangle practically embraced in Arkansas. While the north received an area capable of being organized into many free states, the south could expect from the remaining territory awarded her only one state.

Among the immediate effects of the contest was its influence upon Monroe, who was the more ready to relinquish the American claim to Texas in the negotiations over Florida, because he feared that the acquisition of this southern province would revive the antagonism of the northern antislavery forces.[3]

The south learned also the lesson that slavery needed defence against the power of the majority,

---

[1] Adams, *Memoirs*, IV., 531.    [2] *Ibid.*, V., 210.
[3] Monroe, *Writings*, VI., 127; cf. Adams, *Memoirs*, V., 25, 54, 68.

and that it must shape its political doctrine and its policy to this end. But it would be a mistake to emphasize too strongly the immediate effect in this respect. Slavery was not yet accepted as the foundation of southern social and economic life. The institution was still mentioned with regret by southern leaders, and there were still efforts in the border states to put it in the process of extinction. South Carolina leaders were still friendly to national power, and for several years the ruling party in that state deprecated appeals to state sovereignty.[1] In the next few years other questions, of an economic and judicial nature, were even more influential, as a direct issue, than the slavery question. But the economic life of the south was based on slavery, and the section became increasingly conscious that the current of national legislation was shaped by the majority against their interests. Their political alliances in the north had failed them in the time of test, and the Missouri question disclosed the possibility of a new organization of parties threatening that southern domination which had swayed the Union for the past twenty years.[2]

The slavery struggle derived its national significance from the west, into which expanding sections carried warring institutions.

[1] See chap. xviii. below.

[2] Adams, *Memoirs*, IV., 529; King, *Life and Corresp. of King*, VI., 501; Jefferson, *Writings*, X., 175, 193 *n.*; cf. chap. xi. below; Hart, *Slavery and Abolition* (*Am. Nation*, XVI.), chap. xviii.

# CHAPTER XI

## PARTY POLITICS

### (1820–1822)

TO the superficial observer, politics might have seemed never more tranquil than when, in 1820, James Monroe received all but one of the electoral votes for his second term as president of the United States. One New Hampshire elector preferred John Quincy Adams, although he was not a candidate, and this deprived Monroe of ranking with Washington in the unanimity of official approval. But in truth the calm was deceptive. The election of 1820 was an armistice rather than a real test of political forces. The forming party factions were not yet ready for the final test of strength, most of the candidates were members of the cabinet, and the reelection of Monroe, safe, conciliatory, and judicious, afforded an opportunity for postponing the issue.

As we have seen, the Missouri contest had in it the possibility of a revolutionary division of the Republican party into two parties on sectional lines. The aged Jefferson, keen of scent for anything that threatened the ascendency of the triumphant democ-

racy, saw in the dissolution of the old alliance between Virginia and the "fanaticized" Pennsylvania,[1]
in the heat of the Missouri conflict, the menace of a
revived Federalist party, and the loss of Virginia's
northern following.   So hotly did Virginia resent the
Missouri Compromise, that while the question was
still pending, in February, 1820, her legislative caucus, which had assembled to nominate presidential
electors, indignantly adjourned on learning that
Monroe favored the measure.   "I trust in God,"
said H. St. George Tucker, "if the president does
sign a bill to that effect, the Southern people will
be able to find some man who has not committed
himself to our foes; for such are, depend on it,
the Northern Politicians."[2]   But the sober second
thought of Virginia sustained Monroe.   On the other
side, Rufus King believed that the issue of the Missouri question would settle "forever the dominion
of the Union."   "Old Mr. Adams," said he, "as he
is the first, will on this hypothesis be the last President from a free state."[3]

The truth is that the individual interests of the
south were stronger in opposing than those of the
north in supporting a limitation of slavery;[4] the
northern phalanx had hardly formed before it began

[1] Jefferson, *Writings* (Ford's ed.), X., 161, 171, 172, 177, 179,
192, 193 *n*., 279; King, *Life and Corresp. of King*, VI., 279, 282,
299; *Cong. Globe*, 30 Cong., 2 Sess., App. 63–67.
   [2] *William and Mary College Quarterly*, X., 11, 15.
   [3] King, *Life and Corresp. of King*, 267; cf. Adams, *Memoirs*,
IV., 528.                                    [4] Adams, *Memoirs*, IV., 533.

to dissolve.[1] Nevertheless, the Missouri question played some part in the elections in most of the states. In Pennsylvania, under the leadership of Duane, the editor of the *Aurora*, electors favorable to Clinton were nominated on an antislavery ticket,[2] but, outside of Philadelphia and the adjacent district, this ticket received but slight support. With few exceptions, the northern congressmen who had voted with the south failed of re-election.

The elections in the various states in this year showed more political division than was revealed by the vote for president, and they showed that in state politics the Federalist party was by no means completely extinct. In the congressional elections the flood of Republicanism left only isolated islands of Federalism unsubmerged. In Massachusetts eight of the thirteen members professed this political faith; New York returned some half - dozen men whose affiliations were with the same party; from Pennsylvania came a somewhat larger number; and they numbered nearly half of the delegation of Maryland. The cities of New York and Philadelphia were represented by Federalists, and there were three or four other districts, chiefly in New England, which adhered to the old party. There were also a few congressmen from the south who had been members of

[1] Benton, *Thirty Years' View*, I., 10.

[2] *Niles' Register*, XIX., 129; *National Advocate*, October 27, 1820; *Franklin Gazette*, October 25, November 8, 1820 (election returns); Ames, *State Docs. on Federal Relations*, No. 5, p. 5.

this organization. On the whole, however, the Fed-eralists awaited the new development of parties, determined to secure the best terms from those to whom they should transfer their allegiance. In New England, as has already been pointed out,[1] the toleration movement was completing its work of transferring power to democracy.

More important than local issues or the death throes of federalism, was the democratic tendency revealed in the constitutional conventions of this period. Between 1816 and 1830, ten states either established new constitutions or revised their old ones. In this the influence of the new west was peculiarly important. All of the new states which were formed in that region, after the War of 1812, gave evidence in their constitutions of the demo-cratic spirit of the frontier. With the exception of Mississippi, where the voter was obliged either to be a tax-payer or a member of the militia, all the western states entered the Union with manhood suffrage, and all of them, in contrast with the south, from which their settlers had chiefly been drawn, pro-vided that apportionment of the legislature should be based upon the white population, thus accepting the doctrine of the rule of the majority rather than that of property. As the flood of population moved towards the west and offered these attractive exam-ples of democratic growth, the influence reacted on the older states. In her constitution of 1818, Con-

[1] See chap. ii. above.

necticut gave the franchise to tax-payers or members of the militia, as did Massachusetts and New York in their constitutions of 1821. Maine provided in her constitution of 1820 for manhood suffrage, but by this time there was but slight difference between manhood suffrage and one based upon tax-paying.

Webster in Massachusetts and Chancellor Kent in New York viewed with alarm the prospect that freehold property should cease to be the foundation of government. Kent particularly warned the landed class that "one master capitalist with his one hundred apprentices, and journeymen, and agents, and dependents, will bear down at the polls an equal number of farmers of small estates in his vicinity, who cannot safely unite for their common defence." [1] It was the new counties of New York, particularly those of the western and northeastern frontier, which were the stronghold of the reform movement in that state. The abolition of the council of appointments and the council of revision by the New York convention contributed to the transfer of power to the people. But under the leadership of Van Buren a group of politicians, dubbed "The Albany Regency," controlled the political machinery as effectively as before.[2]

The campaign for the presidency of 1824 may be

[1] Carter and Stone, *Reports of the Proceedings and Debates of the Convention of 1821*, 222.

[2] McMaster, *United States*, V., 373–432; *ibid.*, *Rights of Man*, 61; MacDonald, *Jacksonian Democracy* (*Am. Nation*, XV.), chap. iv.

said to have begun as early as 1816.[1] Adams observed in 1818 that the government was assuming daily the character of cabal, "and preparation, not for the next Presidential election, but for the one after";[2] and by 1820, when the political sea appeared so placid, and parties had apparently dissolved, bitter factional fights between the friends of the rival candidates constituted the really significant indications of American politics. From the details of the personal struggles (usually less important to the student of party history) one must learn the tendency towards the reappearance of parties in this period, when idealists believed that all factions had been fused into one triumphant organization. In all of the great sections, candidates appeared, anxious to consolidate the support of their own section and to win a following in the nation. It is time that we should survey these men, for the personal traits of the aspirants for the presidency had a larger influence than ever before or since in the history of the country. Moreover, we are able to see in these candidates the significant features of the sections from which they came.

New England was reluctantly and slowly coming to the conclusion that John Quincy Adams was the only available northern candidate. Adams did not fully represent the characteristics of his section, for he neither sprang from the democracy of the interior of New England nor did he remain loyal to the Fed-

[1] Adams, *Memoirs*, V., 89.      [2] *Ibid.*, IV., 193.

eralist ideas that controlled the commercial interests of the coast. Moreover, of all the statesmen whom the nation produced, he had had the largest opportunity to make a comparative study of government. As an eleven-year-old boy, he went with his father to Paris in 1778, and from then until 1817, when he became Monroe's secretary of state, nearly half his time was spent at European courts. He served in France, Holland, Sweden, Russia, Prussia, and England, and had been senator of the United States from Massachusetts.

Thus Adams entered on the middle period of his career, a man of learning and broad culture, rich in experience of national affairs, familiar with the centres of Old-World civilization and with methods of European administration. He had touched life too broadly, in too many countries, to be provincial in his policy. In the minds of a large and influential body of his fellow-citizens, the Federalists, he was an apostate, for in the days of the embargo he had warned Jefferson of the temper of his section, had resigned, and had been read out of the party. The unpopularity, as well as the fame, of his father, was the heritage of the son. Perhaps the most decisive indication of the weakening of sectional bias by his foreign training is afforded by his diplomatic policy. An expansionist by nature, he had been confirmed in the faith by his training in foreign courts. "If we are not taken for Romans we shall be taken for Jews," he exclaimed to one who questioned the wisdom of the bold utterances of his diplomatic correspondence.

In one important respect Adams was the personification of his section. He was a Puritan, and his whole career was deeply affected by the fact. A man of method and regularity, tireless in his work (for he rose before the dawn and worked till midnight), he never had a childhood and never tried to achieve self-forgetfulness. His diary, printed in twelve volumes, is a unique document for the study of the Puritan in politics. Not that it was an entirely unreserved expression of his soul, for he wrote with a consciousness that posterity would read the record, and its pages are a compound of apparently spontaneous revelation of his inmost thought and of silence upon subjects of which we would gladly know more. He had the Puritan's restraint, self-scrutiny, and self-condemnation. "I am," he writes, "a man of reserved, cold, austere, and forbidding manners." Nor can this estimate be pronounced unjust. He was a lonely man, communing with his soul in his diary more than with a circle of admiring friends. It was not easy for men to love John Quincy Adams. The world may respect the man who regulates his course by a daily dead-reckoning, but it finds it easier to make friends with him who stumbles towards rectitude by the momentum of his own nature. Popularity, in any deep sense, was denied him. This deprivation he repaid by harsh, vindictive, and censorious judgments upon his con-

temporaries, and by indifference to popular prejudices.

With the less lovely qualities of the Puritan
aggravated by his own critical nature, Adams found
himself in a struggle for the presidency against some
of the most engaging personalities in American history. He must win over his enemies in New England and attach that section to his fortunes; he must
find friends in the middle states, conciliate the
south, and procure a following in the west, where
Clay, the Hotspur of debate, with all the power of
the speakership behind him, and Jackson, "Old
Hickory," the hero of New Orleans, contested the
field. And all the time he must satisfy his conscience, and reach his goal by the craft and strength
of his intellect rather than by the arts of popular
management. No statesman ever handled the problems of his public career with a keener understanding of the conditions of success.

The middle region was too much divided by the
game of politics played by her multitude of minor
leaders to unite upon a favorite son in this campaign; but De Witt Clinton, finding elements of
strength in the prestige which his successful advocacy of the Erie Canal had brought to him throughout the region where internal improvements were
popular, and relying upon his old connections with
the Federalists, watched events with eager eye,
waiting for an opportunity which never came.
Although the south saw in Rufus King's advocacy

of the exclusion of slavery from Missouri a deep design to win the presidency by an antislavery combination of the northern states, there was little ground for this belief. In truth, the middle region was merely the fighting-ground for leaders in the other sections.

In the south, Calhoun and Crawford were already contending for the mastery. Each of them represented fundamental tendencies in the section. Born in Virginia in 1772, Crawford had migrated with his father in early childhood to South Carolina, and soon after to Georgia.[1] Here he became the leader of the Virginia element against the interior democracy. But in his coarse strength and adaptability the burly Georgian showed the impress which frontier influences had given to his state. His career in national politics brought him strange alliances. This Georgia candidate had been no mere subject of the Virginia dynasty, for he supported John Adams in his resistance to France in 1798; challenged the administration of Jefferson by voting with the Federalists in the United States Senate against the embargo; and ridiculed the ambiguous message of Madison when the issue of peace or war with Great Britain was under consideration. A fearless supporter of the recharter of the national bank, he

[1] Phillips, "Georgia and State Rights," in Am. Hist. Assoc., *Report* 1901, II., 95; Cobb, *Leisure Labors;* Miller, *Bench and Bar of Georgia;* West, "Life and Times of William H. Crawford," in *National Portrait Gallery*, IV.; Adams, *Life of Gallatin.* 598.

had championed the doctrine of implied powers and denied the right of a state to resist the laws of Congress except by changing its representation or appealing to the sword under the right of revolution.

Nevertheless, in the period of this volume, Crawford joined the ranks of the southerners who demanded a return to strict construction and insistence on state rights. In the congressional caucus of 1816, he obtained 54 votes for the presidency against 65 for Monroe. Had not the influence of Madison been thrown for the latter, it seems probable that Crawford would have obtained the nomination; but his strength in building up a following in Congress was much greater than his popularity with the people at large. Controlling the patronage of the treasury department, he enlarged his political influence. As the author of the four-years'-tenure-of-office act, in 1820, he has been vehemently criticised as a founder of the spoils system. But there are reasons for thinking that Crawford's advocacy of this measure was based upon considerations of efficiency at least as much as those of politics,[1] and the conduct of his department was marked by sagacity. The administration of such a man would probably have been characterized by an accommodating spirit which would have carried on the traditions of Monroe.

In the career of Calhoun are strikingly exhibited the changing characteristics of the south in this era.

[1] Fish, *Civil Service and Patronage*, 66 et seq.

His grandfather was a Scotch-Irishman who came to Pennsylvania with the emigration of that people in the first half of the eighteenth century, and thence followed the stream of settlement that passed up the Great Valley and into South Carolina to the frontier, from which men like Daniel Boone crossed the mountains to the conquest of Kentucky and Tennessee.[1] The Calhoun family were frontier Indian fighters, but, instead of crossing the mountains as did Andrew Jackson, Calhoun remained to grow up with his section and to share its changes from a community essentially western to a cotton-planting and slave-holding region. This is the clew to his career.

In his speech in the House of Representatives in 1817, on internal improvements, Calhoun warned his colleagues against "a low, sordid, selfish, and sectional spirit," and declared that "in a country so extensive, and so various in its interests, what is necessary for the common good, may apparently be opposed to the interests of particular sections. It must be submitted to as the condition of our greatness." [2] This was the voice of the nationalistic west, as well as that of South Carolina in Calhoun's young manhood.

In view of his later career, it is significant that many of those who described him in these youthful years of his nationalistic policy found in him

[1] Cf. Howard, *Preliminaries of the Revolution* (*Am. Nation*, VIII.), chap. xiii.

[2] *Annals of Cong.*, 14 Cong., 2 Sess., 854, 855.

a noticeable tendency to rash speculation and novelty. "As a politician," said Senator Mills, of Massachusetts, about 1823, he is "too theorizing, speculative, and metaphysical,—magnificent in his views of the powers and capacities of the government, and of the virtue, intelligence, and wisdom of the *people*. He is in favor of elevating, cherishing, and increasing all the institutions of the government, and of a vigorous and energetic administration of it. From his rapidity of thought, he is often wrong in his conclusions, and his theories are sometimes wild, extravagant, and impractical. He has always claimed to be, and is, of the Democratic party, but of a very different class from that of Crawford; more like Adams, and his schemes are sometimes denounced by his party as ultra-fanatical." [1]

Another contemporary, writing prior to 1824, declared: "He wants, I think, consistency and perseverance of mind, and seems incapable of long-continued and patient investigation. What he does not see at the first examination, he seldom takes pains to search for; but still the lightning glance of his mind, and the rapidity with which he analyzes, never fail to furnish him with all that may be necessary for his immediate purposes. In his legislative career, which, though short, was uncommonly luminous, his love of novelty, and his apparent solicitude to astonish were so great, that he has occasionally been known to go beyond even the

[1] Mass. Hist. Soc., *Proceedings*, XIX., 37 (1881–1882).

dreams of political visionaries, and to propose schemes which were in their nature impracticable or injurious, and which he seemed to offer merely for the purpose of displaying the affluence of his mind, and the fertility of his ingenuity."[1] "Calhoun," said William Wirt, in 1824, "advised me the other day to study less and trust more to genius; and I believe the advice is sound. He has certainly practised on his own precepts, and has become, justly, a distinguished man. It may do very well in politics, where a proposition has only to be compared with general principles with which the politician is familiar."[2]

At the beginning of the campaign, Calhoun was the confidant and friend of Adams, apparently considering the alternative of throwing his influence in the latter's favor, if it proved impossible to realize his own aspirations.

From beyond the Alleghanies came two candidates who personified the forces of their section. We can see the very essence of the west in Henry Clay and Andrew Jackson. Clay was a Kentuckian, with the characteristics of his state; but, in a larger sense, he represented the stream of migration which had occupied the Ohio Valley during the preceding half-century. This society was one which, in its

[1] Quoted by Hodgson, *Letters from North Am.*, I., 81.
[2] Kennedy, *William Wirt*, II., 143; other views of Calhoun in MacDonald, *Jacksonian Democracy*, chaps. v., ix.; Hart, *Slavery and Abolition*, chap. xix.; Garrison, *Westward Extension* (*Am. Nation*, XV., XVI., XVII.).

composition, embraced elements of the middle region as well as of the south. It tended towards freedom, but had slaves in its midst, and had been accustomed, through experience, to adjust relations between slavery and free labor by a system of compromise. Economically, it was in need of internal improvements and the development of manufactures to afford a home market. It had the ideal of American expansion, and in earlier days vehemently demanded the control of the Mississippi and the expulsion of the Spaniard from the coasts of the Gulf. In the War of 1812 it sent its sons to destroy English influence about the Great Lakes and had been ambitious to conquer Canada.

It is an evidence of the rapidity with which the west stamped itself upon its colonists, that although Clay was born, and bred to the law, in Virginia, he soon became the mouth-piece of these western forces. In his personality, also, he reflected many of the traits of this region. Kentucky, ardent in its spirit, not ashamed of a strain of sporting blood, fond of the horse-race, partial to its whiskey, ready to "bluff" in politics as in poker, but sensitive to honor, was the true home of Henry Clay. To a Puritan like John Quincy Adams, Clay was, "in politics, as in private life, essentially a gamester." [1] But if the Puritan mind did not approve of Henry Clay, multitudes of his fellow-countrymen in other sections did. There was a charm about him that

[1] Adams, *Memoirs*, V., 59.

fastened men to him.   He was "Harry of the West,"
an impetuous, wilful, high-spirited, daring, jealous,
but, withal, a lovable man.  He had the qualities of
leadership; was ambitious, impulsive, often guided
by his intuitions and his sensibilities, but, at the
same time, an adroit and bold champion of con-
structive legislation.  He knew, too, the time for
compromise and for concession.  Perhaps he knew
it too well; for, although no statesman of this era
possessed more courageous initiative and construct-
ive power, his tact and his powers of management
were such that his place in history is quite as much
that of the "great compromiser" as it is that of the
author of the "American system."

It is not too much to say that Clay made the
speakership one of the important American institutions.  He was the master of the House of Representatives, shaping its measures by the appointment
of his committees and his parliamentary management.[1]  By the period of our survey, with the power of this office behind him, Clay had fashioned a
set of American political issues reflective of western
and middle-state ideas, and had made himself a
formidable rival in the presidential struggle.  He
had caught the self-confidence, the continental aspirations, the dash and impetuosity of the west.   But
he was also, as a writer of the time declared, "able
to captivate high and low, *l'homme du salon* and the
'squatter' in the Western wilderness."   He was a

[1] Follett, *Speaker of the House,* §§ 41-46.

mediator between east and west, between north and south—the "great conciliator." [1]

If Henry Clay was one of the favorites of the west, Andrew Jackson was the west itself. While Clay was able to voice, with statesman-like ability, the demand for economic legislation to promote her interests, and while he exercised an extraordinary fascination by his personal magnetism and his eloquence, he never became the hero of the great masses of the west; he appealed rather to the more intelligent — to the men of business and of property. Andrew Jackson was the very personification of the contentious, nationalistic democracy of the interior. He was born, in 1767, of Scotch-Irish parents, who had settled near the boundary-line between North and South Carolina, not far from the similar settlements from which, within a few years of Jackson's birth, Daniel Boone and Robertson went forth to be the founders of Kentucky and Tennessee. In 1788, with a caravan of emigrants, Jackson crossed the Alleghanies to Nashville, Tennessee, then an outpost of settlement still exposed to the incursions of Indians. During the first seven or eight years of his residence he was public prosecutor—an office that called for nerve and decision, rather than legal acumen, in that turbulent country.

[1] Grund, *Aristocracy in America*, II., 213. For other views of Clay, cf. Babcock, *Am. Nationality*, chap. xii.; MacDonald, *Jacksonian Democracy*, chap. xi.; Garrison, *Westward Extension*, chap. iii. (*Am. Nation*, XIII., XV., XVII.).

The appearance of this frontiersman on the floor
of Congress was an omen full of significance.  He
reached Philadelphia at the close of Washington's
administration, having ridden on horseback nearly
eight hundred miles to his destination.  Gallatin
(himself a western Pennsylvanian) afterwards graph-
ically described Jackson, as he entered the halls of
Congress, as "a tall, lank, uncouth-looking person-
age, with long locks of hair hanging over his face,
and a cue down his back tied in an eel-skin; his
dress singular, his manners and deportment those
of a rough backwoodsman."[1]   Jefferson afterwards
testified to Webster: "His passions are terrible.
When I was President of the Senate, he was a
Senator, and he could never speak, on account of
the rashness of his feelings.  I have seen him attempt it repeatedly, and as often choke with rage."[2]
At length the frontier, in the person of its leader,
had found a place in the government.  This six-foot
backwoodsman, angular, lantern-jawed, and thin,
with blue eyes that blazed on occasion; this choleric,
impetuous, Scotch-Irish leader of men; this expert
duellist and ready fighter; this embodiment of the
contentious, vehement, personal west, was in politics
to stay.[3]

In the War of 1812, by the defeat of the Indians

[1] Hildreth, *United States*, iv., 692.

[2] Webster, *Writings* (National ed.), XVII., 371.

[3] For other appreciations, see Babcock, *Am. Nationality*,
chap. xvii.; MacDonald, *Jacksonian Democracy*, chaps. ii., xviii.
(*Am. Nation*, XIII., XV.).

of the Gulf plains, he made himself the conqueror of a new province for western settlement, and when he led his frontier riflemen to the victory of New Orleans he became the national hero, the self-made man, the incarnation of the popular ideal of democracy.

The very rashness and arbitrariness which his Seminole campaign displayed appealed to the west, for he went to his object with the relentless directness of a frontiersman. This episode gave to Adams the opportunity to write his masterly state paper defending the actions of the general. But Henry Clay, seeing, perhaps, in the rising star of the frontier military hero a baneful omen to his own career, and hoping to break the administration forces by holding the government responsible for Jackson's actions, led an assault upon him in the Seminole debates on the floor of the House of Representatives.[1] Leaving Tennessee when he heard of the attack which was meditated against him, the general rushed (1819) to this new field of battle, and had the satisfaction of winning what he regarded as "the greatest victory he ever obtained"—a triumph on every count of Clay's indictment. This contest Jackson considered "the Touchstone of the election of the next president."[2] From this time the personality of the "Old Hero" was as weighty a factor

[1] Babcock, *Am. Nationality* (*Am. Nation*, XIII.), chap. xvii.
[2] N. Y. Publ. Library, *Bulletin*, IV., 160, 161; Parton, *Jackson*, II., chap. xl.

in American politics as the tariff or internal improvements.

He had now outgrown the uncouthness of his earlier days and had become stately and dignified in his manner. Around this unique personality there began to gather all those democratic forces which we have noted as characteristic of the interior of the country, reinforced by the democracy of the cities, growing into self-consciousness and power. A new force was coming into American life. This fiery Tennesseean was becoming the political idol of a popular movement which swept across all sections, with but slight regard to their separate economic interests. The rude, strong, turbulent democracy of the west and of the country found in him its natural leader.

All these candidates and the dominant element in every section professed the doctrines of republicanism; but what were the orthodox tenets of republicanism at the end of the rule of the Virginia dynasty? To this question different candidates and different sections gave conflicting answers. Out of their differences there was already the beginning of a new division of parties.

The progress of events gave ample opportunity for collision between the various factions. The crisis of 1819 and the depression of the succeeding years worked, on the whole, in the interests of Jackson, inclining the common people to demand a leader and a new dispensation. Not, perhaps, without a malicious joy did John Quincy Adams write in his diary at that time that "Crawford has labors and perils enough before him in the management of the finances for the three succeeding years."[1]   From the negotiation of the Florida treaty in 1819, and especially from the relinquishment by Spain of her claims to the Pacific coast north of the forty-second parallel, the secretary of state expected to reap a harvest of political advantage.[2]   But Clay, as well as Benton and the west in general, balked his hopes by denouncing the treaty as an abandonment of American rights; and, although Adams won friends in the south by the acquisition of Florida, Spain's delay of two years in the ratification of the treaty so far neutralized the credit that the treaty was, after all, but a feast of Tantalus.   In these intervening years, when the United States was several times on the verge of forcibly occupying Florida, the possibility of a war with Spain, into which European powers might be drawn, increased the importance of General Jackson as a figure in the eyes of the public.

Next the Missouri controversy, like "a flaming sword,"[3] cut in every direction and affected the future of all the presidential candidates.   The hope of Crawford to reap the reward of his renunciation in 1816 was based, not only upon his moderation in his earlier career, which had brought him friends

---

[1] Adams, *Memoirs*, IV., 391.
[2] *Ibid.*, IV., 238, 273, 451, V., 53, 109, 290; Monroe, *Writings*, VI., 127.   [3] Adams, *Memoirs*, V., 91.

among the Federalists, but also upon the prospect of attracting a following in Pennsylvania, with the aid of the influence of Gallatin, and in New York as the regular candidate of the party. These hopes of northern support demanded that Crawford should trim his sails with care, attacking the policies of his rivals rather than framing issues of his own. But for a time the Missouri controversy alienated both Pennsylvania and New York from the south, and it brought about a bitterness of feeling fatal to his success in those two states. To Clay, too, the slavery struggle brought embarrassments, for his attitude as a compromiser failed to strengthen him in the south, while it diminished his following in the north. Calhoun suffered from the same difficulty, although his position in the cabinet enabled him to keep in the background in this heated contest. Jackson stood in a different situation. At the time he was remote from the controversy, having his own troubles as governor of Florida, and, as a slave-holding planter he was not suspected by the south, while at the same time his popularity as the representative of the new democracy was steadily winning him friends in the antislavery state of Pennsylvania.

To Adams all the agitation was a distinct gain, since it broke the concert between Virginia and New York and increased his chances as the only important northern candidate. He saw—none more clearly—the possibility of this issue as a basis for a new

party organization,[1] but he saw also that it menaced a dissolution of the Union.[2] He was not dis-
posed to alienate the south, and he contented himself with confiding his denunciation of slavery to the
secret pages of his diary, while publicly he took his
stand on the doctrine that the proposed restriction
upon Missouri was against the Constitution.[3] As
early as 1821 he recognized that the number of
candidates in the field made it almost certain that
the election would be decided by the vote of states
in the House of Representatives, where the vote of
the single member from Illinois would count as much
as that of the whole delegation of New York or Pennsylvania. What Adams needed, therefore, was to
combine New England in his support, obtain, if possible, a majority in New York, and add the votes of
a sufficient number of smaller states to win the
election.

The seventeenth Congress, which met in December, 1821, and lasted until the spring of 1823, was
one of the most ineffective legislative bodies in the
country's history. Henry Clay had returned to
Kentucky to resume the practice of the law as a
means of restoring his financial fortunes, and the
importance of his leadership was emphasized by his
absence. Without mastery, and in the absence of
party discipline, Congress degenerated into a mere
arena for the conflicts of rival personal factions, each

[1] Adams, *Memoirs*, IV., 529.        [2] *Ibid.*, V., 12, 13, 53.
[3] *Ibid.*, IV., 529.

anxious to destroy the reputation of the candidate favored by the other.

In December, 1821, Barbour, of Virginia, was chosen speaker, by a close vote, over Taylor, the favorite of Adams, thus transferring the control of the congressional committees again to the south, aided by its New York allies. The advantage to Crawford arising from this election was partly neutralized by the fact that in this year his partisans in Georgia were defeated by the choice of his bitterest enemy for the governorship. It may have been this circumstance which aroused the hope of Crawford's southern rivals and led to the calling of a legislative caucus in South Carolina, which, on December 18, 1821, by a close vote, nominated William Lowndes instead of Calhoun for the presidency. Many of Calhoun's partisans refused to attend this caucus, and the vote was a close one (57 to 53).[1] Lowndes was a wealthy South Carolina planter, judicious and dispassionate, with a reputation for fair-mindedness and wisdom that gained him the respect of his foes as well as his friends. According to tradition, Clay once declared that among the many men he had known he found it difficult to decide who was the greatest, but added, "I think the wisest man I ever knew was William Lowndes."[2]  His death, in less than a year, removed from the presidential contest

[1] Ravenel, *William Lowndes*, chap. x.; Adams, *Memoirs*, V., 468, 470; *National Intelligencer*, January 19, 1822.
[2] Ravenel, *William Lowndes*, 238.

an important figure, and from the south one of the most gifted of her sons.

As soon as the news of the nomination of Lowndes reached Washington, a delegation of members of Congress, from various sections, secured Calhoun's consent to avow his candidacy. His career as a tariff man and as a friend of internal improvements had won him northern supporters, especially in Pennsylvania, although, as South Carolina's action showed, he was not able to control his state. The announcement of Calhoun's candidacy turned against him all the batteries of his rivals. Pleading the depleted condition of the treasury, Crawford's partisans in Congress attacked the measures of Calhoun as secretary of war. Retrenchment in the expenditures for the army was demanded, and finally, under the leadership of Crawford's friends, the Senate refused to ratify certain nominations of military officers made by the president on the recommendation of the secretary of war, giving as a reason that they were not in accordance with the law for the reduction of the army. In the cabinet discussion, Crawford openly supported this opposition, and his relations with the president became so strained that, in the spring of 1822, reports were rife that his resignation would be demanded.[1] Crawford himself wrote to Gallatin that it would not be to his disadvantage to be removed from office.[2]

[1] Cf. Adams, *Memoirs*, V., 525.
[2] Gallatin, *Writings*, II., 241.

In the summer the matter was brought to a head by a correspondence in which Monroe indignantly intimated that Crawford had given countenance to the allegation that the president's principles and policy were not in sympathy with the early Jeffersonian system of economy and state rights. Believing that Crawford was aiming at the creation of a new party (a thing which distressed Monroe, who regarded parties as an evil),[1] he made it clear that it was the duty of a cabinet officer, when once the policy of the executive had been determined, to give that policy co-operation and support.[2] In his reply Crawford denied that he had personally antagonized the measures of the administration;[3] but he took the ground that a cabinet officer should not attempt to influence his friends in Congress either for or against the policy of the government.

His assurances of loyalty satisfied Monroe and averted the breach. It is easy to see, however, that Crawford's attitude strengthened the feeling on the part of his rivals that he was intriguing against the administration. They believed, whether he instigated his partisans to oppose measures favored by the president or was unable to restrain them, in either case he should be forced into open opposi-

---

[1] Monroe, *Writings*, VI., 286–291.

[2] Monroe to Crawford, August 22, 1822, MS. in N. Y. Pub. Library.

[3] Crawford to Monroe, September 3, 1822, MS. in N. Y. Pub. Library; cf. Adams, *Memoirs*, VI., 390.

tion.[1] The truth is that the government was so divided within itself that it was difficult to determine with certainty what its policy was. Monroe's greatest weakness was revealed at this time in his inability to create and insist upon a definite policy. The situation was aggravated by the president's determination to remain neutral between the rival members of his official family, and by the loss of influence which he suffered through the knowledge that he was soon to lay down the presidential power.

Meanwhile, John Quincy Adams watched these intrigues with bitterness of soul. Debarred by his Puritan principles from the open solicitation of votes which his rivals practised, he yet knew every move in the game and gauged the political tendencies with the astuteness of the politician, albeit a Puritan politician. Nor did he disdain to make such use of his position as would win friends or remove enemies. He proposed to Calhoun a foreign mission, suggested the same to Clay, favored an ambassadorship for Clinton, and urged the appointment of Jackson to Mexico. These overtures were politely declined by the candidates, and Adams was forced to fight for the presidency against the men whom he would so gladly have sent to honor their country abroad.

[1] Cf. Poinsett to Monroe, May 10, 1822, *Monroe MSS.*, in Library of Cong.; Adams, *Memoirs*, V., 315, VI., 57.

## CHAPTER XII

### THE MONROE DOCTRINE

### (1821–1823)

THE place of slavery in the westward expansion of the nation was not the only burning question which the American people had to face in the presidency of Monroe. Within a few years after that contest, the problem of the independence of the New World and of the destiny of the United States in the sisterhood of new American republics confronted the administration. Should the political rivalries and wars of Europe to acquire territory be excluded from the western hemisphere? Should the acquisition of new colonies by European states in the vast unsettled spaces of the two Americas be terminated? These weighty questions were put to the mild Virginian statesman; history has named his answer the Monroe Doctrine.

From the beginning of our national existence, the United States had been pushing back Europe from her borders, and asserting neutrality and the right to remain outside of the political system of the Old World. Washington's farewell address of 1796, with its appeal to his fellow-citizens against "interweaving our destiny with that of any part of Europe," sank deep into the popular consciousness. It did not interfere with the process by which, piece by piece, the United States added to its domains fragments from the disintegrating Spanish empire; for so long as European states held the strategic positions on our flanks, as they did in Washington's day, the policy of separation from the nations of the Old World was one difficult to maintain; and France and England watched the enlargement of the United States with jealous eye. Each nation, in turn, considered the plans of Miranda, a Venezuelan revolutionist, for the freeing of Spanish America. In 1790 the Nootka Sound affair threatened to place England in possession of the whole Mississippi valley and to give her the leadership in Spanish America.[1] Two years later, France urged England to join her in freeing the colonies of Spain in the New World;[2] and when Pitt rejected these overtures, France sent Genêt to spread the fires of her revolution in Louisiana and Florida.[3]

When this design failed, France turned to diplomacy, and between 1795 and 1800 tried to persuade Spain to relinquish Florida and Louisiana to herself, as a means of checking the expansion of the United States and of rendering her subservient to

---

[1] Turner, in *Am. Hist. Rev.*, VII., 704, VIII., 78; Manning, *Nootka Sound Controversy*, in Am. Hist. Assoc., *Report*, 1904, p. 281; cf. Bassett, *Federalist System* (*Am. Nation*, XI.), chap. vi.
[2] Sorel, *L'Europe et la Révolution Française*, II., 384, 418, III., 17. [3] Turner, in *Am. Hist. Rev.*, III., 650, X. 259.

France.   The growing preponderance of France over Spain, and the fear that she would secure control of Spanish America, led England again in 1798 to listen to Miranda's dream of freeing his countrymen, and to sound the United States on a plan for joint action against Spain in the New World.[1]   The elder Adams turned a deaf ear to these suggestions, and when at last Napoleon achieved the possession of Louisiana, it was only to turn it over to the United States.[2] Jefferson's threat that the possession of Louisiana by France would seal the union between England and the United States and "make the first cannon which shall be fired in Europe the signal for the tearing up of any settlement she may have made, and for holding the two continents of America in sequestration for the common purposes of the united British and American nations,"[3] showed how unstable must be the American policy of isolation so long as Europe had a lodgment on our borders.[4]

The acquisition of Louisiana by the United States was followed by the annexation of West Florida; and the Seminole campaign frightened Spain into the abandonment of East Florida.[5]   While the United States was thus crowding Europe back from

[1] Turner, in *Am. Hist. Rev.*, X., 249 et seq., 276.
[2] Sloane, in *Am. Hist. Rev.*, IV., 439.
[3] Jefferson, *Writings* (Ford's ed.), VIII., 145.
[4] Cf. Channing, *Jeffersonian System* (*Am. Nation*, XII.), chap. v.
[5] Babcock, *American Nationality* (*Am. Nation*, XIII.), chap. xvii.

its borders and strengthening its leadership in the New World, Spanish America was revolting from the mother-country. When Napoleon made himself master of Spain in 1807, English merchants, alarmed at the prospect of losing the lucrative trade which they had built up in the lands which Spain had so long monopolized, supported the revolutionists with money, while various expeditions led by English officers aided the revolt.[1] At first, failure met the efforts of the loosely compacted provinces, made up of sharply marked social classes, separated by race antagonisms, and untrained in self-government. Only in Buenos Ayres (later the Argentine Confederation), where representatives of the United Provinces of the Rio de la Plata declared their independence in 1816, were the colonists able to hold their ground.

A new era in the revolt began, however, in 1817, when General San Martin surprised the Spaniards by his march, from a frontier province of La Plata, over a pass thirteen thousand feet above the sea across the Andes to Chili. In the course of four years, with the co-operation of Lord Cochrane (who relinquished the British service in order to command the fleet of the insurgents on the Pacific), he effected the liberation of Chili and of Peru. Meanwhile, in the northern provinces the other great South American revolutionist, Bolivar, aided by a legion of

[1] Paxson, *Independence of the So. Am. Republics*, chap. iii.; *Am. Hist. Rev.*, IV., 449, VI., 508.

Irish and English veterans, won the independence of Venezuela and Colombia. In July, 1822, these two successful generals met in Ecuador; and San Martin, yielding the leadership to the more ambitious Bolivar, withdrew from the New World. By this date, America was clearly lost to the Latin states of Europe, for Mexico became an independent empire in 1821, and the next year Brazil, while it chose for its ruler a prince of the younger line of the royal house of Portugal, proclaimed its independence.[1]

Although the relations between these revolutionary states and England, both on the military and on the commercial side, were much closer than with the United States, this nation followed the course of events with keen interest. Agents were sent, in 1817 and 1820, to various South American states, to report upon the conditions there; and the vessels of the revolutionary governments were accorded belligerent rights, and admitted to the ports of the United States.[2] The occupation of Amelia Island and Galveston, in 1817, by revolutionists, claiming the protection of the flags of Colombia and Mexico respectively, gave opportunity for piratical forays upon commerce, which the United States was unable to tolerate, and these establishments were broken up by the government.[3]

[1] Paxson, *Independence of the So. Am. Republics*, chap. i.
[2] *Ibid.*, 121; *Am. State Paps., Foreign*, IV., 217, 818.
[3] McMaster, *United States*, IV., chap. xxxiv.; Reeves, in *Johns Hopkins Univ. Studies*, XXIII., Nos. 9, 10.

President Monroe seems to have been inclined to recognize the independence of these states on the earliest evidence of their ability to sustain it; but the secretary of state, John Quincy Adams, favored a policy of delay. He had slight confidence in the turbulent, untrained republics of Latin-America, and little patience with the idea that their revolution had anything in common with that of the United States. At the close of 1817 he believed it inexpedient and unjust for the United States to favor their cause, and he urged a friend to publish inquiries into the political morality and the right of the United States to take sides with a people who trampled upon civil rights, disgraced their revolution by buccaneering and piracy, and who lacked both unity of cause and of effort.[1] His own system was based on the theory that the United States should move in harmony with England, and, if possible, with the other European powers in the matter of recognition;[2] and he perceived that Spain would be more likely to yield Florida to the United States if the president did not acknowledge the independence of her other provinces.

Henry Clay now came forward as the advocate of immediate recognition of the revolutionary republics. In this he was undoubtedly swayed by a real sympathy with the cause of freedom and by the

---

[1] Letter to A. H. Everett, in *Am. Hist. Rev.*, XI., 112.

[2] Paxson, *Independence of the So. Am. Republics*, 149 (citing MSS. in State Dept.)

natural instincts of a man of the west, where antagonism to Spain was bred in the bone. But his insistence upon immediate action was also stimulated by his opposition to Monroe and the secretary of state. Clay's great speech on recognition was made May 24 and 25, 1818. His imagination kindled at the vastness of South America: "The loftiest mountains; the most majestic rivers in the world; the richest mines of the precious metals; and the choicest productions of the earth." "We behold there," said he, "a spectacle still more interesting and sublime—the glorious spectacle of eighteen millions of people struggling to burst their chains and be free." He appealed to Congress to support an American system by recognizing these sister republics, and argued that, both in diplomacy and in commerce they would be guided by an American policy and aid the United States to free itself from dependence on Europe. His motion was lost by an overwhelming majority, but the speech made a deep impression.[1]

In the two years which elapsed between the negotiation and the ratification of the Florida treaty, the president was several times on the point of recommending the forcible occupation of Florida, but he withheld the blow, hoping that the liberal Spanish government established under the constitution of 1820 might be brought to give its consent to the cession. The impetuous Clay chafed under this

[1] *Annals of Cong.*, 15 Cong., 1 Sess., II., 1474.

delay, and on May 10, 1820, he broke forth in
another speech, in support of a resolution declaring
the expediency of sending ministers to the South
American states. Charging the administration, and
especially John Quincy Adams, with subserviency
to Great Britain, he demanded that the United
States should become the centre of a system against
the despotism of the Old World and should act on
its own responsibility. "We look too much abroad,"
said he. "Let us break these commercial and political fetters; let us no longer watch the nod of any
European politician; let us become real and true
Americans, and place ourselves at the head of the
American system." [1]

Clay was steadily gaining support in his efforts to
force the hands of the administration: his resolutions won by a fair majority, and again, in February,
1821, he secured the almost unanimous assent of the
House to a resolution of sympathy with South America. Another resolution, expressing the readiness of
that body to support the president whenever he
should think it expedient to recognize the republics,
passed by a vote of 86 to 68, and the triumphant
Clay was placed at the head of a committee to wait
on the president with this resolution. [2]

Although the victory was without immediate effect
on the administration, which refused to act while

[1] *Annals of Cong.*, 16 Cong., 1 Sess., II., 2727.
[2] *Ibid.*, 2229, and 2 Sess., 1081, 1091; Adams, *Memoirs*, V.,
268.

the Florida treaty was still unratified, Adams perceived that the popular current was growing too strong to be much longer stemmed; the charge of dependence upon England was one not easy to be borne, and Clay's vision of an independent American system guided by the United States had its influence on his mind. Five months after Clay's speech, in 1820, extolling such a system, Adams set forth similar general ideas in a discussion between himself and the British minister over the regulation of the slave-trade.[1] By 1822, Florida was in our possession. The success of the arms of the revolutionists was unmistakable; several governments of sufficient stability to warrant recognition had been erected; and it was patent to the world that Spain had lost her colonies. Acting on these considerations, Monroe sent a message to Congress, March 8, 1822, announcing that the time for recognition had come, and asking for appropriations for ministers to South America.[2]

In the mean time, the secretary of state was confronted with important diplomatic questions which complicated the South American problem. As Spanish America broke away from the mother-country, its possessions in North America on the Pacific were exposed to seizure by the rival powers. In 1821, when Stratford Canning, the British minister to the United States, protested against a motion,

---

[1] Adams, *Memoirs*, V., 182.
[2] Richardson, *Messages and Papers*, II., 116

in the House of Representatives, that the United
States should form an establishment on the Columbia, Adams challenged any claim of England to the
shores of the Pacific. "I do not *know*," said he,
"what you claim nor what you do not claim. You
claim India ; you claim Africa ; you claim—"
"Perhaps," said Canning, "a piece of the moon."
"No," said Adams, "I have not heard that you
claim exclusively any part of the moon; but there
is not a spot on *this* habitable globe that I could
affirm you do not claim; and there is none which
you may not claim with as much color of right as
you can have to Columbia River or its mouth."[1]

The time had arrived when Adams's familiarity
with foreign diplomacy, his belief that a new nation
must assert its rights with vigor if it expected to
maintain them, his very testiness and irascibility,
his "bull-dog fighting qualities"—in short, the characteristics that were sources of weakness to him in
domestic politics—proved to be elements of strength
in his conduct of foreign relations. The individualism, the uncompromising nature, the aggressiveness,
and the natural love of expansion, which were traits
of John Quincy Adams, became of highest service
to his country in the diplomatic relations of the next
few years.

Hardly a year elapsed after this defiance to England when Adams met the claims of Russia likewise
with a similar challenge. On September 4, 1821,

[1] Adams, *Memoirs*, V., 252.

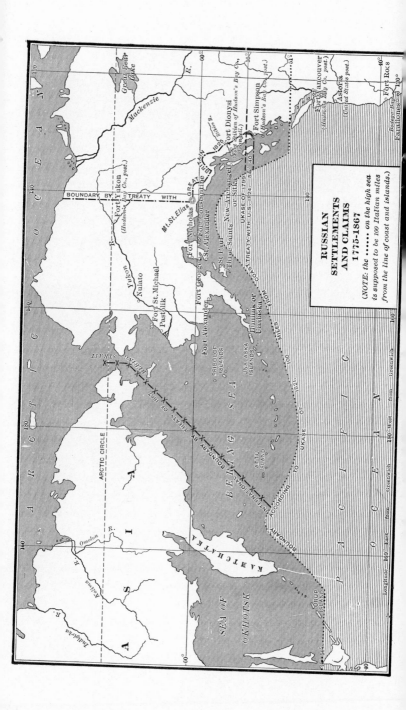

RUSSIAN
SETTLEMENTS
AND CLAIMS
1775-1867

(NOTE: the ...... on the high sea
is supposed to be 100 Italian miles
from the line of coast and islands.)

the Russian czar issued a ukase announcing the claim of Russia on the Pacific coast **north** of the fifty-first degree, and interdicting to the commercial vessels of other powers the approach on the high seas within one hundred Italian miles of this claim.[1] This assertion of Russian monopoly, which would, in effect, have closed Bering Sea, met with peremptory refusal by Adams, and on July 17, 1823, having in mind Russia's posts in California, he informed the minister, Baron Tuyl, "that we should contest the right of Russia to *any* territorial establishment on this continent, and that we should assume distinctly the principle that the American continents are no longer subjects for *any* new European colonial establishments."[2]  After negotiations, Russia concluded the treaty of April 17, 1824, by which she agreed to form no establishments on the northwest coast south of latitude 54° 40', and the United States reciprocally agreed to make no establishments north of that line.  At the same time Russia abandoned her extreme claim of maritime jurisdiction.

While the Russian claims were under consideration, the question of the future of Cuba was also giving great concern.  The Pearl of the Antilles remained in the possession of Spain when she lost her main-land colonies.  By its position, commanding both the Gulf of Mexico and the Caribbean Sea, it was of the highest importance to the United States

[1] *U. S. Foreign Relations* (1890), 439.
[2] Adams, *Memoirs*, VI., 163.

as well as to the West Indian powers, England and France. From a party in Cuba itself, in September, 1822, advances were made to the United States for annexation, and Monroe sent an agent to investigate, meanwhile refraining from encouraging the movement.[1]

George Canning, who became premier of England in September, 1822, was convinced that no questions relating to continental Europe could be more immediately and vitally important to Great Britain than those which related to America.[2] Alarmed lest the United States should occupy Cuba, Canning, in a memorandum to the cabinet in November, questioned whether any blow that could be struck by any foreign power in any part of the world would more affect the interests of England.[3] He contented himself, however, with sending a naval force to the waters of Cuba and Puerto Rico, with the double purpose of checking American aggressions and protecting English commerce. This action created suspicion on the part of the United States, and Adams issued instructions (April 28, 1823) to the American minister at Madrid, declaring that, within a half-century, the annexation of Cuba to the United States would be indispensable to the continuance and integrity of the Union itself. The laws of political

[1] Adams, *Memoirs*, VI., 69, 72.
[2] Stapleton, *Official Corresp. of George Canning*, I., 48.
[3] *Ibid.*, 52; Royal Hist. Soc., *Transactions* (new series), XVIII., 89.

gravitation would, in his opinion, ultimately bring Cuba to this country, if, in the mean time, it were not acquired by some other power. Adams's immediate policy, therefore, favored the retention of Cuba and Puerto Rico by Spain, but he refused to commit the United States to a guarantee of the independence of Cuba against all the world except that power.[1]

The mutual jealousies of the nations with respect to the destiny of Cuba became, at this time, entangled with the greater question of the intervention of the Holy Alliance in the New World. At the Congress of Verona, in November, 1822, Austria, France, Russia, and Prussia signed a revision of the treaty of the Holy Alliance,[2] which had for its objects the promotion of the doctrine of legitimacy in support of the divine right of rulers, and the doctrine of intervention, for the purpose of restoring to their thrones those monarchs who had been deposed by popular uprisings, and of rehabilitating those who had been limited by written constitutions. At Verona, the allies agreed to use their efforts to put an end to the system of representative government in Europe, and to prevent its further introduction. Having already suppressed uprisings in Naples and Piedmont, the Alliance empowered France to send troops into the Spanish peninsula to restore the

---

[1] Wharton, *Digest of Am. Int. Law*, I., 361–366; Latané, *Diplomatic Relations with Lat. Am.*, chap. iii.

[2] Snow, *Treaties and Topics;* Seignobos, *Pol. Hist. of Europe since 1814*, 762.

authority of the king of Spain and to put down the
revolutionary constitution of 1820. Châteaubriand,
the French representative, desired the congress to
go further and intervene in Spanish America, but
this question was postponed.

Alarmed by the prospect of French power in Spain
and by the proposed extension of the system of the
allies to the New World, Canning protested against
the doctrine of intervention, and determined that,
if France was to become the mistress of Spain, she
should at least not control the old Spanish empire.
In the spring of 1823 he made an unsuccessful effort
to secure a pledge from France not to acquire any
Spanish-American possessions, either by conquest
or by cession from Spain. But the French government maintained its reserve, even after England
disclaimed for herself the intention of acquiring
Spanish-American territory.[1]

Having broken with the concert of the European
powers, it was natural that England should turn to
the United States, and it is very likely that the next
step of Canning was influenced by the despatches of
the British minister to the United States, who reported a conversation with Adams, in June, 1823, in
which the secretary strongly set forth his belief that,
in view of the virtual dissolution of the European
alliance, England and the United States had much
in common in their policy. "With respect to the
vast continent of the West," said he, "the United

[1] Stapleton, *Political Life of Canning*, I., 19.

States must necessarily take a warm and decided interest in whatever determined the fate or affected the welfare of its component members." But he disclaimed any wish on the part of this country to obtain exclusive advantages there. He urged that England ought to recognize the independence of the revolted provinces, and he deprecated the conquest or cession of any part of them.[1]

The first impression of the British minister, on hearing Adams's emphasis on the community of interests between the two nations, was that the secretary was suggesting an alliance; and it may well have been that Canning was encouraged by the American attitude to make overtures to Rush, the American minister, shortly after these despatches must have reached him. On August 16, 1823, and three times thereafter, Canning proposed a joint declaration by England and the United States against any project by a European power of "a forcible enterprise for reducing the colonies to subjugation, on the behalf or in the name of Spain; or which meditates the acquisition of any part of them to itself, by cession or by conquest."[2] Canning was willing to make public announcement that the recovery of the colonies by Spain was hopeless; that the matter of recognition was only a question of

[1] Stratford Canning to George Canning, June 6, 1823, *MSS. Foreign Office, America*, CLXXVI.; Adams, *Memoirs*, VI., 151; cf. Reddaway, *Monroe Doctrine*, 83.

[2] Stapleton, *Political Life of Canning*, II., 24; W. C. Ford, in Mass. Hist. Soc. *Proceedings* (2d series), XV., 415.

time; and that Great Britain did not aim at the possession of any portion of them, but that it "could not see any part of them transferred to any other power with indifference." These professions Canning desired that the United States and England should mutually confide to each other and declare "in the face of the world."

Confronted with Canning's important proposition, Rush, who doubted the disinterestedness of England, prudently attempted to exact a preliminary recognition of the Spanish-American republics; if Canning would agree to take this action, he would accept the responsibility of engaging in such a declaration.[1] Having failed in four successive efforts to persuade Rush to join in an immediate declaration, irrespective of prior recognition by England, Canning proceeded alone, and, in an interview with Polignac, the French minister in London, on October 9, 1823, he announced substantially the principles which he had expressed to the American minister.[2] Polignac thereupon disclaimed for France any intention to appropriate Spanish possessions in America, and abjured any design, on the part of his country, of acting against the colonies by force; but he significantly added that the future relations between Spain and her colonies ought to form a subject of discussion between the European powers. Acting on this idea, and in opposition to England's

[1] Ford, in Mass. Hist. Soc. *Proceedings* (2d series), XV., 420, 423.    [2] Stapleton, *Political Life of Canning*, II., 26.

wishes, an invitation was sent to Russia, Prussia, and Austria to confer at Paris on the relations of Spain and her revolted provinces.

Rush's despatches relating the overtures of Canning reached President Monroe [1] October 9, 1823, on the same day that Canning was interviewing Polignac. Adams was absent from Washington at the time, and Monroe, returning to Virginia, consulted ex-Presidents Jefferson and Madison. He clearly intimated his own belief that the present case might be an exception to the general maxim against entanglement in European politics, and was evidently willing to accept the proposal of the British government.[2]

To Jefferson [3] the question seemed the most momentous since the Declaration of Independence. One nation, most of all, he thought, could disturb America in its efforts to have an independent system, and that nation, England, now offered "to lead, aid, and accompany us in it." He believed that by acceding to her proposition her mighty weight would be brought into the scale of free government, and "emancipate a continent at one stroke." Construing the English proposition to be a maintenance of our own principle of "keeping out of our land all foreign powers," he was ready to accept Canning's invitation. He was even ready to yield his desire for the annexation or independence of Cuba, in

[1] Ford, in *Am. Hist. Rev.*, VII., 684.
[2] Monroe, *Writings*, VI., 323.
[3] *Ibid.*, VI., 394.

order to obtain England's co-operation. Madison,[1] also, was prepared to accept the English proposal, and to invite that government to join in disapproval of the campaign of France in Spain and in a declaration in behalf of the Greeks.

Thus, by a strange operation of fate, members of the "Virginia dynasty," the traditional antagonists of England, were now willing to accept her leadership in American affairs, and were inclined to mingle in European concerns in opposition to the Holy Alliance. By an equally strange chance, it was a statesman from New England, the section traditionally friendly to British leadership, who prevented the United States from casting itself into the arms of England at this crisis, and who summoned his country to stand forth independently as the protector of an American system.

When John Quincy Adams learned of Canning's proposals, he had just been engaged in a discussion with the representative of the czar, who informed him of the refusal of Russia to recognize the Spanish-American republics, and expressed the hope that America would continue her policy of neutrality.

While the cabinet had Rush's despatches under consideration, Adams received a second communication from the Russian minister, expounding the reactionary ideas of the Holy Alliance.[2] To the

[1] Madison, *Writings* (ed. of 1865), III., 339–341.
[2] Ford, in Mass. Hist. Soc. *Proceedings* (2d series), XV., 378, 395, 402–408.

secretary of state this was a challenge to defend the American ideas of liberty. Convinced that his country ought to decline the overture of Great Britain and avow its principles explicitly to Russia and France, "rather than to come in as a cock-boat in the wake of the British man-of-war," Adams informed the president that the reply to Russia and the instructions to Rush in England must be part of a combined system of policy. "The ground that I wish to take," he said, "is that of earnest remonstrance against the interference of European powers by force with South America, but to disclaim all interference on our part with Europe; to make an American cause and adhere inflexibly to that." [1]

In the cabinet he stood firmly against giving guarantees to England with respect to Cuba. He heartened up his colleagues, who were alarmed at the possibility of the spread of war to the United States; but at the same time that he dismissed this danger as remote he pictured to the cabinet the alarming alternatives in case the allies subjugated Spanish America: California, Peru, and Chili might fall to Russia; Cuba, to England; and Mexico, to France. The danger was even at our doors, he declared, for within a few days the minister of France had openly threatened to recover Louisiana. [2] Such suggestions exhibit the real significance of the prob-

[1] Adams, *Memoirs*, VI., 178, 194, 197, 199–212.
[2] *Ibid.*, VI., 207; cf. Reeves, in *Johns Hopkins Univ. Studies*, XXIII., Nos. 9, 10.

lem, which in truth involved the question of whether America should lie open to seizure by rival European nations, each fearful lest the other gain an undue advantage. It was time for the United States to take its stand against intervention in this hemisphere.

Monroe was persuaded by Adams to change the first draught of his message, in which the president criticised the invasion of Spain by France and recommended the acknowledgment of the independence of the Greeks, in terms which seemed to threaten war with Europe on European questions. Even Webster and Clay, in fervent orations, showed themselves ready to go far towards committing the United States to an unwise support of the cause of the Greeks, which at this time was deeply stirring the sympathy of the United States. On the other hand, Adams stood firmly on the well-established doctrine of isolation from Europe, and of an independent utterance, by the United States, as the leader in the New World, of the principles of a purely American system. In the final draught, these ideas were all accepted, as well as the principles affirmed by Adams in his conferences with the Russian minister.

When sent to Congress, on December 2, 1823, Monroe's message asserted "as a principle in which the rights and interests of the United States are involved, that the American continents, by the free and independent condition which they have assumed and maintain, are henceforth not to be considered as subjects for future colonization by any European powers." This was in effect the proclamation of the end of a process that began with Columbus, Cabot, and Cartier — the rivalry of the nations of the Old World in the discovery, occupation, and political control of the wild lands of the western hemisphere. The interpretation by the next administration left the enforcement of this general principle to the various American states according to their interests.[1]

The message further dealt with the determination of the United States not to meddle with European affairs. "It is only when our rights are invaded or seriously menaced," said Monroe, "that we resent injuries or make preparation for our defense. With the movements in this hemisphere we are of necessity more immediately connected, and by causes which must be obvious to all enlightened and impartial observers. The political system of the allied powers is essentially different in this respect from that of America." This declaration expressed the consciousness that there was a real American system contrasted with that of Europe and capable of separate existence.

Finally, the message met the immediate crisis by a bold assertion of the policy of the United States: "We owe it, therefore, to candor and to the amicable relations existing between the United States and

[1] See chap. xvi. below.

those powers to declare that we should consider any attempt on their part to extend their system to any portion of this hemisphere as dangerous to our peace and safety. With the existing colonies or dependencies of any European power we have not interfered and shall not interfere. But with the Governments who have declared their independence and maintained it, and whose independence we have, on great consideration and on just principles, acknowledged, we could not view any interposition for the purpose of oppressing them, or controlling in any other manner their destiny, by any European power in any other light than as the manifestation of an unfriendly disposition toward the United States." [1] Herein was the assertion of the well-established opposition of the United States to the doctrine of intervention as violating the equality of nations. It was the affirmation also of the equality of the Old and the New World in diplomatic relations, and the announcement of the paramount interest of the United States in American affairs. [2]

This classic statement of the position of the United States in the New World, therefore, applied an old tendency on the part of this country to a particular exigency. Its authorship can hardly be attributed to any single individual, but its peculiar

---

[1] Richardson, *Messages and Papers*, II., 207–218; cf. Hart, *Foundations of Am. Foreign Policy*, chap. vii.

[2] Moore, "Non-Intervention and the Monroe Doctrine," in *Harper's Mag.*, CIX., 857.

significance at this juncture lay in the fact that the United States came forward, unconnected with Europe, as the champion of the autonomy and freedom of America, and declared that the era of European colonization in the New World had passed away. The idea of an American system, under the leadership of the United States, unhampered by dependence upon European diplomacy, had been eloquently and clearly voiced by Henry Clay in 1820. But John Quincy Adams also reached the conception of an independent American system, and to him belongs the credit for the doctrine that the two Americas were closed to future political colonization. His office of secretary of state placed him where he was able to insist upon a consistent, clear-cut, and independent expression of the doctrine of an American system. Monroe's was the honor of taking the responsibility for these utterances.[1]

Canning afterwards boasted, "I called the New World into existence to redress the balance of the Old."[2] Unquestionably his determination that "if France had Spain it should not be Spain with the Indies," materially contributed to make effective the protest of the United States, and he recognized the value of the president's message in putting an end to the proposal of a European congress. "It was broken," said he, "in all its limbs before,

[1] Cf. Reddaway, *Monroe Doctrine*, chap. v.; and Ford, in *Am. Hist. Rev.*, VII., 676, VIII., 28.

[2] Stapleton, *Political Life of Canning*, III., 227.

but the president's message gives it the *coup de grâce*." [1]

Nevertheless, the assertion by the United States of an American system independent of Europe, and the proposed exclusion of Europe from further colonization were, in truth, as obnoxious to England as they were to France.[2] "The great danger of the time," declared Canning in 1825, shortly after the British recognition of Mexico, "—a danger which the policy of the European system would have fostered—was a division of the world into European and American, republican and monarchical; a league of wornout governments on the one hand and of youthful and stirring nations, with the United States at their head, on the other. *We* slip in between, and plant ourselves in Mexico. The United States have gotten the start of us in vain, and we link once more America to Europe." On December 17, 1824, Canning wrote: "Spanish America is free; and if we do not mismanage our matters sadly, she is English, and *novus saeclorum nascitur ordo*." [3]

Later events were to reveal how unsubstantial were the hopes of the British minister. For the present, his hands were tied by the fact that England and the United States had a common interest in safeguarding Spanish America; and the form of Monroe's

[1] Stapleton, *George Canning and His Times*, 395.

[2] Reddaway, *Monroe Doctrine*, 98.

[3] Festing, *J. H. Frere and His Friends*, 267, quoted by E. M. Lloyd, in Royal Hist. Soc. *Transactions* (new series), XVIII., 77, 93.

declaration seemed less important than its effective-
ness in promoting this result. In the United States
the message was received with approbation. Although Clay, from considerations of policy, withdrew a resolution which he presented to Congress
(January 20, 1824), giving legislative endorsement to
the doctrine,[1] there was no doubt of the sympathy of
the American people with its fundamental principles.
Together with the attitude of England, it put an end
to the menace of the Holy Alliance on this side of the
ocean, and it began a new chapter, yet unfinished,
in the history of the predominance of the United
States in the New World.

[1] *Annals of Cong.*, 18 Cong., 1 Sess., I., 1104, II., 2763.

## CHAPTER XIII

### INTERNAL IMPROVEMENTS

#### (1818–1824)

THE transformation by which the slender line of the Indian trail became the trader's trace, and then a road, superseded by the turnpike and canal, and again replaced by the railroad, is typical of the economic development of the United States. As the population of the west increased, its surplus products sought outlets. Improved means of communication became essential, and when these were furnished the new lines of internal trade knitted the nation into organic unity and replaced the former colonial dependence upon Europe, in the matter of commerce, by an extensive domestic trade between the various sections. From these changes flowed important political results.[1]

Many natural obstacles checked this process. The Appalachian mountain system cut off the seaboard of the United States from the interior. From the beginning, the Alleghanies profoundly influenced the course of American history, and at one time even

[1] For the earlier phase of internal improvements, cf. Babcock, *Am. Nationality* (*Am. Nation*, XIII.), chap. xv.

endangered the permanency of the Union.  In our own day the railroad has so reduced the importance of these mountains that it is difficult for us to realize the part which they once played in our development. Although Webster boasted that there were no Alleghanies in his politics, we have already seen[1] that in the twenties they exercised a dominant influence on the lines of internal commerce, and compelled the pioneer farmers to ship their surplus down the Mississippi to New Orleans and around the coast, and thence abroad and to the cities of the north.  The difficult and expensive process of wagoning goods from Philadelphia and Baltimore across the mountains to the Ohio Valley raised the price of manufactured goods to the western farmer; while, on the other hand, the cost of transportation for his crops left him little profit and reduced the value of his lands.[2]

Under these circumstances, it was inevitable that the natural opportunities furnished by the water system of the Great Lakes and the widely ramifying tributaries of the Mississippi should appeal to statesmen who considered the short distances that intervened between these navigable waters and the rivers that sought the Atlantic.  Turnpikes and canals had already shown themselves practicable and profitable in England, so a natural effort arose to use them in aid of that movement for connecting east and west by ties of interest which Washington had so much at

---

[1] See chaps. iii., vi., above.

[2] *Journ. of Polit. Econ.*, VIII., 36–41.

heart. New York, Pennsylvania, Maryland, and Virginia, all subdivided by the mountains into eastern and western sections, fostered roads and chartered turnpike and canal companies. Pennsylvania was pre-eminent in this movement even before the close of the eighteenth century, subscribing large amounts to the stock of turnpike companies in order to promote the trade between Philadelphia and the growing population in the region of Pittsburg. So numerous were the projects and beginnings of roads and canals in the nation, that as early as 1808 the far-sighted Gallatin made his famous report for a complete national system of roads and canals.[1]

When New York undertook the Erie Canal in 1817 as a state enterprise, and pushed it to such a triumphant conclusion that before a decade after its completion its tolls repaid the cost of construction, a revolution was effected in transportation. The cheapness of water carriage not only compelled the freighters on the turnpike roads to lower their charges, but also soon made it probable that canals would supersede land transportation for heavy freights, and even for passengers. For a time the power of Pittsburg and the activity of Philadelphia merchants sustained the importance of the Pennsylvania turnpike. Until Great Lake steam navigation developed and population spread along the shore of Lake Erie and canals joined the Ohio and the lakes, the Erie Canal did not reap its harvest

[1] Cf. Hart, *Slavery and Abolition* (*Am. Nation*, XVI.), chap. iii.

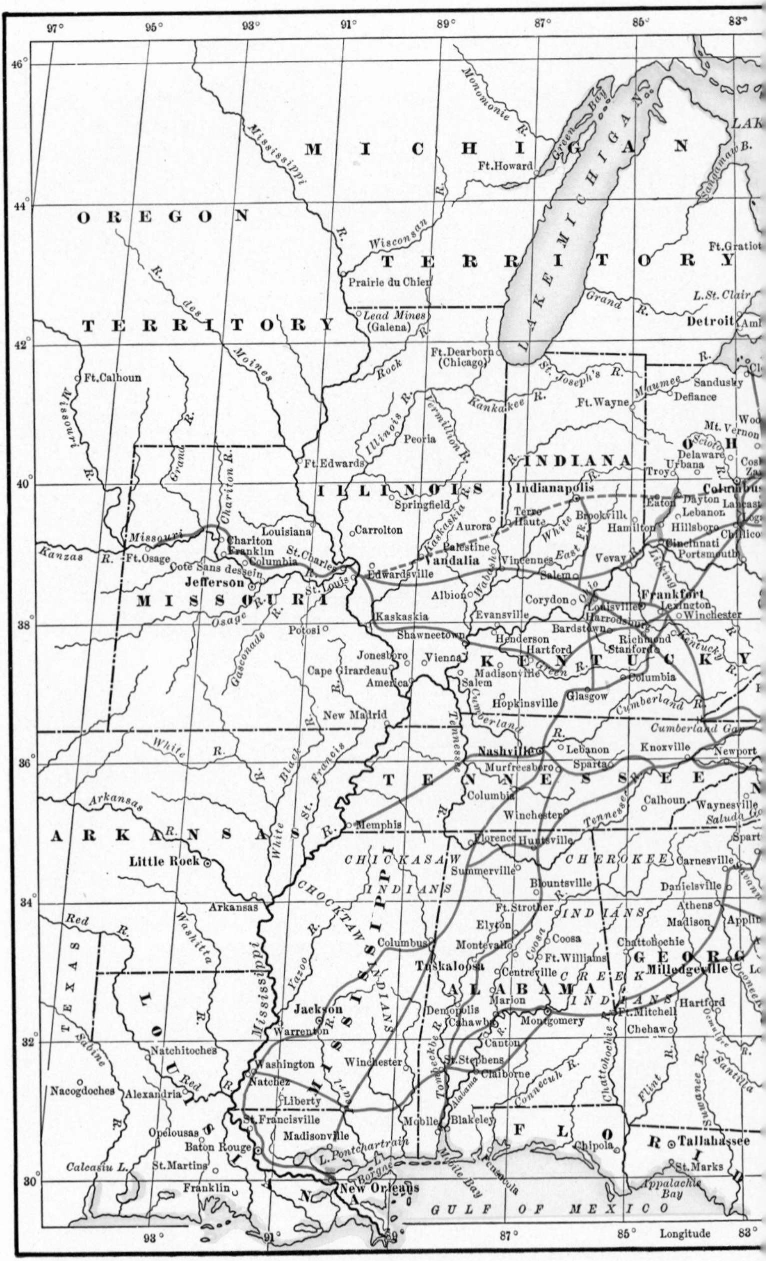

97° 95° 93° 91° 89° 87° 85° 83°
46° 44° 42° 40° 38° 36° 34° 32° 30°
MICHIGAN TERRITORY
OREGON TERRITORY
LAKE MICHIGAN
Green Bay
Monomonie R.
Mississippi R.
Ft.Howard
Wisconsan R.
Prairie du Chien
Lead Mines (Galena)
Rock R.
Grand R.
L.St. Clair
Detroit
Ft.Gratiot
Sanganaw B.
LAK
des Moines R.
Ft.Dearborn (Chicago)
St. Joseph's R.
Maumee
Sandusky
Defiance
Ft. Wayne
Kankakee R.
Ft.Calhoun
Missouri R.
Illinois R.
Vermillion R.
Peoria
Ft.Edwards
Grand R.
Chariton R.
INDIANA
OHIO
Mt. Vernon
Scioto
Delaware
Urbana
Troy
Columbus
ILLINOIS
Indianapolis
Springfield
Eaton
Dayton
Lebanon
Brookville
Hamilton
Hillsboro
Chillicothe
Cincinnati
Portsmouth
Terre Haute
White R.
Aurora
Carrolton
Louisiana
Chariton
Franklin
Columbia
Missouri
Kanzas R.
Ft.Osage
Cote Sans dessein
Jefferson
MISSOURI
St.Charles
St.Louis
Edwardsville
Kaskaskia R.
Palestine
Vandalia
Wabash
Vincennes
East Fk.
Vevay
Salem
Licking R.
Frankfort
Lexington
Winchester
Ohio
Corydon
Louisville
Harrodsburg
Albion
Kaskaskia
Evansville
Bardstown
Osage R.
Gasconade R.
Potosi
Shawneetown
Henderson
Hartford
Richmond
Stanford
Kentucky R.
Jonesboro
Vienna
Cape Girardeau
America
Madisonville
Salem
Green R.
KENTUCKY
Columbia
Glasgow
Hopkinsville
Cumberland R.
New Madrid
Cumberland Gap
Tennessee R.
White R.
Black R.
St. Francis R.
Nashville
Lebanon
Knoxville
Newport
Murfreesboro
Sparta
TENNESSEE
Columbia
Calhoun
Waynesville
Arkansas
Winchester
Saluda
Memphis
ARKANSAS
Florence
Huntsville
Little Rock
CHICKASAW INDIANS
CHEROKEE
Carnesville
Summerville
Blountsville
Danielsville
Arkansas
Athens
Red R.
Washitta
CHOCKTAW INDIANS
MISSISSIPPI
Ft.Strother
INDIANS
Madison
Elyton
Yazoo R.
Columbus
Montevallo
Coosa
Chattohochie
Ft.Williams
GEORGIA
Milledgeville
Oconee
Tuskaloosa
Centreville
CREEK
TEXAS
LOUISIANA
Jackson
Marion
ALABAMA
INDIANS
Demopolis
Cahawba
Montgomery
Ft.Mitchell
Hartford
Warrenton
Chehaw
Ocmulgee R.
Sabine
Natchitoches
Canton
Washington
Winchester
St.Stephens
Natchez
Claiborne
Nacogdoches
Alexandria
Red R.
Tombeckbe R.
Alabama R.
Connecuh R.
Chattohochie R.
Flint R.
Suwanee R.
Santilla
Liberty
St.Francisville
Mobile
Blakeley
Opelousas
Madisonville
FLORIDA
Chipola
Tallahassee
Baton Rouge
L. Pontchartrain
Mobile Bay
Pensacola
Calcasiu L.
St.Martins
L. Borgne
St.Marks
Franklin
New Orleans
Appalachie Bay
GULF OF MEXICO
93° 91° 89° 87° 85° 83°
Longitude

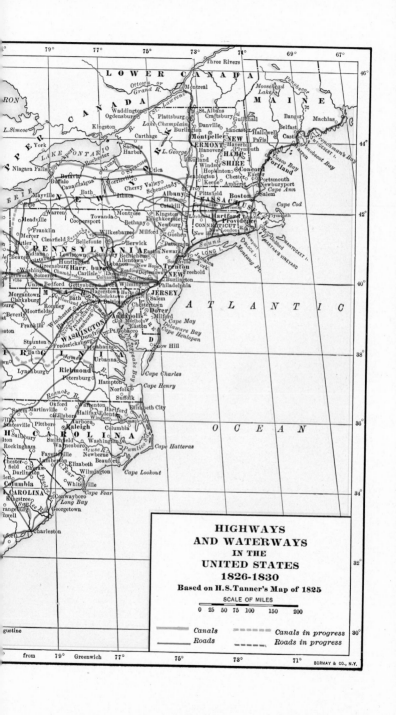

HIGHWAYS
AND WATERWAYS
IN THE
UNITED STATES
1826-1830

Based on H.S.Tanner's Map of 1825

SCALE OF MILES

0  25  50  75  100      150        200

Canals                 Canals in progress
Roads                  Roads in progress

BORMAY & CO., N.Y.

of trade in the west.    But already Pennsylvania was
alarmed at the prospect of losing her commercial
ascendency.

While New York and Philadelphia were developing canals and turnpikes to reach the west, Baltimore was placed in an awkward position.    The attempts to improve the waters of the upper Potomac
engaged the interests of Maryland and Virginia from
the days of Washington.    But the success of the
Potomac Company, chartered jointly by these two
states in an effort to reach the Ohio trade, would
have turned traffic towards the city of Washington
and its outlying suburbs instead of towards Baltimore, which was already connected by a turnpike
with the Cumberland Road, so as to share with Philadelphia in the wagon trade to the Ohio.    On the
other hand, Baltimore was interested in the development of the Susquehanna's navigation, for this
river had its outlet in Chesapeake Bay, near enough
to Baltimore to make that city its entrepôt; and
it tapped the great valley of Pennsylvania as well
as the growing agricultural area of south-central
New York, which was not tributary to the Erie
Canal.    But it was not possible to expect New York,
Pennsylvania, or even that part of Maryland interested in the Potomac to aid these ambitions of
Baltimore; and that city found itself at a disadvantage and Maryland's interests were divided.[1]

[1] Hulbert, *Historic Highways*, XIII., 69 et seq.; Mills, *Treatise
on Inland Navig.*; see chap. xvii., below.

Meantime, Virginia, anxious to check the western exodus from the interior of her state, established a state fund and a board of public works for the improvement of her rivers, including the project of connecting the James and Kanawha.[1] North Carolina was agitating similar plans;[2] and South Carolina made appropriations for extensive improvements.

New England devoted her attention to canals along the seaboard and up the Connecticut Valley, to give the products of the interior of that section an outlet on the coast. Boston was feeling the isolation from the western trade that was enriching New York, and some voices were raised in favor of a canal to reach the Hudson; but the undertaking was too difficult, and the metropolis of New England devoted its energies to the ocean commerce.

Meantime, the west was urging the federal government to construct those interstate roads and canals which were essential to the prosperity of that section and which could not be undertaken by jealous and conflicting states. The veto by Madison of Calhoun's bonus bill, in 1817,[3] was followed nine months later by Monroe's first annual message,[4] in which he stated his belief that the Constitution did not empower

---

[1] Babcock, *Am. Nationality* (*Am. Nation*, XIII.), chap. xv.; Adams, *United States*, IX., 164.

[2] Murphy, *Memorial on Internal Improvements*; Weaver, *Internal Improvements in N. C.*, in *Johns Hopkins Univ. Studies*, XXI., 113.

[3] Cf. Babcock, *Am. Nationality* (*Am. Nation*, XIII.), chap. xvii.      [4] Richardson, *Messages and Papers*, II., 18.

Congress to establish a system of internal improvements, and recommended an amendment to convey the power. To Clay and the friends of internal improvements, these constitutional scruples of the Virginia dynasty, although accompanied by approval of the plan of a system of internal improvements at federal expense, came as a challenge. In an important debate on the constitutionality of national internal improvements, in 1818, the House of Representatives, voting on four resolutions submitted by Lowndes, of South Carolina,[1] declared that Congress had power to appropriate money for the construction of military roads, and of other roads, and of canals, and for the improvement of watercourses (89 ayes to 75 nays).[2] But after a debate which turned on the significance of the word "establish" in the Constitution, the House decided against the power to construct post-roads and military roads (81 to 84); against the power to construct roads and canals necessary to commerce between the states (71 to 95); and against the power to construct canals for military purposes (81 to 83).

It was clear after this debate that there was not a sufficient majority to override the veto which might be expected from the president. On the other hand, the majority were unwilling to hazard the rights which they claimed to possess, by appealing to the states for a constitutional amendment. The

---

[1] *Annals of Cong.*, 15 Cong., 1 Sess., I., 1249
[2] By count of names; the *Journal* gives ayes 90.

next year Calhoun, the secretary of war, responding
to an invitation of Congress, submitted a report out-
lining a comprehensive system of internal improvements requisite for the defence of the United States.
While avoiding an opinion on the question of constitutionality, he declared that a judicious system
of roads and canals, constructed for commerce and
the mail, would be "itself among the most efficient
means for the more complete defense of the United
States"; [1] and he favored the use of the engineering
corps for surveying the routes and of federal troops
for the actual work of construction.

By 1818 the National Road [2] had been constructed from Cumberland, on the Potomac, across the
mountains to Wheeling, on the Ohio, and two years
later Congress made appropriations for a survey of
the road westward to the Mississippi River. The
panic of 1819, however, left the treasury in such a
condition that it was not until 1822 that the preservation and construction of this highway was again
taken up with vigor. In that year a bill was introduced authorizing the president to cause toll-houses,
gates, and turnpikes to be erected on the Cumberland Road, and to appoint toll-gatherers, with power
to enforce the collection of tolls to be used for the
preservation of the road. The bill further provided

[1] *Am. State Paps., Miscellaneous*, 534.
[2] Cf. Babcock, *Am. Nationality* (*Am. Nation*, XIII.), chap.
xv.; Young, *Cumberland Road*, 15; Hulbert, *Historic Highways*,
X., chap. i.

for a system of fines for violation of the laws of the road. It therefore involved the question of the right of jurisdiction as well as of construction.

The measure passed the House of Representatives by a vote of 87 to 68. The districts along the line of the Potomac and the Ohio, and the regions tributary to the road in Pennsylvania and western Virginia, were almost a unit in favor of the bill. Indeed, the whole vote of the western states, with the exception of two members from Tennessee, was given in the affirmative. But Pittsburg, which feared the diversion of her western trade to Baltimore, opposed the bill. The area along the Susquehanna which looked to Baltimore also voted in the negative, as did the majority of the delegation from New York, who were apprehensive of the effect of the National Road as a rival to the Erie Canal. The Senate passed the bill by the decisive vote of 29 to 7.

Monroe vetoed this measure, on the ground that it implied a power to execute a complete system of internal improvements, with the right of jurisdiction and sovereignty. Accompanying his veto (May 4, 1822), he submitted "Views on the Subject of Internal Improvements." [1] In this elaborate disquisition, he rehearsed the constitutional history of internal improvements, and expounded his concep-

---

[1] Richardson, *Messages and Papers*, II., 142–183; Monroe, *Writings*, VI., 216; Mason, *Veto Power*, § 85; Nelson, *Presidential Influence on Int. Imp. (Iowa Journal of Hist. and Politics)*, IV., 29, 30.

tion of the construction of the Constitution, and of
the relation of the states and the nation under the
theory of divided sovereignty. Although he denied
to the federal government the right of jurisdiction
and construction, he asserted that Congress had un-
limited power to raise money, and that "in its appropriation, they have a discretionary power, restricted
only by their duty to appropriate it to purposes of
common defense and of general, not local, national,
not state, benefit." Nevertheless, he strongly recommended a system of internal improvements, if it
could be established by means of a constitutional
amendment. Both houses sustained the president's
veto.

Acting upon Monroe's intimation of the power to
appropriate money, and following the line of least
resistance, the next year an act was passed making
appropriations for repairs of the Cumberland Road.
On March 3, 1823, also, was signed the first of the
national acts for the improvement of harbors.[1]
The irresistible demand for better internal com-
munications and the development of a multitude of
local projects, chief among them a new plan for uniting Chesapeake Bay with the Ohio by a canal along
the Potomac, resulted, in 1824, in the introduction of
the general survey bill, authorizing the president to
cause surveys to be made for such roads and canals
as he deemed of national importance for commercial,
military, or postal purposes. The evident intention

[1] *U. S. Statutes at Large*, III., 780.

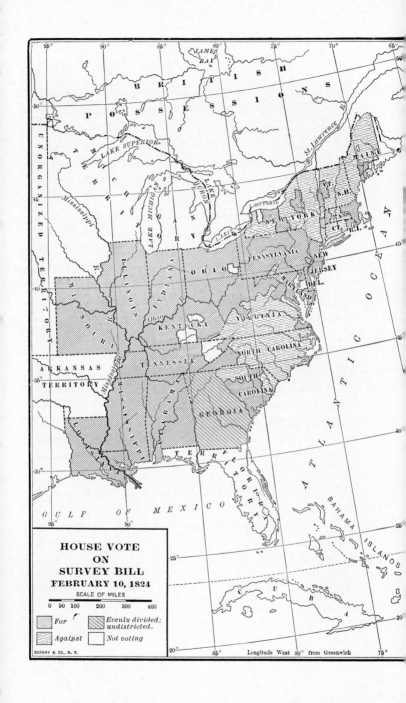

HOUSE VOTE
ON
SURVEY BILL
FEBRUARY 10, 1824

SCALE OF MILES

0  50 100    200    300    400

For

Evenly divided;
undistricted.

Against

Not voting

BORMAY & CO., N. Y.

Longitude West 80° from Greenwich

of the bill was to prepare a programme for appropriations for internal improvements on a national scale, and for subscription to the stock of companies engaged in these enterprises. The discussion of the general survey bill brought out the significance of the problem of transportation, and revealed the sectional divisions of the nation in clear light.

Henry Clay made an earnest effort to commit Congress to the exercise of the power of construction of interstate highways and canals which could not be undertaken by individual states or by combinations of states, and which, if built at all, must be by the nation. He recounted the attention given by Congress to the construction of public buildings and light-houses, coast surveys, erection of sea-walls in the Atlantic states—"everything on the margin of the ocean, but nothing for domestic trade; nothing for the great interior of the country."[1] "Not one stone," he said, "had yet been broken, not one spade of earth removed, in any Western State." He boldly claimed that the right to regulate commerce granted as fully the power to construct roads and canals for the benefit of circulation and trade in the interior as it did the power to promote coastwise traffic. His speech was a strong assertion of the right of the west to equality of treatment with the old sections of the country. "A new world," said he, "has come into being since the Constitution was adopted. Are the narrow, limited necessities of the old thirteen states,

[1] *Annals of Cong.*, 18 Cong., 1 Sess., I., 1035.

of, indeed, parts only of the old thirteen states, as they existed at the formation of the present Constitution, forever to remain the rule of its interpretation?"[1]

In contrast with the united attitude of the west upon internal improvements, which Henry Clay voiced with such lofty accent, the south showed divisions which reflected opposing economic interests in the section. Not only were the representatives of Maryland almost a unit in support of the bill, but also the western districts of Virginia and North Carolina, as well as a considerable fraction of the representatives from South Carolina and Georgia, supported the cause of the west on this occasion.

The opposition in the south found, perhaps, its most inflexible expression in the speech of John Randolph,[2] who, with characteristic recklessness and irresponsibility, dragged from its closet the family skeleton of the south, and warned his fellow slaveholders that, if Congress possessed power to do what was proposed by the bill, they might emancipate every slave in the United States, "and with stronger color of reason than they can exercise the power now contended for." He closed by threatening the formation of associations and "every other means short of actual insurrection." "We shall keep on the windward side of treason," said he.[3]

---

[1] *Annals of Cong.*, 18 Cong., 1 Sess., I., 1315; Colton, *Private Corresp. of Clay*, 81.

[2] *Annals of Cong.*, 18 Cong., 1 Sess., I., 1296–1311.

[3] Cf. Macon's identical views in 1818 and 1824, Univ. of North Carolina, *James Sprunt Hist. Monographs*, No. 2, pp. 47, 72.

On the other hand, McDuffie, of South Carolina, the friend and protégé of Calhoun and a later leader of the nullification forces, supported the measure and spoke as earnestly in favor of a liberal construction of the Constitution as any of the most enthusiastic supporters of the bill.  He declared that the constitutional convention "did not regard the state governments as sentinels upon the watch-towers of freedom, or in any respect more worthy of confidence than the general government."

When the bill came to the final vote in the House of Representatives, New England gave 12 votes in favor and 26 against; the middle states, 37 to 26 (New York, 7 to 24); the south, 23 to 34; the west, 43 to 0.  Thus the bill carried by 115 to 86.  As the map shows, the opposition was chiefly located in New England and New York and in a fragment of the old south.  The entire west, including the south-western slave states, with Pennsylvania and the Potomac Valley, acted together.  In the Senate, the vote stood 24 to 18.  Here New England gave an almost solid vote against the bill.

Thus by the close of Monroe's administration the forces of nationalism seemed to have triumphed in the important field of internal improvements.  It was the line of least resistance then, as it had been in the days of the Annapolis Convention.[1]

[1] McLaughlin, *Confederation and Constitution* (*Am. Nation,* X.), chap. xi.

# CHAPTER XIV

## THE TARIFF OF 1824

### (1820–1824)

AS has been shown in the last chapter, the attitude of portions of the south towards strict
construction was not inveterate upon measures
which promised advantages to that section. But
the tariff struggle revealed the spirit which arose
when powers were asserted unfavorable to any section. The failure of the tariff bill of 1820[1] was followed by other unsuccessful attempts to induce a
majority of Congress to revive the subject. The
messages of Monroe favored a moderate increase of
duties; but it was not until 1824, after the return of
Henry Clay and his triumphant election to the speakership, that Congress showed a protectionist majority ably disciplined and led.[2]

The tariff bill of 1824 was supported, not as a
revenue, but as a protective measure. It proposed
an increase of the duty upon iron, hemp, cotton
bagging, woollens, and cottons. Upon woollen goods,

[1] See above, chap. ix.
[2] For previous tariff history, cf. Babcock, *Am. Nationality*
(*Am. Nation*, XIII.), chap. xiv.

the friends of protection desired to apply the minimum principle which the tariff of 1816 had provided for cotton goods. But the cheap woollens were mostly used for the clothing of southern slaves, and the proposition for an increase of duty met with so strenuous a resistance that in the outcome the cheap foreign goods bore a lower rate of duty than did the high-priced products. Although the act somewhat increased the protection upon woollen fabrics as a whole, this was more than offset by the increased duty which was levied upon raw wool in response to the demand of the wool-raising interests of the country.[1]

Another struggle occurred over the protection of hemp. This product was used both for the manufacture of the ropes essential to New England shipping and for the cotton bagging used in the south. Thus the shipping and the slave-holding sections were brought into union in opposition to the provision. Nevertheless, this important Kentucky interest received a substantial protection. The attempt to secure a marked increase of the duty on iron bars resulted in a compromise proposition which satisfied neither party and had little effect upon domestic manufacture, while it increased the cost to the consumer. The Senate amendments reduced the proposed rates on the most important articles, so that, on the whole, the extreme protectionists failed to carry their programme, although the bill

[1] Taussig, *Tariff Hist.*, 75.

increased the duties upon the articles most essential to the shipping and planting sections sufficiently to leave great discontent.[1]

In the debates upon this tariff, Henry Clay led the protectionist forces, basing his arguments upon the general distress of the country, which he explained by the loss of the foreign market for agricultural products, and which he would remedy by building up a home market by means of the support of manufactures—the creation of an "American system." "We must naturalize the arts in our country," said he. Not the least significant portion of his plea for protection was that in which he called attention to the great diversity of interests—"agricultural, planting, farming, commercial, navigating, fishing, manufacturing"—within the United States. Some of these interests were, as he said, peculiar to particular sections. "The inquiry should be in reference to the great interests of every section of the Union (I speak not of minute subdivisions); what would be done for those interests if that section stood alone and separated from the residue of the Republic? If they come into absolute collision with the interests of another section, a reconciliation, if possible, should be attempted, by mutual concession, so as to avoid a sacrifice of the prosperity of either to that of the other."[2]

[1] Stanwood, *Amer. Tariff Controversies*, I., chap. vii.

[2] *Annals of Cong.*, 18 Cong., 1 Sess., II., 1997; cf. Clay's letter to Brooke, August 28, 1823, Clay, *Private Corresp.*, 81.

Perhaps the ablest speech on the other side was that of Webster,[1] who ridiculed Clay's discovery. "This favorite American policy," said he, "is what America has never tried, and this odious foreign policy is what, as we are told, foreign states have never pursued." He denied the existence of general depression, although he admitted that profits were lower and prices considerably depressed. Webster's argument included an analysis of the theory of protection as against free-trade, in which he made a classical statement of the opposition to protection. In short, he represented the attitude of the commercial classes, particularly those of New England, whose interests were injured by any restraint of the freedom of exchange. As yet these classes exercised a dominant influence in Massachusetts.

Senator Hayne, of South Carolina, also argued the case against the tariff with a grasp and power of presentation that was hardly second to that of Webster. In particular he protested against compelling the planting regions to pay the cost of a protective system. Two-thirds of the whole amount of the domestic exports of the United States, he argued, were composed of cotton, rice, and tobacco, and from this trade arose the imports of manufactured goods which paid the revenues of the United States, and which the protective system rendered expensive and burdensome to his section. He warned the manufacturers that the south would repeal the system at the

[1] Webster, *Writings* (National ed.), V., 94-149.

first opportunity, regardless of interests that might accrue under the proposed measure.[1]

In the speeches of some of the representatives of the south was a note of revolt not to be found in Webster's argument. For the first time in the discussion of the tariff, the constitutional objection was made prominent. It was argued that the power to impose taxes and duties was given for the purpose of raising revenue, not for the purpose of protection. If not the letter, at least the spirit, of the Constitution was violated, so it was charged, by this distortion of the power of taxation. The proceedings of the constitutional convention were recited to show that a proposition conferring the alleged power was voted down. To this, Clay gave the reply that the clause on which the protectionists relied was the power to regulate commerce with foreign nations.

Even the south, however, laid less stress upon the constitutional argument than upon the injustice to the section. McDuffie, for example, replying to Clay,[2] argued that no one of the great sections of the country, if it were a separate nation, could advantageously apply the system of protection. He warned the western states that the system would make them tributary to the Atlantic states,[3] and that they had more to lose by alienating the friendship of the south for a system of internal improve-

---

[1] *Annals of Cong.*, 18 Cong., 1 Sess., I., 618.
[2] *Ibid.*, II., 2400 et seq.          [3] *Ibid.*, II., 2423.

ments which should facilitate the sale of their meat products to the south than by a union with the manufacturing interests. With respect to the south itself, he declared that cotton, which alone constituted one-third of the whole export of the Union, was in danger of losing the market of England if we ceased to take the manufactures of that country. Protesting that the protective system would strike at the root of their prosperity, by enhancing the cost of the clothing of their slaves and the bagging used to cover their cotton-bales, while at the same time it put to hazard the sale of their great staple in the English market, he yet declared that, if the bill should pass, "even with a majority of a single vote, I shall, as bound by my allegiance, submit to it as one of the laws of my country."

But if this South Carolina leader represented the attitude of his state in showing moderation at this time,[1] not so did the free-lance John Randolph, of Virginia. "I do not stop here, sir," said he, "to argue about the constitutionality of this bill; I consider the Constitution a dead letter; I consider it to consist, at this time, of the power of the General Government and the power of the States—that is the Constitution." "I have no faith in parchment, sir; . . . I have faith in the power of the commonwealth of which I am an unworthy son." "If, under a power to regulate trade, you prevent exportation; if, with the most approved spring lancets, you draw

[1] See Ames, *State Docs. on Federal Relations*, No. 4, p. 6.

the last drop of blood from our veins; if, *secundum artem*, you draw the last shilling from our pockets, what are the checks of the Constitution to us? A fig for the Constitution! When the scorpion's sting is probing to the quick, shall we stop to chop logic? . . . There is no magic in this word *union*." While he threatened forcible resistance, he rejoiced in the combination of the shipping and commercial classes of New England with the south in opposition to the measure. "The merchants and manufacturers of Massachusetts, New Hampshire, the province of Maine and Sagadahock," said he, "repel this bill, whilst men in hunting-shirts, with deer-skin leggings and moccasins on their feet, want protection for manufactures."

The bill passed the House of Representatives on April 16, 1824, by the close vote of 107 to 102, and subsequently passed the Senate by a small majority:

| | New England | | | | | | | Middle Region | | | | | South | | | | | |
|---|---|---|---|---|---|---|---|---|---|---|---|---|---|---|---|---|---|---|
| | Me. | N. H. | Vt. | Mass. | R. I. | Conn. | Total | N. Y. | N. J. | Pa. | Del. | Total | Md. | Va. | N. C. | S. C. | Ga. | Total |
| Ayes.... | 1 | 1 | 5 | 1 | 2 | 5 | **15** | 26 | 6 | 24 | 1 | **57** | 3 | 1 | 0 | 0 | 0 | **4** |
| Nays.... | 6 | 5 | 0 | 11 | 0 | 1 | **23** | 8 | 0 | 1 | 0 | **9** | 6 | 21 | 13 | 9 | 7 | **56** |

| | Northwest and Kentucky | | | | | | Southwest | | | | | Total |
|---|---|---|---|---|---|---|---|---|---|---|---|---|
| | Ohio | Ind. | Ill. | Mo. | Ky. | Total | Tenn. | Ala. | Miss. | La. | Total | |
| Ayes..... | 14 | 2 | 1 | 1 | 11 | **29** | 2 | 0 | 0 | 0 | **2** | **107** |
| Nays .... | 0 | 0 | 0 | 0 | 0 | **0** | 7 | 3 | 1 | 3 | **14** | **102** |

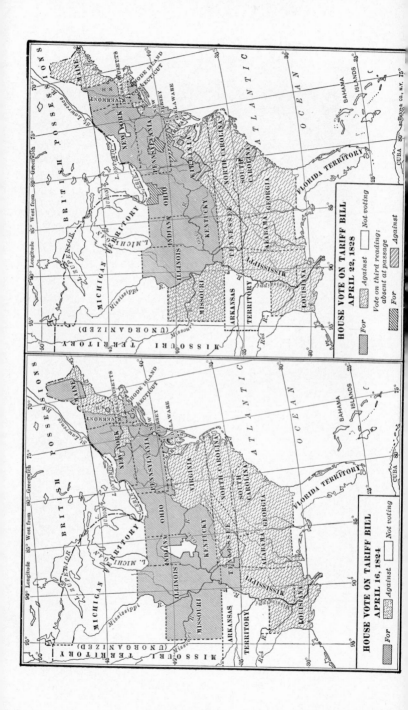

HOUSE VOTE ON TARIFF BILL
APRIL 22, 1828

For    Against    Not voting

Vote on third reading;
absent at passage

For    Against

HOUSE VOTE ON TARIFF BILL
APRIL 16, 1824

For    Against    Not voting

By this analysis and the map, it is clear that the navigating states were in opposition, while the manufacturing states were generally in favor of the bill. The most important textile manufacturers of Massachusetts, however, were not advocates of protection at this time. The grain and wool producing states gave an overwhelming vote (91 to 9) in favor of the attempt to provide a home market. The planting states gave but 3 votes in favor to 64 against.[1] By comparison with the map of the general survey bill, it is seen that the southern half of the west was in a state of unstable equilibrium on these sectional issues. It joined the Ohio Valley and the middle states in supporting a system of internal improvements, while it transferred its support to the old south on the question of the tariff. New England, on the other hand, although divided, tended to unite its strength with that of the south on both these measures. In general, the map reveals the process of forming a northern section in opposition to the south — the union of the Ohio Valley with the middle states against the alliance of the south Atlantic seaboard with the Gulf states. The division of forces exhibited in the Missouri struggle was strikingly like the division now revealed on the tariff question.

On the whole, the tariff of 1824 was distinctly a compromise measure. Although the ad valorem duties on cotton and woollen goods were raised,

[1] See the analysis in *Niles' Register*, XXVI., 113.

this was balanced by the doubled duty on raw wool. Nevertheless, it aroused the opposition of the entire planting section, at the same time that the manufacturers of woollen goods felt that their interests had been sacrificed. The tariff question was, in fact, only postponed. In the history of party development, however, Clay's system of internal improvements and tariff, as shown in this session of Congress, had a significance not easily missed; and state sovereignty sentiment in the south grew steadily after these measures.[1]

[1] See chapter xviii, below; cf. Ames, *State Docs. on Federal Relations*, No. 4, pp. 4-12.

# CHAPTER XV

## THE ELECTION OF 1824

### (1822–1825)

AS we have seen,[1] the dissensions in Monroe's cabinet approached the point of rupture by the spring and summer of 1822, when the spectacle was presented of the friends of the secretary of the treasury making war upon the measures of the secretary of war, and even antagonizing the president himself. Crawford's followers gained the name of the "radicals," and declared as their principles, democracy, economy, and reform.[2] Professing to represent the pure Jeffersonian republicanism of the "Revolution of 1800," they appealed to the adherents of the Virginia school of politics for support.[3] Jefferson, although refusing to come out openly, was clearly in sympathy with Crawford's candidacy: he believed that the old parties still continued, although under different names, and that the issue would finally be reduced to a contest between a northern and a southern candidate.

[1] See above, chap. x.
[2] Adams, *Memoirs*, VI., 56; Mass. Hist. Soc., *Proceedings*, XIX., 40.           [3] Edwards, *Illinois*, 489.

"You see," said he, in a letter to Gallatin, "many calling themselves Republicans and preaching the rankest doctrine of the old Federalists.  One of the prominent candidates [Adams] is presumed to be of this party; the other [Crawford] a Republican of the old school, and a friend to the barrier of state rights, as provided by the Constitution against the danger of consolidation." [1]  Pennsylvania and New York, he thought, would decide the question, and the issue would depend upon whether or not the "Missouri principle" became involved.

At this time parties and principles were still plastic.  This is illustrated by a letter written in the spring of 1823 to Monroe, by John Taylor, of Caroline, the leading exponent of the orthodox Virginia tenets of state sovereignty.  The writer was evidently stirred by the recent publication, in Calhoun's Washington organ, of a series of letters signed A. B., [2] in which Crawford was denounced for corrupt dealings with the banks, collusion with slave-traders, and intrigues in general.  Calhoun himself had just ended a visit with Taylor when the latter wrote, bitterly condemning the "example of obtaining the presidency by crafty intrigues and pecuniary influence," as tending to transfer power to a moneyed aristocracy.  Neither Calhoun nor Adams, in his opinion,

[1] Jefferson, *Writings* (Ford's ed.), X., 235; cf. 225–227, 237, 261, 264. 280.

[2] Edwards, *Illinois*, 525; *National Intelligencer*, April 21–23, 1823; *Am. State Paps.. Finance*, V., 1–145.

was open to this objection, and neither of them, he thought, would prefer a protective tariff to a navy as a means of national defence. While he admitted his ignorance of Adams's views on the subject of division of power between the federal and state governments, he declared that Calhoun had no advantage on this point, for although the latter professed to consider the distribution of powers between the states and the central authority as "a distinguishing pre-eminence in our form of government," yet, in the opinion of Taylor, he destroyed "this pre-eminence by endowing the federal government with a supremacy over the state governments whenever they come in conflict." This was important testimony, following immediately on Calhoun's visit, and coming from the pen of a man who was primarily interested in the question.

In spite of these objections, which would seem to be insuperable from the point of view of this distinguished expositor of state sovereignty, Taylor was ready to take the initiative in a movement against Crawford, if Monroe, Jefferson, and Madison agreed. Although as between Calhoun and Adams, he intimated that "the Missouri question" made a distinction of considerable weight,[1] he did not press the point. James Barbour, the other senator from Vir-

---

[1] Taylor to Monroe, April 29, 1823, *Monroe Papers*, MSS. in Cong. Libr.; cf. "Farmer's" attacks on Crawford as a protectionist, in *Richmond Enquirer*, noted in *Niles' Register*, XXIV., 306. See Calhoun to Gouverneur, April 28, 1823, N. Y. Publ. Libr., *Bulletin*, 1899, p. 324; Adams, *Memoirs*, VI., 356.

ginia, also seriously thought of supporting Adams,[1] and it is clear that the secretary of state at this time was not regarded as unsafe in the Old Dominion.

In the spring and summer of 1823, however, Crawford seemed to be clearly in the lead. He was supported by a well-organized press, which took its tone from the Washington newspapers; and until Calhoun, in retaliation, established a paper of his own to denounce Crawford's management of his department, he had effective control of the most influential organs of public opinion.[2] He was a master of political manipulation; but among his rivals were men of almost equal skill in this respect.

Clay was again chosen speaker, on his return to the House of Representatives in December, 1823, by a triumphant majority, and, as the session advanced, he and Calhoun, with all the arts of fascinating conversation, plied the old and new members. At this critical period in his campaign, Crawford was overwhelmed by a stroke of paralysis (September, 1823), which wrecked his huge frame and shattered his career. Shut in a darkened room, threatened with blindness and the loss of speech, bled by the doctors twenty-three times in three weeks, unable to sign his official papers with his own hand, he was prevented from conducting his own political battle.

[1] Adams, *Memoirs*, VI., 242, 450–452; see also Taylor's interview with Adams, May 26, 1824, *ibid.*, 356, 357.

[2] *Ibid.*, 47, 56, 57, 60, 62–64, 66.

But he kept his courage and his purpose, concealing his real condition from all but his most trusted intimates. Not until April, 1824, was he able to attend cabinet meetings, and within a month after that he suffered a relapse, which prevented his active participation in his duties until the fall.[1]

Adams had the New England scruples against urging his cause personally, and took the attitude that the office of president should come from merit, not from manipulation.[2] Moreover, he saw that the practice of soliciting votes from members of Congress would render the executive subservient to that body. Although his uncompromising temper unfitted him for the tactics of political management, he was an adept in the grand strategy of the contest, and he noted every move of his adversaries. His replies to attacks were crushing, for he had the gift of clear and forcible exposition.[3] But his greatest strength in the presidential contest lay in the fact that he was the only promising northern candidate.

Early in the campaign, Calhoun commented on the fact that five candidates were from the slave-holding states—a circumstance which, in his opinion, would

[1] *National Intelligencer*, September 15, 1824; *Life of W. W. Seaton*, 160; King, *Life and Corresp. of King*, VI., 539; Adams, *Memoirs*, VI., 130, 270, 275, 356, 357, 387, 428, 435, 439; Univ. of North Carolina, *James Sprunt Hist. Monographs*, No. 2, pp. 69, 71; Edwards, *Illinois*, 492.

[2] Adams, *Memoirs*, IV., 64, 242, 298, V., 89, 129, 298, 525; Dwight, *Travels*, I., 266.

[3] Adams, *Memoirs*, V., 361, 496–535, VI., 116–118; King, *Life and Corresp. of King*, VI., 475; Gallatin, *Writings*, II., 246.

give Adams great advantages if he knew how to improve them.[1]   Naturally, therefore, Adams gained the influential support of Rufus King, the chief antagonist of the slave section.  At first decidedly hostile, King's final adhesion was given to him, not out of personal regard, but because he believed that the public should be aroused against "longer submission to a Southern Master. . . . He is the only northern Candidate, and as between him and the black Candidates I prefer him."[2]   Steadily Adams increased his following in reluctant New England.[3] In New York he had an element of strength in the fact that the population was nearly evenly divided between the natives of that state and the settlers from New England.  Of the delegation from the state of New York in the seventeenth Congress, for example, those who were born in New England were about equal to those born in the state itself. Nearly forty per cent. of the members of the New York constitutional convention of 1821 were born in New England.[4]   The adhesion of ex-Speaker Taylor, another of the champions of restriction in the Missouri struggle, furnished an able manager in New York.

Even the attitude of Van Buren was for a time in

[1] Edwards, *Illinois*, 492.
[2] King, *Life and Corresp. of King*, VI., 508, 510.
[3] *Niles' Register*, XXIII., 322, 342; Clay, *Private Corresp.*, 98; Adams, *Memoirs*, VI., 235.
[4] King, *Life and Corresp. of King*, VI., 413; Carter and Stone, *Reports of New York Convention*, 637; Force, *Calendar* (1823).

doubt, for he would gladly have retired from politics
to accept a place on the bench of the supreme court
of the United States; but Adams and King pressed
his candidacy for this position in vain upon the
president, and Van Buren finally gave his full support to Crawford.[1]

So little did Adams appreciate the popular movement that was gathering about Jackson's name, that
he advised his followers to support the "Old Hero"
for the vice-presidency, "a station in which the General could hang no one, and in which he would need
to quarrel with no one.  His name and character
would serve to restore the forgotten dignity of the
place, and it would afford an easy and dignified retirement to his old age."[2]  In January, 1824, on the
anniversary of the victory of New Orleans, Adams
gave a great ball, attended by over a thousand people, in honor of his rival.[3]

After Jackson's return from the governorship of
Florida, in 1821, his star steadily rose in the political
horizon.  His canvass was conducted by his neighbor, Major Lewis, who was one of the most astute
politicians in American history, able subtly to influence the attitude of his volcanic candidate and to
touch the springs of political management.  On July

[1] King, *Life and Corresp. of King*, VI., 512–517, 520–527;
Adams, *Memoirs*, VI., 168, 173; Crawford to Van Buren, August
1, 1823, *Van Buren Papers* (MSS.); Am. Hist. Assoc., *Report*
1904, p. 178.
[2] Adams, *Memoirs*, VI., 333.
[3] *Ibid.*, 229; Sargent, *Public Men and Events*, I., 48–51.

20, 1822, the legislature of Tennessee formally nominated the general for the presidency.[1]

This gave the signal of revolt by the states against the congressional caucus.   Clay rallied his own forces, and in 1822 and 1823 was nominated[2] by members of the legislatures of Missouri, Kentucky, Ohio, and Louisiana.[3]   Alabama nominated Jackson; and Mississippi, by a tie vote, proposed both Adams and Jackson.[4]   These nominations by states showed that, however the west might be divided, it was a unit in resistance to the selection of a president by a combination of congressmen.   It was believed that the spirit of the Constitution was violated by this method, which made the executive depend on the legislative body for nomination; and that a minority candidate might win by the caucus.   This became the rallying cry of Jackson, whose canvass was conducted on the issue of the right of the people to select their president;[5] and the prevalent discontent and industrial depression made the voters responsive to this idea. The movement was one of permanent significance in American history, for it represented the growth of democracy, and led the way to the institution of the national nominating convention.

[1] Parton, *Jackson*, III., 20; *Niles' Register*, XXII., 402.

[2] *Niles' Register*, XXIII., 245, 342; *Ohio Monitor*, January 4, 1823; *National Republican* (Cincinnati), January 14, 1823; King, *Life and Corresp.*, VI., 487; Clay, *Private Corresp.*, 70.

[3] *National Intelligencer*, April 12, 1823; *Ky. Reporter*, April 21, 1823.          [4] McMaster, *United States*, V., 68.

[5] Sargent, *Public Men and Events*, I., 57; Parton, *Jackson*, III., 17, 40, 41.

In the fall of 1823, Tennessee returned Jackson to the Senate, having chosen him over one of the prominent leaders of the Crawford party, and, shortly afterwards, the legislature sent to the other states a vigorous resolution, asking them to unite in putting down the congressional caucus.[1] In Virginia and many other states the Tennessee resolutions gave rise to agitation which strengthened the popular feeling against congressional dictation.[2] Although Adams at first considered the congressional caucus as one of the "least obnoxious modes of intrigue," he also finally threw his influence against the system and announced that he would not accept a nomination by that body.[3]

Realizing that, in spite of his illness, Crawford could command the largest following in Congress, the friends of all the other candidates united their forces in an effort to prevent the meeting of the caucus. Already it was evident to the Georgian's supporters that the only thing that could bring him the victory was insistence upon party unity and discipline, and on February 14, 1824, sixty-six of the two hundred and sixteen Democrats in Congress gathered for the last congressional caucus which nominated a president. That these were practically all Crawford men was shown by his nomination with

[1] Parton, *Jackson*, III., 21; *Niles' Register*, XXV., 114, 137, 197, 292; McMaster, *United States*, V., 60; Tyler, *Tylers*, I., 341; *Richmond Enquirer*, January 1, 6, 13, 1824.

[2] McMaster, *United States*, V., 60–62, 64; Dallinger, *Nominations*, 19 n., 54.        [3] Adams, *Memoirs*, VI., 191, 236.

only four opposing votes.[1]  Gallatin had been persuaded to return from Paris, and he received the
nomination for vice-president, in order to hold the
state of Pennsylvania in Crawford's column; but
it proved a forlorn hope, for this old companion-in-
arms of Jefferson found Pennsylvania "Jackson mad."

Calhoun, seeing that he had lost the northern
state on which he had founded his hopes of success,
and despairing of making inroads upon Crawford's
southern forces after the congressional caucus, sought
his political fortunes in an alliance with his rival.[2]
The result was that, in a state nominating convention held at Harrisburg, Pennsylvania (March 4,
1824), Jackson was almost unanimously nominated
by that state for president, and Calhoun was named
for the vice-presidency.  In vain the managers of
Crawford sought to throw discredit upon Jackson
by the publication of his correspondence with Monroe, in which he had pleaded for recognition of the
Federalists;[3] the letters added to his strength, and
finally Gallatin was induced to withdraw from the
unequal contest, in order that an attempt might be
made to persuade Henry Clay to accept the vice-
presidency under Crawford.[4]

[1] Dallinger, *Nominations*, 19; *Niles' Register*, XXV., 388–392,
403; Hammond, *Pol. Hist, of N. Y.*, II., 149; McMaster, *United
States*, V., 64; *Life of W. W. Seaton*, 173; *Annals of Cong.*, 18
Cong., 1 Sess., I., 358.     [2] Clay, *Private Corresp.*, 87.

[3] Parton, *Jackson*, II., 357, III., 20; Monroe, *Writings*.

[4] Gallatin, *Works*, II., 297–300; Adams, *Life of Gallatin*, 604;
Clay, *Private Corresp.*, 100–103; Sargent, *Public Men and
Events*, I., 57.

The conflict was not entirely a matter of personal politics. Jackson had raised the popular movement against the congressional caucus into a distinct issue —the right of the people to choose their own president. Clay's "American system" of internal improvements and the protective tariff furnished others. We have seen that these subjects were hotly debated in Congress during the spring months of 1824. As the pre-eminent champion of these interests, Clay had a large following in the states of the Ohio Valley, as well as in New York  The early popularity of Calhoun in Pennsylvania was also due, in part, to his record as a friend of tariff and internal improvements. Upon that subject, on July 3, 1824, he gave an exposition of his constitutional principles to Garnett, of Virginia, in which he showed some tendency to moderate his position.[1] When interrogated upon his views in respect to the tariff, Jackson replied, in a letter to Coleman, avowing himself a moderate protectionist and a supporter of the doctrine of the promotion of manufactures in order to create a home market; and in the Senate he voted for the tariff of 1824, and in favor of internal improvements.[2] Crawford was embarrassed by the need of reconciling his southern support with his following in the middle states upon these subjects. While his treasury reports indicated a preference for a revenue tariff, they

[1] Houston, *Nullification in S. C.*, 143.

[2] Parton, *Jackson*, III., 34, 35; *Niles' Register*, XXVI., 245; Wheeler, *Hist. of Cong.*, II., 231.

were sufficiently ambiguous to create opposition in the south and a loss of support in the north. The issue of internal improvements he evaded by professing himself in favor of a constitutional amendment, for which he tried in vain to secure the support of his friends in the Georgia legislature.[1]

Adams announced that his policy with reference to the opposing interests of the country was "*conciliation*, not *collision*"; but he declared that there was no constitutional question involved, either in the tariff or in internal improvements,[2] and he was frankly in favor of the latter, while he professed himself satisfied with the tariff of 1824, as a reasonable compromise between the conflicting interests. If changed at all, he believed that the tariff should be reduced. An attempt was made to bring him into disrepute in the south for his negotiation of a convention in 1824 with England for the international regulation of the slave-trade. This subject had been forced upon his reluctant attention early in his career as secretary of state. While he was willing to join in declaring that traffic piracy, he was very proud of his record as a steadfast opponent of the right of search in any form. It was too valuable political capital to be given up, even if he had not espoused the cause with all his energy. To all propositions, therefore, for conceding the right of search of suspected slavers,

[1] King, *Life and Corresp. of King*, VI., 496, 500; *Niles' Register*, XXIV, 306; Gilmer, *Sketches*, 294.
[2] Adams, *Memoirs*, VI., 353, 451; cf. 343.

Adams had turned a deaf ear, as he did to proposals of mixed courts to try cases of capture. But in the convention of 1824, declaring the slave-trade piracy under the law of nations, he had offered to concede the right of British vessels to cruise along our coasts to intercept slavers, and this clause the Senate struck out, whereupon England refused to ratify it.[1]

On the whole, however, while candidates were forced to declare themselves on important questions, and while there were distinct sectional groupings in Congress, which revealed conflicting interests in economic policy, issues were not clearly drawn in this campaign. Indeed, it was difficult for any one of the candidates to stand on a clear-cut platform without losing some of the support essential to his success. "Could we hit upon a few great principles, and unite their support with that of Crawford," wrote his friend Cobb, shortly before the election, "we could succeed beyond doubt." [2]

As the year 1824 drew towards its close, the heat of the struggle was transferred to New York. Nowhere was the revulsion of popular feeling against caucus control more clearly manifested than in that state. The feeling was aggravated by the fact that the Albany Regency, under Van Buren, stubbornly

---

[1] Adams, *Memoirs*, VI., 321, 338, 345; Monroe, *Writings*, VII., 22; King, *Life and Corresp. of King*, 571, 572; DuBois, *Slave Trade*, 139, 140.

[2] Cobb, *Leisure Labors*, 216; Shepard, *Van Buren*, 92.

refused to concede the popular demand for the repeal of the state law for choice of presidential electors by the legislature. The political machine's control of the legislature insured New York's vote to Crawford; but if the choice were confided to the people, no one could predict the result. Out of these conditions a new combination sprang up in New York, which took the name of the "People's party," and sought not only to transfer the choice of electors to the people, but to overturn the Albany Regency. So rapidly did the discordant elements of New York Clintonians and anti-Clintonians combine in this party, that Crawford's managers, in an effort to break the combination, introduced a resolution in the legislature removing DeWitt Clinton from his office of canal commissioner. The purpose was to split the People's party by compelling its members to revive their old antagonisms by taking sides for or against Clinton. Although the resolution was carried by a decisive majority, the indignity placed upon the champion of the Erie Canal aroused popular resentment and increased the revolt against the Regency. In September, 1824, the People's party met in a state convention at Utica and nominated Clinton for governor.[1]

While this campaign (which resulted in an over-

---

[1] On the New York campaign, see Rammelkamp, Am, Hist. Assoc., *Report* 1904, p. 177; Hammond, *Pol, Hist. of N. Y.*, II., chaps. xxix.–xxxii.; Weed, *Autobiography*, chap. xv.; McMaster, *United States*, V., 71–73.

whelming victory for the People's party) was in
progress, the legislature met to choose electors. So
clearly marked was the trend of public opinion that
many members broke away from their allegiance to
Crawford. The Senate nominated electors favorable to him, but in the Assembly the Adams men
predominated, although they were not in a majority.
After several days of deadlock, a combination ticket,
made up of Adams electors and certain Clay men
who had been named on the Senate's ticket, was
suddenly presented to the Assembly and passed, with
the aid of Crawford men, who thought that if the
matter could be brought to a joint ballot they could
then win and exclude Clay from the contest. But
the Adams men had conciliated the supporters of
Clay by guaranteeing to them five electoral votes,
which were expected, if the ultimate choice of the
president should come to the House of Representatives, to make Clay one of the three candidates before that body.[1]  The Clay following, therefore, supported the Adams ticket on the joint ballot, with the
result that Adams secured 25 electors, Clay 7, and
Crawford 4. When the electoral college met in
December, Clay lost three of his votes, so that
New York finally gave 26 to Adams, 5 to Crawford,
4 to Clay, and 1 to Jackson. Thus the Adams
men had failed to carry out their agreement with

[1] Clay, *Private Corresp.*, 99, 104, 106; *National Intelligencer*,
September 15, 1824; Van Buren to Crawford, November 17,
1824; *Van Buren Papers* (Cong. Libr.).

the followers of Clay; had not these three Clay votes been withdrawn he would have tied Crawford for third place. Louisiana, although New York's electoral college voted in ignorance of the fact, had already deserted Clay.[1] The choice of electors in Louisiana was made by the legislature, in the absence of several Clay men, and the combined Jackson and Adams ticket received a majority of only two votes over Clay.[2] Thus vanished the latter's hopes of becoming one of the three candidates to be voted on by the House of Representatives.

In the country as a whole, Jackson received 99 electoral votes, Adams 84, Crawford 41, and Clay 37. For the vice-presidency, Calhoun was chosen by a vote of 182, while Sanford, of New York, received the vote of Ohio, together with a portion of that of Kentucky and New York; Virginia voted for Macon, of North Carolina; Georgia for Van Buren; and scattering votes were given for Jackson and Clay. No presidential candidate had a majority, and, in accordance with the Constitution, the House of Representatives was to decide between the three highest candidates.

To Clay, powerful in Congress, fell the bitter honor of deciding between his rivals. Jackson had a decisive plurality of the electoral vote, and even

[1] *N. Y. American*, December 3, 1824; *N. Y. Com. Adv.*, December 14, 1824; Weed, *Autobiography*, 128, is in error; L. E. Aylsworth, *Clay in Elec. of 1824* (MS. thesis).

[2] Sargent, *Public Men and Events*, I., 67; *Niles' Register*, XXVII., 257; Adams, *Memoirs*, VI., 446.

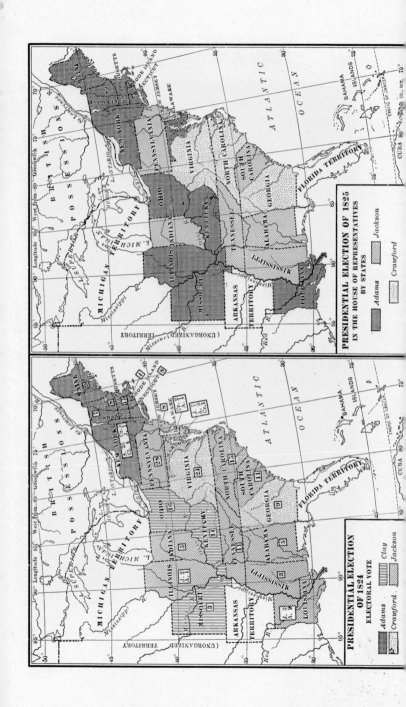

PRESIDENTIAL ELECTION OF 1825
IN THE HOUSE OF REPRESENTATIVES
BY STATES

Adams
Crawford
Jackson

PRESIDENTIAL ELECTION
OF 1824
ELECTORAL VOTE

Adams
Crawford
Clay
Jackson

the Kentucky legislature, under the dominance of
the "relief party," urged the representatives from
that state to cast their vote in his favor.[1]    But
although Jackson was popular in the west, Clay
had long been hostile to the candidacy of this military chieftain, and could not well alter his opinion.
Moreover, Clay's presidential ambitions stood in
the way of this choice.    It would not have been
easy for him to become Jackson's successor, both
because of the difficulty of electing two successive
candidates from the west and because Calhoun
had already anticipated him in the alliance.    With
Crawford, he was on better terms; but that candidate was clearly in the minority, his health was
gravely impaired, and his following was made up
largely of the opponents of the policies which Clay
represented.[2]

He determined, therefore, to use his influence in
behalf of Adams—the rival who had borne away
from him the secretaryship of state and whose foreign policy had been the target of his most persistent attacks.    On the other hand, the recognition of
the Spanish-American republics and the announcement of the Monroe Doctrine had made Adams in
a sense the heir of Clay's own foreign policy, and,
in the matter of tariff and internal improvements,
Adams was far more in accord with him than was
Crawford.

[1] Adams, *Memoirs*, VI., 446.
[2] *Ibid.*, VII., 4; *Niles' Register*, XXVII., 386.

As the day approached on which the House was to make its choice, friends of Clay, including his "messmate," Letcher, of Kentucky, sought Adams to convey to him the friendly attitude of Clay and their hope that their chieftain might serve himself by supporting Adams.[1] They made it perfectly clear that by this they intended to suggest for Clay a membership in his cabinet. Without giving explicit promises, Adams made it equally clear to these visitors that, if he were chosen by the votes of western delegations, he should naturally look to the west for much of the support that he should need. In short, Adams's diary, like a book of judgment, shows that he walked perilously, if safely, along the edge of his conscience at this time. "*Incedo super ignes*,"[2] he wrote—"I walk over fires." But his diary records no vulgar bargaining with Clay, although he talked over with him the general principles which he would follow in his administration.

The adhesion of Clay by no means assured Adams's election: the result was not fully certain until the actual vote was given. Missouri and Illinois were long in doubt,[3] and in the case of both of these states the vote was cast by a single person. Cook, of Illinois, was a personal friend of Adams, and, although the plurality of the electoral vote of that state had been in favor of Jackson, Cook, giving a strained interpretation of his pre-election promises to

---

[1] Adams, *Memoirs*, VI., 447, 457, 473–475.
[2] *Ibid.*, 453.    [3] *Ibid.*, 469.

follow the will of his constituency, cast his vote in
favor of Adams.[1]  With Scott, of Missouri, Adams
made his peace in an interview wherein he gave him
assurances with respect to newspaper patronage and
the retention of his brother, a judge in Arkansas territory, who was threatened with the loss of his office
because he had killed his colleague in a duel.  He
also secured the vote of Louisiana, by the one dele-
gate who held the balance of power; and he won
the Maryland member who had its decisive vote, by
the statement given through Webster, that his administration would not proscribe the Federalists.[2]
Friends of all the other candidates were busy in
proposing combinations and making promises which
cannot be traced to their principals.[3]

When the vote was taken, Adams was found to
have thirteen states, Jackson seven, and Crawford
four.[4]  Adams controlled New England, New York,
and the Ohio Valley, with the exception of Indiana, together with Maryland, Missouri, and Louisiana.  The
grouping of the Jackson vote showed a union of the
states of Pennsylvania and New Jersey with South
Carolina, Tennessee, and the cotton states of the
southwest.  The Crawford territory included Georgia, North Carolina, Virginia, and Delaware.  Van

[1] Adams, *Memoirs*, VI., 443, 473, 476, 495; Edwards, *Illinois*,
261–265.

[2] Adams, *Memoirs*, VI., 492, 499; Webster, *Writings* (National
ed.), XVII., 378.

[3] Adams, *Memoirs*, VI., 476, 495, 513; Clay, *Private Corresp.*,
109, 111; Parton, *Jackson*, III., 56.          [4] See map.

Buren had received the electoral vote of Georgia for the vice-presidency, and he still exercised a powerful influence in New York. Adams had to face, therefore, the possibility of a union between two of the ablest politicians in the nation, Calhoun and Van Buren, both of whom saw that their political fortunes were involved in the triumph of Andrew Jackson; and Jackson's popularity was extraordinary even in the western states which voted for Adams. Even as he saw victory approaching, the New England leader was filled with gloomy forebodings over the prospects. "They are flattering for the immediate issue," he recorded in his diary, "but the fearful condition of them is that success would open to a far severer trial than defeat."

# CHAPTER XVI

## PRESIDENT ADAMS AND THE OPPOSITION

### (1825–1827)

FOR eight years President Monroe had adminis-
tered the executive department of the federal
government—years that have been called the "Era
of Good Feeling." The reader who has followed the
evidences of factional controversy among the rival
presidential candidates in the cabinet, and noted the
wide-spread distress following the panic of 1819, the
growing sectional jealousies, the first skirmishes in
the slavery struggle, and the clamor of a democracy
eager to assert its control and profoundly distrustful
of the reigning political powers, will question the
reality of this good feeling. On the other hand, in
spite of temporary reverses, the nation as a whole
was bounding with vigor in these years of peace after
war; and if in truth party was not dead, and a golden
age had not yet been given to the American people,
at least the heat of formal party contest had been for
a time allayed. The bitterness of political warfare
in the four years which we are next to consider might
well make the administration of the last of the Virginia dynasty seem peaceful and happy by contrast.

Monroe's presidential career descended to a close in a mellow sunset of personal approval, despite the angry clouds that gathered on the horizon. He had grown in wisdom by his experiences, and, although not a genius, he had shown himself able, by patient and dispassionate investigation, to reach judgments of greater value than those of more brilliant but less safe statesmen. Candor, fair-mindedness, and magnanimity were attributed to him even by those who were engaged in bitter rivalry for the office which he now laid down. He was not rapid or inflexible in his decisions between the conflicting views of his official family; but in the last resort he chose between policies, accepted responsibility, and steered the ship of state between the shoals and reefs that underlay the apparently placid sea of the "Era of Good Feeling." How useful were his services in these transitional years appeared as soon as John Quincy Adams grasped, with incautious hands, the helm which Monroe relinquished.[1]

"Less possessed of your confidence in advance than any of my predecessors," wrote President Adams, in his first annual message, "I am deeply conscious of the prospect that I shall stand more and oftener in need of your indulgence." In his reply to the notification of his election by the House, after adverting to the fact that one of his competitors

---

[1] On Monroe's personal traits, see Adams, *Memoirs*, IV., 240 et passim; J. Q. Adams, *Eulogy on the Life and Character of James Monroe;* Schouler, *United States*, IV., 201–207.

had received a larger minority of the electoral vote than his own, he declared that, if his refusal of the office would enable the people authoritatively to express their choice, he should not hesitate to decline; [1] he believed that perhaps two-thirds of the people were adverse to the result of the election.[2]

In truth, the position of the new president was a delicate one, and he was destined neither to obtain the indulgence asked nor the popular ratification which he craved. By receiving his office from the hands of the House of Representatives in competition with a candidate who had a larger electoral vote, he fell heir to the popular opposition which had been aroused against congressional intrigue, and especially against the selection of the president by the congressional caucus. More than this, it was charged that Clay's support was the result of a corrupt bargain, by which the Kentucky leader was promised the office of secretary of state. This accusation was first publicly made by an obscure Pennsylvania member, George Kremer, who, in an unsigned communication to a newspaper, when Clay's decision to vote for Adams was first given out, reported that overtures were said to have been made by the friends of Adams to the friends of Clay, offering him the appointment of secretary of state for his aid to elect Adams; and that the friends of Clay gave this information to the friends of Jackson, hinting that for the same price

[1] Richardson, *Messages and Papers*, II., 293.
[2] Adams, *Memoirs*, VII., 98; cf. *ibid.*, VI., 481.

they would close with the Tennesseean.    When these overtures, said the writer, were rejected, Clay transferred his interest to Adams.[1]

Stung to the quick, Clay rushed into print with a denunciation of the writer as a dastard and a liar, and held him responsible to the laws which govern men of honor.[2]  In reply to this evident invitation to a duel, Kremer avowed his authorship and his readiness to prove his charges.  If Clay had known the identity of his traducer, he would hardly have summoned him to the field of honor, for Kremer was a well-meaning but credulous and thick-headed rustic noted solely for his leopard-skin overcoat.  The speaker, therefore, abandoned his first idea, and asked of the House an investigation of the charges, which Kremer reiterated his readiness to prove. But when the investigating committee was ready to take testimony, the Pennsylvania congressman refused to appear.  He was, in fact, the tool of Jackson's managers, who greatly preferred to let the scandal go unprobed by Congress.  If Clay transferred his following to Adams, the charge would gain credence with the masses; if he were not made secretary of state, it would be alleged that honest George Kremer had exposed the bargain and prevented its consummation.  In vain, in two successive and elaborate addresses,[3] did Clay marshal evidence

---

[1] *Niles' Register*, XXVII., 353.          [2] *Ibid.*, 355.
[3] Address of 1825 and of 1827, in Clay, *Works* (Colton's ed.), V., 299, 341.

that, before he left Kentucky, he had determined to
vote for Adams in preference to Crawford or Jackson, and that there was no proof of Kremer's charge.[1]
In vain was evidence produced to show that friends
of Jackson[2] and Crawford[3] solicited Clay's support
by even more unblushing offers of political reward
than those alleged against Adams. To the end of
his career, the charge remained a stumbling-block
to Clay's ambitions, and the more he denounced and
summoned witnesses[4] the more the scandal did its
poisonous work.

After all, it was Adams who gave the charge im-
mortality. Even if he had appreciated the power
of public feeling he would not have hesitated. If
the accusation was a challenge to the spirited Kentuckian, it was a call to duty to the Puritan. Two
days after his election, Adams, asking Monroe's advice about the composition of the cabinet, announced
that he had already determined to appoint Clay
secretary of state, "considering it due," said he, "to
his talents and services to the western section of the
Union, whence he comes, and to the confidence in
me manifested by their delegations."[5] Clay spoke
lightly of the threatened opposition as a mere tem-

[1] Clay, *Address to the Public* (1827), 52; *ibid., Works* (Colton's
ed.), IV., 109; Adams, *Memoirs*, VII., 4.
[2] Clay, *Works* (Colton's ed.), I., chaps. xvi., xvii.; Parton,
*Jackson*, III., 56, 110–116.
[3] Adams, *Memoirs*, VI., 464, 513, VII., 91.
[4] See, for example, testimony of congressmen, *Niles' Register*,
XXVIII., 69, 133, 134, 203; *Address of David Trimble* (1828).
[5] Adams, *Memoirs*, VI., 508.

porary ebullition of disappointment at the issue of the election,[1] and after a short interval accepted the appointment.[2]

Up to this time Jackson had kept his temper remarkably; but now that Adams had called to the department of state the man who made him president, the man who justified his choice by the statement that Jackson was a "military chieftain," the great deep of his wrath was stirred. Clay seemed to him the "Judas of the West," and he wrote a letter, probably for publication, passionately defending the disinterestedness of his military services, calling attention to the fact that Clay had never yet risked himself for his country, and soothing himself in defeat by this consolation: "No midnight taper burnt by me; no secret conclaves were held; no cabals entered into to persuade any one to a violation of pledges given or of instructions received. By me no plans were concerted to impair the pure principles of our republican institutions, nor to prostrate that fundamental maxim, which maintains the supremacy of the people's will."[3]

On his way back to Tennessee, he spread broadcast in conversation his conviction that "honest George Kremer" had exposed a corrupt bargain between Clay and Adams,[4] and to this belief he stuck

---

[1] Adams, *Memoirs*, VI., 509.
[2] For his reasons, see Clay, *Works* (Colton's ed.), IV., 114, 192.
[3] *Niles' Register*, XXVIII., 20; Parton, *Jackson*, III., 77.
[4] Parton, *Jackson*, III., 107.

through the rest of his life, appealing, when his witnesses failed him, to the stubborn fact of Clay's appointment.[1]   In October, 1825, Tennessee renominated Jackson, who accepted, and resigned his seat in the Senate, accompanying his action with a plea for a constitutional amendment rendering congressmen ineligible to office during their term of service and for two years thereafter, except in cases of judicial appointment.   The purpose was evidently to wage a new campaign to give effect to "the will of the people."[2]

Although he realized that an organized opposition would be formed, Adams sought to give a non-partisan character to his administration.[3]   In spite of the low opinion expressed in his diary for the honesty and political rectitude of the secretary of the treasury, he asked him to retain his office, but Crawford refused.[4]   Ascertaining that Gallatin would also decline the place,[5] he appointed Richard Rush, of Pennsylvania, then serving as minister to England.   Jackson's friends made it clear that he would take unkindly the offer of the department of war, and Adams gave that office to James Barbour, of Virginia.[6]   He retained Southard, of New Jersey, as secretary of the navy, William Wirt, of Virginia, as

[1] Parton, *Jackson*, III., 110–116.
[2] *Ibid.*, III., 95; *Niles' Register*, XXIX., 155.
[3] Richardson, *Messages and Papers*, II., 295–297.
[4] Adams, *Memoirs*, VI., 506, 508.
[5] *Ibid.*, *Life of Gallatin*, 607; Gallatin, *Writings*, II., 301.
[6] Adams, *Memoirs*, VI., 510; cf. *ibid.*, 450.

attorney-general, and McLean, of Ohio, as postmaster-general. The latter selection proved peculiarly
unfortunate, since it gave the influence and the patronage of the post-office to the friends of Jackson.
For the mission to England, he first selected Clinton,
and after his refusal he persuaded Rufus King to
take the post.[1]   Since King's acceptance of the sena-
torship at the hands of the Van Buren element in
New York, he had been less a representative of the
Federalists than in his earlier days; but the appointment met in some measure the obligations which
Adams owed to supporters in that party.

Far from organizing party machinery and using
the federal office-holders as a political engine, he
rigidly refused to introduce rotation in office at the
expiration of the term of the incumbent—a principle which "would make the Government a perpetual
and unintermitting scramble for office."[2]   He determined to renominate every person against whom
there was no complaint which would have warranted
his removal. By this choice he not only retained
many outworn and superfluous officers and thus fostered a bureaucratic feeling,[3] but he also furnished
to his enemies local managers of the opposition, for
these office-holders were, in general, appointees of
Crawford, in his own interest, or of McLean, in the
interest of Calhoun and Jackson.

So rigidly did Adams interpret his duty in the mat-

[1] Adams, *Memoirs*, VI., 523.          [2] *Ibid.*, 521.
[3] Fish, *Civil Service*, 76–78.

ter that only twelve removals altogether were made during his term.[1]   He even retained the surveyor of the port of Philadelphia, whose negligence had occasioned the loss of large sums of money to the government and whose subordinates were hostile to Adams.  Under such conditions, the friends of the administration had to contend not only against their enemies, but against the Adams administration itself, which left its power in the hands of its enemies to be wielded against its friends.[2]   Binns, the editor of one of the leading administration papers, in an interview was informed that the president did not intend to make any removals.   "I bowed respectfully," said the editor, "assuring the president that I had no doubt the consequence would be that he himself would be removed so soon as the term for which he had been elected had expired.  This intimation gave the president no concern."[3]

Another illustration of his tenacity in this matter, even in opposition to the wishes of Henry Clay, was his refusal to remove a naval officer at New Orleans who had made preparations for a public demonstration to insult a member of Congress who had assisted in electing Adams.  Clay believed that the administration "should avoid, on the one hand, political persecution, and, on the other, an appearance of pusillanimity."   But the president refused to remove

[1] Fish, *Civil Service*, 72.
[2] Adams, *Memoirs*, VII., 163.
[3] Parton, *Jackson*, III., 92; Adams, *Memoirs*, VII., 154.

a man for an intention not carried into effect, and particularly because he could frame no general policy applicable to this case which would not result in a clean sweep. Four-fifths of the custom officers throughout the Union, he thought, were opposed to his election. To depart in one case from the rule which he had laid down against removals would be to expose himself to demands from all parts of the country.[1]

The president who rejected these favorite instruments of political success was unable to find compensation in personal popularity or the graces of manner. Cold and repellent, he leaned backward in his desire to do the right, and alienated men by his testy and uncompromising reception of advances. And yet there never was a president more in need of conciliating, for already the forces of the opposition were forming. Even before his election he had been warned that the price of his victory would be an organized opposition to the measures of the administration,[2] and that Calhoun and his friends in South Carolina and Pennsylvania would be the leaders.[3]

The union of the opposition forces into a party was perfected slowly, for between Crawford, Jackson, and Calhoun there had been sharp rivalry. Virginia by

---

[1] Adams, *Memoirs*, VI., 546.

[2] *Ibid.*, 476, 481, 495, 506, 510.

[3] Am. Hist. Assoc., *Report* 1899, II., 230, 231; Calhoun, *Works*, III., 51; Sargent, *Public Men and Events*, I., 106, 109.

no means relished the idea of the promotion of the
military hero; and in New York Jackson had been
sustained by Clinton in 1824 against Crawford, the
candidate of Van Buren. The Senate ratification of
the nomination of Clay (March 7, 1825) foreshad-
owed the alliance of southern interests with those
of Pennsylvania;[1] but only fourteen votes, including
that of Jackson, were mustered against him, while
among the twenty-seven who ratified the nomination
was Van Buren. By the opening of the nineteenth
Congress, in December, 1825, however, the situation
might well have convinced Adams of the need of
caution. Taylor, the administration candidate for
speaker, was elected by a majority of only five
against his opponents' combined vote, and, in the
Senate, Calhoun appointed committees unfriendly to
the president.

Nevertheless, in his first annual message[2] Adams
challenged his critics by avowing the boldest doctrines of loose construction. The tide of sentiment
in favor of internal improvements was so strong[3]
that, to insure its complete success, it would have
been necessary only for the executive to cease to
interpose the checks which Monroe had placed
upon this movement. Prudence would have dic-
tated to a president anxious to enlarge his following the avoidance of irritating utterances upon this

[1] Adams, *Memoirs*, VI., 525, VII., 69.
[2] Richardson, *Messages and Papers*, II., 299.
[3] Jefferson, *Writings* (Ford's ed.), X., 348.

point. But Adams characteristically threw away his opportunity, choosing rather to make extreme proposals which he realized had slight chance of success, and to state broad principles of national power.

In this respect he went even further than Clay approved.[1] Defining the object of civil government as the improvement of the condition of those over whom it is established, not only did he urge the construction of roads and canals, but, in his enlarged view of internal improvements, he included the establishment of a national university, the support of observatories, "light-houses of the skies," and the exploration of the interior of the United States and of the northwest coast. Appealing to the example of European nations, as well as of various states of the Union, he urged Congress to pass laws for the promotion of agriculture, commerce, and manufactures, the "encouragement of the mechanic and of the elegant arts, the advancement of literature, and the progress of the sciences, ornamental and profound." "Were we," he asked, "to slumber in indolence or fold up our arms and proclaim to the world that we are palsied by the will of our constituents, would it not be to cast away the bounties of Providence and doom ourselves to perpetual inferiority?" Such a profession of faith as this sounded strangely in the ears of Americans, respectful of their constituents and accustomed to regard government as a necessary evil. At

[1] Adams, *Memoirs*, VII., 59, 61–63.

a stroke, Adams had destroyed his fair prospects of winning the support of Virginia, and, what is more, he had aroused the fears of the whole slave-holding section.

At the beginning of 1824 the legislature of Ohio passed a resolution in favor of the emancipation and colonization of the adult children of slaves, and was supported by the legislatures of at least six northern states, including Pennsylvania, while the proposal was attacked by all the states of the lower south.[1] This followed soon after the excitement aroused by an attempted negro insurrection in Charleston,[2] in 1822, and from the fears aroused by this plot the south had not yet recovered. Already Governor Wilson, of South Carolina, was sounding the alarm in a message[3] denouncing the Ohio proposition, and declaring that there would be more "glory in forming a rampart with our bodies on the confines of our territory than to be the victims of a successful rebellion or the slaves of a great consolidated government." Governor Troup, of Georgia, stirred by the same proposition, and especially by a resolution which Senator King, of New York, submitted (February 18, 1825) for the use of the funds arising from the public lands to aid in emancipating and removing the slaves, warned his constituents that very soon

[1] Ames, *State Docs. on Federal Relations*, No. 5, p. 11 (with citations); McMaster, *United States*, V., 204.

[2] McMaster, *United States*, V., 199; *Atlantic Monthly*, VII., 728.

[3] December 1, 1824. Ames, *State Docs. on Federal Relations*, No. 5, p. 13; *Niles' Register*, XXVII., 263, 292.

" the United States government, discarding the mask, will openly lend itself to a combination of fanatics for the destruction of everything valuable in the southern country "; and he entreated the legislature, " having exhausted the argument, to stand by its arms." [1] While Georgia was in this frame of mind, the administration, as we shall see,[2] completed the breach by refusing to permit the survey of the Indian lands by the state, and thus forced the followers of Crawford in Georgia to unite with their former opponents in South Carolina.

Even in North Carolina, where there had been a considerable sentiment in favor of Adams,[3] the conviction grew strong that, under such a loose construction of the Constitution as that which his message advocated, the abolition of slavery might be effected. The venerable Senator Macon, to whom Adams had at one time looked as a possible candidate for the vice-presidency, believed that the spirit of emancipation was stronger than that for internal improvements; and that the president's loose-construction doctrine would render it possible for Congress to free every slave.[4] One of the senators of South Carolina, desirous of supporting the administration in opposition to the Calhoun faction, begged Adams to include in his message some passage reas-

[1] Ames, *State Docs. on Federal Relations*, No. 5, p. 17; *House Exec. Docs.*, 19 Cong., 2 Sess., IV., No. 59, pp. 69, 70.

[2] Chap. xviii., below.

[3] Univ. of North Carolina, *James Sprunt Hist. Monographs*, No. 2, pp. 79, 88, 106.          [4] *Ibid.*, 76, 106, 107.

suring the south in the matter of slavery, but he received a chilling reply.[1]  The speaker, Taylor, already obnoxious because of his previous championship of the proposed exclusion of slavery from Missouri, aroused the wrath of the south by presenting to the House a memorial from a "crazy Frenchman," who invited Congress to destroy all the states which should refuse to free their slaves.[2]  In short, there was a wide-spread though absolutely unfounded fear that the administration favored emancipation, and that the doctrines avowed in the message of the president gave full constitutional pretext for such action.

On the other hand, the opposition was in no agreement on principles.[3]  It was dangerous for the south to marshal its forces on an issue which might alienate the support of Pennsylvania.  Much more safely could the enemies of the president press the charge that the favorite of the people had been deprived of his rights by a corrupt political intrigue.  Consequently, a flood of proposed amendments to the Constitution poured upon both branches of Congress day after day, demanding the abolition of the choice of president by the House of Representatives and the exclusion of members of Congress from appointment to executive office during their term of service.[4]

[1] Adams, *Memoirs*, VII., 57.                    [2] *Ibid.*, 103.

[3] Univ. of North Carolina, *James Sprunt Hist. Monographs*, No. 2, p. 79.

[4] Ames, *Amendments to the Const.*, in Am. Hist. Assoc., *Report* 1896, II., 21, 106, 339, 343.

These measures were championed by McDuffie, Benton, and other friends of Calhoun and Jackson. Although they were undoubtedly called out in part by a sincere desire to effect a change in a system which was regarded as dangerous, they also served admirably the purpose of popular agitation. In pursuance of the same policy, a report proposing restrictions upon the executive patronage was made in the Senate (1826) by a committee which included Benton and Van Buren. This was accompanied by six bills, transferring a large share of the patronage from the president to the congressmen, and proposing the repeal of the four-year tenure of office act.[1] Six thousand copies of this report were printed for distribution, and the Puritan president, so scrupulous in the matter of the civil service that he disgusted his own followers, found himself bitterly attacked throughout the country as a corrupt manipulator of patronage.

The first fully organized opposition, however, was effected in the debates over Adams's proposal to send delegates to the Panama Congress, for here was a topic that permitted combined attack under many flags. In the spring of 1825 the ministers of Mexico and Colombia sounded Clay to ascertain whether the United States would welcome an invitation to a congress[2] initiated by Bolivar, with the design of

[1] Fish, *Civil Service*, 73; McMaster, *United States*, V., 432.
[2] Adams, *Memoirs*, VI., 531, 536, 542; International Am. Conference, *Reports*, etc., IV., "The Congress of 1826 at Panama," 23.

consolidating the Spanish-American policy, though
at first the United States had not been included
among the states invited.[1]   Clay was predisposed to
accept the overture, for he saw in the congress an
opportunity to complete the American system, which
he had long advocated and which appealed strongly
to his idealistic view of the destiny of the new republics.[2]   But Adams was sceptical of the future of these
new nations, and, as for an American system, he had
once (1820) declared that we had one already, "we
constituted the whole of it; there is no community of
interests or of principles between North and South
America." [3]

Adams had learned something from Clay in the
mean time, however, and his own share in announcing the Monroe Doctrine inclined him to favor the
idea of such a congress, under careful restrictions, to
safeguard our neutrality and independence.   So the
inquiries were met in a friendly spirit, and formal
invitations were received from Mexico, Colombia, and
Central America in the fall of 1825, defining more
clearly the purposes of the congress and the mode of
procedure.[4]   The explanations still left much to be
desired, and it may be doubted whether the president would have accepted the invitation had not
Clay's zeal influenced his decision.

[1] International Am. Conference, *Reports*, etc., IV., " The Congress of 1826 at Panama," 155.          [2] See chap. xi., above.
[3] Adams, *Memoirs*, V., 176; cf. *Am. Hist. Rev.*, XII., 113.
[4] International Am. Conference, *Report*, IV., 24–34.

As its proceedings finally showed, the real purpose of the congress was to form a close union of the new republics against Spain or other nations which might attack them or make colonial settlements in violation of their territory, and to determine the troops and funds to be contributed by each state for this end. Its general assembly was to meet every two years, and, during the war, its members were to be bound by the action of the majority.[1] Such an organization was manifestly dangerous to the predominance of the United States, and participation in it was incompatible with our neutrality and independence. Having reason to apprehend that the congress might go to this extent, the president, in determining to accept the invitation, also determined so to limit our representatives that they should have no power to commit either our neutrality or our independent action, unless their action were ratified by the government.

Nevertheless, the prospect of an American system from which the United States was excluded was not a pleasing one, and certain topics which were suggested for consideration made the situation really critical. The presence of a large French fleet off the coast of Cuba, in the summer of 1825, revived the apprehension of an invasion of that island, and both Colombia and Mexico contemplated an attack upon

[1] International Am. Conference, *Report*, IV., 169 (Bolivar's instructions); 184 (Treaty of Confederation framed by the Panama Congress).

this remaining stronghold of Spain. The annexation of Cuba and Puerto Rico by any of the South American republics would unquestionably have meant the emancipation of the slaves, and already the spectacle of the black republic of Haiti had brought uneasiness to the south. In this juncture the administration endeavored to persuade the South American republics to suspend their expedition, and made overtures for Russian influence to induce Spain to recognize the revolted republics and thus avoid the danger of loss of her remaining possessions.

Adams sent a special message to the Senate (December 26, 1825), nominating two delegates to the Panama Congress. He attempted to disarm the gathering opposition by declaring that, although the commissioning of these delegates was regarded as within the rights of the executive, he desired the advice and consent of the Senate and the House of Representatives to the proposed mission. Among the topics named by Adams as suitable for discussion at the congress were the principles of maritime neutrality, and " an agreement between all of the parties represented at the meeting that each will guard by its own means against the establishment of any future European colony within its borders." This was a striking qualification of a portion of the Monroe Doctrine, and it indicates the anxiety of the executive not to commit the United States to any permanent defensive alliance of the American republics. Seeing their opportunity, however, the opposition brought in a report strongly antagonizing the recommendation of this congress, on the ground that it involved a departure from our time-honored policy of avoiding entangling alliances, that the congress would really constitute a government, and that the topics of discussion might better be handled by negotiation with the respective states. The opposition considered rather the purposes of the congress as contemplated by the South American promoters than the propositions which the United States was willing to discuss in the purely consultative body which Adams and Clay had in mind.

The knowledge, ignored in the executive message, that the congress proposed to deal with the problem of the slave-trade and of the destiny of Cuba, Puerto Rico, and Haiti, kindled southern indignation at the idea of submitting the subject of slavery to the discussion of an international tribunal. In a notable speech, Hayne declared this an entirely "domestic question." "With respect to foreign Nations," said he, "the language of the United States ought to be, that it concerns the peace of our own political family, and therefore we cannot permit it to be touched; and in respect to the slave-holding States, the only safe and constitutional ground on which they can stand, is, that they will not permit it to be brought into question either by their sister States, or by the Federal Government." [1]  "The peace of eleven States

---

[1] *Register of Debates*, 19 Cong., 1 Sess., II., pt. i., 165.

in this Union," said Benton, "will not permit the fruits of a successful negro insurrection to be exhibited among them." [1]

This southern resentment against the submission of the question of our connection with slavery and with the insurrectionary negro republics to the discussion of a foreign tribunal, was combined with the opposition of northern men like Van Buren to engaging the United States in a system for the control of American affairs by a congress. Thus the enemies of the administration were brought into unison. Nevertheless, the Senate assented to the mission (March 14, 1826) by a vote of 24 to 19; and, after an animated debate, the House, by a vote of 134 to 60, made the necessary appropriations. It was a barren victory, however, for one of the delegates died while on his way, and the other reached Panama after the Congress had adjourned. Although a subsequent session was to have been held at Tacubaya, near the city of Mexico, dissensions among the Spanish-American states prevented its meeting.[2]

[1] *Register of Debates*, 19 Cong., 1 Sess., II., pt. i., 330.
[2] Richardson, *Messages and Papers*, II., 329; International Am. Conference, *Report*, IV., 81, 113, 173–201.

## CHAPTER XVII

### INTERNAL IMPROVEMENTS AND FOREIGN TRADE

#### (1825–1829)

WHAT Adams had nearest at heart in his administration was the construction of a great system of roads and canals, irrespective of local interests, for the nation as a whole.[1] To " exalt the valleys and lay low the mountains and the hills " appealed to his imagination. He hoped that the increased price of the public lands, arising from the improved means of communication, would in turn furnish a large and steadily increasing fund for national turnpikes and canals. But the American people were not anxious for a system of scientific administration, either of the public domain or of internal improvements. Although Benton could not secure sufficient support to carry his measure for graduating the price of the public lands and donating those which found no purchasers at fifty cents an acre,[2] he voiced, nevertheless, a very general antagonism to the management of the domain by the methods of the count-

---

[1] Wheeler, *Hist. of Cong.*, II., 154; Adams, *Memoirs*, VII., 59, VIII., 444; cf. chap. xiii., above.    [2] Meigs, *Benton*, 165–172.

ing-house. Nor was the president able to control legislation on internal improvements. The report of the engineers appointed under the general survey act of 1824 provided for the development of the routes of national importance.[1] But local interests and the pressure of corporations eager to receive federal subscriptions to their stock quickly broke down the unity of the system.

The Senate declined to take action on a resolution introduced December 20, 1825, by Senator Van Buren, of New York, which denied Congress the power to make roads and canals within the respective states, and proposed a constitutional amendment for the grant of the power under limitations.[2] Provision had been made in 1825 for extending the Cumberland Road from Wheeling to Zanesville, Ohio, and for surveys through the other states of the northwest to Missouri, and appropriations were annually made for the road, until by 1833 it was completed as far as Columbus, Ohio. Nevertheless, that highway was rapidly going to destruction, and a counter project, ultimately successful, was already initiated for relinquishing the road to the states through which it passed.[3]

---

[1] *State Papers*, 18 Cong., 2 Sess., V., Doc. 83 (February 14, 1825); cf. *ibid.*, 19 Cong., 2 Sess., II., Ex. Doc. No. 10 (December 7, 1826).

[2] *Register of Debates*, 19 Cong., 1 Sess., II., pt. i., 20; Ames, *Amendments of the Fed. Const.* (Am. Hist. Assoc., *Report* 1896), 71, 261.

[3] Young, *Cumberland Road*, chap. vii.; Hulbert, *Historic Highways*, X.

Over two and a third million dollars was appropriated for roads and harbors during the administration of John Quincy Adams, as against about one million during the administrations of all of his predecessors combined. Acting on the line of least constitutional resistance opened by Monroe, when he admitted the right of appropriation for internal improvements, though not the right of construction or jurisdiction, extensive appropriations were made for roads and canals and for harbors on the Great Lakes and the Atlantic. Far from accepting Adams's ideal of a scientific general system irrespective of local or party interests, districts combined with one another for local favors, corporations eagerly sought subscriptions for their canal stock, and the rival political parties bid against each other for the support of states which asked federal aid for their roads and canals.

By the middle of this administration the popularity of internal improvement appropriations seemed irresistible, although southern states raised their voices against it and complained bitterly that they were neglected. The example of the Erie Canal, which was open by 1825, seemed to furnish proof of the success that awaited state canal construction. States were learning that English capital was ready for investment in such undertakings and that Congress could donate lands and subscribe for stock.

By acts of 1825 and 1826, Pennsylvania initiated its extensive state system of roads and canals to reach the Ohio, the central part of New York, and the Great Lakes.[1] The trunk line of this system united Philadelphia with Pittsburg by a horse railway to Columbia on the Susquehanna, thence by a canal along that river and its tributary, the Juniata, to Hollidaysburg, where stationary engines carried the freight over a series of inclined planes across the thirty-six miles of mountains, to reach the western section of the canal at Johnstown on the Conemaugh, and so by the Allegheny to Pittsburg. Sectional jealousies delayed the work, and piled up a debt incurred partly for branch canals in various parts of the state; but by 1830 over four hundred miles of canal had been built in Pennsylvania and five hundred more projected. Not until 1835 was the trunk line between Philadelphia and Pittsburg fully in operation, however, and in the decade after 1822 the total expenditure for internal improvements in the state amounted to nearly twenty-six million dollars, of which over ten millions was contributed by individual subscription. But the steam railroad proved too strong a competitor, the state was plunged too deeply in debt, and it was not many years before the public works were sold, and the era of the corporation opened.

Meanwhile the Chesapeake and Ohio Canal project[2]

---

[1] Hulbert, *Historic Highways*, XIII., chap. iv.; Worthington, *Finances of Pennsylvania*, 22.

[2] Hulbert, *Historic Highways*, XIII., chap. iii.; Ward, *Chesapeake and Ohio Canal* (*Johns Hopkins Univ. Studies*, XVII.)

had gained great impetus under the efforts of those who wished to turn the tide of western commerce to the Potomac River. The innate difficulties of the task, even more than the opposition of Baltimore, rendered abortive the efforts of the Potomac Company to make the river navigable above tide-water. But in 1823 public interest in Virginia and Maryland was aroused by the plan of a great canal to run alongside of the Potomac to its upper streams, and thence to connect with the Monongahela or Youghiogheny in order to reach the Ohio. At a convention which met in Washington in the fall of 1823, Maryland, Virginia, and the District of Columbia were largely represented by delegates enthusiastic over this new highway to the west. Even Baltimore acquiesced in the undertaking after a provision giving the right to tap the canal by a branch to that city, so that her western trade should not be diverted to the Potomac cities.

By 1826 the company was duly chartered by Virginia and Maryland; Pennsylvania's consent was also obtained; and the financiering of the enterprise seemed feasible by joint subscription to the stock by Maryland, Virginia, the District of Columbia, and the federal government. Under the general survey act of 1824, the route was surveyed, including an extension to Lake Erie by way of a canal from the Ohio. But when, in 1826, the board of engineers published its estimate of the cost of the canal, it was seen that the larger plans were doomed,

for the total cost was placed at over twenty-two
million dollars. This was practically prohibitive, for
the whole capital stock of the Chesapeake and Ohio
Company was only six millions. Congress made a
million-dollar subscription to the stock of the company, but only the eastern section of the canal could
be begun; the completion of navigation between the
coal-fields on the upper Ohio and Cumberland on the
Potomac must be postponed.

Baltimore's interest in the grand design of canal
communication between that city and Pittsburg
quickly disappeared. Nearer to the Ohio Valley
than any other seaport, she had built turnpikes to
connect with the national road, and thus shared with
Philadelphia the western trade. But now New York
and Pennsylvania were undertaking canal systems
which were certain in the long run to destroy the
advantages of Baltimore. In desperation, her far-
sighted and courageous merchants inaugurated the
plan of a railroad across the mountains to the Ohio,
grasping the idea that as the canal had shown its
superiority over the turnpike, so this new device
would win the day over the canal. In 1827 and 1828
charters for the Baltimore and Ohio Railroad were
granted by Maryland, Virginia, and Pennsylvania.

At Washington, on July 4, 1828, President Adams
stripped off his coat, amid the cheers of the crowd,
and thrust the spade into the ground in signal of
the beginning of the Chesapeake and Ohio Canal;
but on the same day a rival celebration was in

progress at Baltimore, where the venerable signer of the Declaration of Independence, Charles Carroll of Carrollton, placed the foundation-stone to commemorate the commencement of the Baltimore and Ohio Railroad, first of the iron bonds between the east and the west. When Adams thus won the plaudits of the people for his evidence of ability to break the conventions of polite society and use a laborer's tool, it was perhaps the only time that he and democracy came into sympathetic touch. But he was aiding in a losing cause, for, though Carroll was a man of the past, destiny was working on the side of the movement which he represented. In the field of transportation, the initiative of individuals and of corporations during the next two generations proved superior to that of state or nation.

In the mean time, Ohio, eager to take advantage of the competition of these rival routes from New York, Philadelphia, Baltimore, and Washington, and wishing to develop the central region of the state, undertook in 1825 a state system of canals connecting the Ohio with Lake Erie.[1] The Ohio Canal began at Portsmouth and followed the valleys of the Scioto and the Cuyahoga to Cleveland, while another canal extended from Cincinnati along the Miami to Dayton. By branches connecting with the Pennsylvania system, this net-work of water-ways was intended to give alternative outlets for the rapidly

---

[1] Morris, *Internal Improvement in Ohio* (Am. Hist. Assoc., *Papers*, III.), 107; see also McClelland and Huntington, *Ohio Canals.*

growing surplus of the state. Wheat which sold for from twenty-five to thirty-seven cents per bushel in central Ohio in 1825 brought double the amount in 1832 when the canal began to be effective; and it sold for a higher price a hundred miles west of Pittsburg than it did sixty miles to the east of that city, where water transportation was lacking.[1] An example of the rivalry of the followers of Adams and of Jackson in conciliating western interests is furnished in the case of Ohio, just prior to the campaign of 1828, when each party in Congress persisted in supporting its own bill donating lands for the canals of that state. Owing to the fear of each that the other party would gain the credit of the measure, both bills were passed, and Ohio received double the amount originally asked.[2] It was small wonder that Indiana, Illinois, and other western states memorialized Congress for aid in their own plans for canals.

The activity of the states, no longer waiting for the federal government to construct a national system; the rapidly growing demand for the relinquishment of the national road to the states within which it lay; and the activity of corporations, all pointed to a new era in internal improvements. The states were ready to receive appropriations, but they preferred to build their own roads and dig their own

[1] *Quar. Jour. of Econ.*, XVII., 15; Dial, in Ohio Archæological and Hist. Soc., *Publications*, XIII., 479.

[2] Benton, *Abridgment*, X., 197 *n*.

canals. The state and the corporation were replacing the national government as the controlling power in internal improvements, and Adams's conception of a national system of turnpikes and canals had failed.

Nor was President Adams successful in carrying out a system of complete maritime reciprocity. After the War of 1812, Great Britain and the United States agreed upon the abolition of discriminating duties on ships or products engaged in the trade between the two countries;[1] but England reserved her right to exempt her American possessions from this reciprocity. By excluding the ships of the United States from the trade with the English West Indies, England denied a profitable avocation to American ship-owners; while, at the same time, the liberal arrangements of the United States permitted her vessels freely to enter the ports of this country with their cargoes of English manufactures, and to carry thence to the West Indies lumber, flour, and provisions to exchange for the molasses and sugar of the islands.

This ability to make a triangular voyage, with profits on each transaction, gave such advantage to British ships that they were able to carry on the trade between the United States and England at a rate below that which American vessels could afford. Driven to seek some remedy, the Yankee merchants and skippers turned to the Orient. The trade with

[1] Cf. Babcock, *Am. Nationality* (*Am. Nation*, XIII.), chap. xvi.

China and the East Indies developed rapidly, and our tonnage registered for foreign trade increased from 583,000 tons in 1820 to 758,000 in 1828.[1] Ninety per cent. of our foreign commerce was carried in our own vessels, and, from this point of view, American shipping enjoyed one of the most prosperous periods in its history.[2] Smuggling was extensively carried on in the West Indies, and a war of retaliatory legislation in regard to shipping characterized the whole decade.

In 1825 Parliament passed a somewhat obscure act which opened the ports on a more liberal system of reciprocity. To nations without colonies she offered the same shipping rights in her colonies which such nations gave to England and her possessions. The act provided that it must be accepted within a year by nations who desired to avail themselves of its provisions. President Adams preferred to deal with the question by diplomacy, and Congress neglected to pass the legislation necessary to accept the offer. When Gallatin, who had been sent to England to treat of this matter, opened his negotiations in 1826, he was informed that it was too late. The stipulated time having elapsed, American vessels were definitely excluded from the West Indies in 1826 by orders in council.[3] In the campaign of

---

[1] Marvin, *American Merchant Marine*, chap. ix.

[2] Pitkin, *Statistical View* (ed. of 1835), 363; Soley, "Maritime Industries," in Shaler (ed. of 1894), *United States*, I., 538.

[3] Adams, *Gallatin*, 615–620; cf. MacDonald, *Jacksonian Democracy* (*Am. Nation*, XV.), 201.

1828 Adams was blamed for the failure to seize this opportunity, but the generally prosperous condition of our shipping not only moderated the discontent, but even led to a law (May 24, 1828) intended to place American vessels in complete control of our foreign commerce by providing for the abolition, by proclamation of the president, of all discriminating duties against such nations as should free ships of the United States from corresponding discriminations. In the long run, this reciprocity act proved a mistake; the end of Adams's administration marked the beginning of a decline in the prosperity of the merchant marine.[1]

American commerce during this period by no means kept pace with the growing wealth and population of the country.[2] As we have seen, the staple states produced the lion's share of the domestic exports, and the internal exchange favored by the protective tariffs restrained the foreign importations. Aside from the depression in 1821, following the panic of 1819, and the extraordinary rise in 1825, the exports in general exhibited no marked increase or decline between 1820 and 1829. Imports showed a value of nearly seventy-four and one-half million dollars in 1820, ninety millions in 1825, and sixty-seven millions in 1829.[3] During the whole of Adams's

---

[1] Soley, in Shaler, *United States*, I., 540.

[2] Sterns, *Foreign Trade of the United States, 1820–1840*, in *Jour. Pol. Econ.*, VIII., 34, 452.

[3] Soley, in Shaler, *United States*, I., 538; cf. Pitkin, *Statistical View* (ed. of 1835), 177; W. C. Ford, in Depew, *One Hundred Years of Am. Commerce*, I., 23.

administration, New York preserved its easy lead in domestic exports, although, as the west leaped up to power, New Orleans rose rapidly to a close second in exports of domestic origin. The southern cities retained merely the same proportion of the exports of domestic origin which they had in 1820, in spite of the great increase of cotton production. New York and New Orleans gained a large fraction of this trade, and Massachusetts changed its proportion of domestic exports only slightly during the whole decade. Over three-fourths of the cotton went to the British Isles, while almost all the pork and beef, and two-thirds of the flour, went to the West Indies, South America, and Great Britain's American colonies.[1]

The statistics of commerce repeat the same story of increasing national self-dependence which was told by the development of manufactures, internal trade, and transportation, and even by the diplomatic policy of the United States. The nation was building an empire of its own, with sections which took the place of kingdoms. The west was already becoming the granary of the whole country. But in the development of this "American system," the navigating portions of New England and the staple states of the south and southwest found themselves at a disadvantage. Their interest lay in a free exchange across the ocean.

Although many minor treaties of commerce and navigation were negotiated by Clay during this ad-

[1] Pitkin, *Statistical View*, 121–137.

ministration, all his other diplomatic efforts met
with failure, among them attempts to purchase
Texas and to procure a treaty with England for the
rendition of fugitive slaves who had escaped to Canada—strange evidences of the political concessions
of the northern president.

# CHAPTER XVIII

## REACTION TOWARDS STATE SOVEREIGNTY
### (1816-1829)

FROM the close of the War of 1812, an increasing reaction was in progress in various states against the ardent nationalism which characterized the country at that time. The assertion of the doctrine of state sovereignty by the Hartford Convention in 1814[1] so aroused the other sections of the country that particularism was for the time discredited. Leaders of Virginia politics even approved a rumor that Madison would march troops against New England; Judge Roane, later a champion of Virginia's sovereignty, denounced the "anarchical principles" of the section.[2] In that period, when Calhoun and the other leading statesmen of South Carolina supported the protective tariff and the bonus bill, when Madison, the author of the Virginia resolutions of 1798, signed the bill for the recharter of the national bank, when Chief-Justice Marshall, a son of Virginia, was welding firm the bonds of nationalism in his great series of decisions

---

[1] Babcock, *Am. Nationality* (*Am. Nation*, XIII.), chap. xv.
[2] Randolph-Macon College, *John P. Branch Hist. Papers*, II., 18.

limiting the powers of the states and developing the doctrine of loose construction of the Constitution,[1] and when New England itself was explaining away the particularistic purposes of the Hartford Convention, it might well seem that the days of state sovereignty had come to an end.

Even then, however, the pendulum was starting to swing in the opposite direction. The crisis of 1819 and the decisions of the supreme court asserting the constitutionality of the national bank under the broad national conception of the Constitution, produced protests and even resistance from various states whose interests were most affected. Ohio in 1819 forcibly collected a tax on the branch bank of the United States, in defiance of Marshall's decision rendered earlier in the year in the case of McCulloch *vs.* Maryland; and in 1821 her legislature reaffirmed the doctrines of the Virginia and Kentucky resolutions, and passed an act withdrawing the protection of the laws of the state from the national bank,[2] and even persisted in her resistance after the decision (Osborn *vs.* Bank of U. S., 1824) against the state. But the proceeds of the tax were ultimately restored. Nor was Ohio alone in her opposition to this decision. Kentucky was almost equally excited, and Senator R. M. Johnson made a vain attempt in 1821 to procure an amendment to the Constitution providing that in controversies in which a state was a party

[1] Babcock, *Am. Nationality* (*Am. Nation*, XIII.), chap. xviii.
[2] Ames, *State Docs. on Federal Relations*, No. 3, p. 5.

the Senate of the United States should have appellate jurisdiction.[1] Judge Roane, chief-justice of Virginia, in a series of papers in the *Richmond Enquirer*, challenging the nationalistic reasoning of the court, asserted that the Constitution resulted from a compact between the states,[2] and in this attack he was heartily supported by Jefferson.[3] Justice Marshall, in *Cohens vs. Virginia*[4] (1821), decided that the supreme court had appellate jurisdiction in a case decided by the state court where the Constitution and the laws of the United States were involved, even though a state was a party.

Virginia's attorneys maintained, on the contrary, that the final construction of the Constitution might be given by the courts of every state in the Union; and Judge Roane, whose own decision had been overturned, again appealed to his fellow - citizens in a strong series of articles. Again Jefferson denounced the consolidating tendencies of the judiciary, "which, working like gravity without any intermission, is to press us at last into one consolidated mass." Virginia entered her solemn protest against the decision, and her House of Delegates reaffirmed the argument of Virginia's counsel, and

[1] *Annals of Cong.*, 17 Cong., 1 Sess., I., 23, 68, 96; Ames, *State Docs.*, No. 3, p. 17; Ames, *Amendments to the Const.*, in Am. Hist. Assoc., *Report* 1896, II., 161; *Niles' Register*, XVII., 289, 311, 447.

[2] Randolph-Macon College, *John P. Branch Hist. Papers*, II., 106-121.

[3] Jefferson, *Writings* (Ford's ed.), X., 140, 189, 229.

[4] 6 Wheaton, 264.

asserted that neither the government of the state
nor of the United States could press the other from
its sphere. In effect, Virginia's position would have
given the state a veto on the will of the federal government, by the protection which her courts could
have extended to the individual subject to her jurisdiction under the interpretation placed by the state
upon the Constitution.[1]

The leading expositor of Virginia reaction in this
period was John Taylor of Caroline, the mover of
the resolutions of 1798. His *Construction Construed*, published in 1820, was introduced by a preface in which the editor said: "The period is indeed
by no means an agreeable one. It borrows new
gloom from the apathy which seems to run over so
many of our sister states. The very sound of State
Rights is scarcely ever heard among them; and by
many of their eminent politicians is only heard to be
mocked at." Taylor himself was led to write the
book by the agitation over the Missouri question
and the case of McCulloch *vs.* Maryland. One of its
purposes was to insist that sovereignty was not divided between the separate spheres of the state and
federal government, but rested rather in the people
of the several states. Two years later, in his *Tyranny Unmasked*, Taylor developed the idea that the

[1] Randolph-Macon College, *John P. Branch Hist. Papers*, II.,
28; Jefferson, *Writings* (Ford's ed.), IX., 184; cf. *ibid.*, X. passim;
Madison, *Writings*, III., 217–224; Ames, *State Docs. on Federal
Relations*, No. 3, p. 15; *Niles' Register*, XX., 118; 6 Wheaton, 385.

division of the power of the people between the federal and state governments would be nugatory if either Congress or the supreme court could exclusively determine the boundaries of power between the states and the general government. His remedy for usurpation was the "state veto," which was to be "no mere didactic lecture," but involved the right of resisting unconstitutional laws. He met the difficulty that the people of one state would construe the Constitution for the people of all the states, by the answer that it was the lesser evil.[1] Again in 1823, in his *New Views of the Constitution*, he expounded the same ideas, and dwelt upon the position of the states as the defenders of separate geographical interests against oppression by the majority of the nation. He saw a grave danger in the relinquishment to Congress of the power to deal with local and dissimilar geographical interests by loose-construction legislation upon such subjects as banks, roads, canals, and manufactures. It would tend to produce geographical combinations; sections by combining would exploit and oppress the minority; "Congress would become an assembly of geographical envoys from the North, the South, and the West." Against these evils, the Constitution, according to his view, had provided by confining geographical interests within state lines instead of "collecting them into one intriguing arena." The states, reposing on their sovereignty, would interpose a check to oppres-

[1] Taylor, *Tyranny Unmasked*, 258, 262.

sive action and to the combination of sectional
interests against the minority.[1]

Not a theory of government, however, but a political exigency called out a working principle of state
rights. When the industrial policy of the government
fell under the complete control of the north, and the
social system of the south seemed to be menaced,
state sovereignty controlled the southern policy. The
increase in popularity of Clay's American system
of internal improvements and a protective tariff
aroused the apprehensions of the whole planting
section; the struggle over the admission of Missouri
taught the south the power of an unfriendly national
majority; and, in 1822, a threatened insurrection of
the negroes at Charleston brought home to the whole
section, and particularly to South Carolina, the dangers arising from an agitation of the question of
slavery.[2] In the irritated condition and depression
of this section, the triumph of loose construction
principles and the possible election of a northern
president seemed to presage not only the sacrifice of
their economic interests, but even the freeing of their
slaves.[3] The colonization society, which in its origin had been supported by southern men, became
an object of denunciation by the lower south after
the Missouri controversy and the insurrection of

---

[1] Taylor, *New Views* (ed. of 1823), 261 et seq.
[2] Cf. Hart, *Slavery and Abolition* (*Am. Nation*, XVI.), chap. viii.
[3] See the resolutions of Virginia, December 23, 1816, in Ames,
*State Docs. on Federal Relations*, No. 5, p. 3.

1822. The opposition was intensified by the disposition of the society, towards the close of the period, to advocate emancipation, as well as the removal of the existing free negroes.[1]

In Virginia the doctrine of state rights was supported by the friends of Crawford, and, in general, by the older portion of the state. In her western counties, however, where a movement was in progress for a constitutional convention to redistribute political power so that the populous interior should not be subordinated to the slave-holding minority of the coast, there was a strong sentiment in favor of the constitutionality and expediency both of federal internal improvements and the tariff. Nevertheless, Virginia's voice was determined by the ascendency of the old-time plantation interests. In 1825, Jefferson suggested that the legislature of Virginia should pass a set of resolutions, declaring the internal-improvement laws null and void. He advised, however, that, at the same time, the issue should be avoided by an act of the Virginia legislature validating these congressional laws[2] until action could be taken on a carefully guarded proposal to amend the Constitution so as to grant the right. This was the last effort of Jefferson to stay the tide of internal improvements which was sweeping opposition before it, and even he withdrew his project

[1] Cf. Hart, *Slavery and Abolition* (*Am. Nation*, XVI.), chap. xiv.
[2] Jefferson, *Writings* (Ford's ed.), X., 348–352; Ames, *State Docs. on Federal Relations*, No. 4, p. 8.

before it was acted on. His death (July 4, 1826) removed from Virginia the most influential advocate of state sovereignty and the greatest of the Virginia dynasty since Washington. On the same day John Adams died. The men who made the declaration of independence were passing away, but the spirit of that epoch was reviving in the south.

South Carolina was the theatre of a conflict between the old-time forces of nationalism, of which Calhoun had been the most prominent exponent, and the newer tendencies which would safeguard the interests of the commonwealth by appealing to the doctrine of state sovereignty.[1] At first, the conservative party was in the ascendency. In 1820 the House of Representatives of South Carolina passed a resolution which deprecated the system of protection as premature and pernicious, but admitted that Congress possessed the power of enacting all laws relating to commerce, and lamented the practice "of arraying upon the questions of national policy the states as *distinct and independent sovereignties* in opposition to, or (what is much the same thing), with a view to exercise a control over the general government";[2] and, as late as 1824, the same body passed resolutions declaring that the man "who disseminates doctrines whose tendency is to give an unconstitutional preponderance to State, or United States' rights,

[1] Houston, *Nullification in S. C.*, chap. iv.
[2] Ames, *State Docs. on Federal Relations*, No. 4, p. 3.

must be regarded as inimical to the forms of government under which we have hitherto so happily lived"; and that "the People have conferred no power upon their state legislature to impugn the Acts of the Federal Government or the decisions of the Supreme Court of the United States." [1] The state Senate was already controlled by the opponents of national power, led by Judge Smith; and the next year the Lower House also fell under their dominance.

The attitude of McDuffie illustrates the transitional conditions in South Carolina. In 1821 he published a pamphlet supporting a liberal construction of the powers of Congress, and refuting the "ultra doctrines respecting consolidation and state sovereignty." [2]  In 1824, also, he supported the constitutionality and expediency of the general survey act, and repudiated the idea that the state governments were "in any respect more worthy of confidence than the General Government." [3] But he opposed the tariff of 1824, and in 1825 he voted against specific measures for internal improvement. Soon after this he joined the ranks of the advocates of state sovereignty, and, together with Hamilton and Hayne, so far outstripped the leaders of that faction that Judge Smith and his friends found them-

---

[1] Ames, *State Docs. on Federal Relations*, No. 4, p. 6.
[2] *Defense of a Liberal Construction*, etc., by "One of the People." Reprinted in Philadelphia, 1831. To this pamphlet, Governor Hamilton had prefixed "an encomiastic advertisement." [3] *Annals of Cong.*, 18 Cong., 1 Sess., 1372.

selves in a conservative minority against the ultra doctrines of their former opponents.

Doubtless the reversal of South Carolina's attitude was accelerated by the slavery agitation which followed the emancipation proposition of Ohio, already mentioned, and by the contest over the negro seamen act,[1] a measure by which South Carolina, in consequence of the plot at Charleston, required that free negroes on vessels entering a port of South Carolina should be imprisoned during the sojourn of the ship. The act brought out protests, both from other states and from Great Britain, whose subjects were imprisoned; and it was declared unconstitutional by Adams's attorney-general and by the federal courts· nevertheless, it remained unrepealed and continued to be enforced.[2] The Senate of South Carolina met the situation, at the close of 1824, by resolutions affirming that the duty of preventing insurrections was "paramount to all *laws*, all *treaties*, all *constitutions*," and protesting against any claims of right of the United States to interfere with her domestic regulations in respect to the colored population.[3]

Georgia, a few years later (December, 1827), in opposition to the Colonization Society,[4] vehemently asserted her rights, and found the remedy no longer

[1] Passed December 21, 1822. See Ames, *State Docs. on Federal Relations*, No. 5, p. 12; cf. Hart, *Slavery and Abolition* (*Am. Nation*, XVI.), chap. xix.

[2] McMaster, *United States*, V., 200–204, 417.

[3] Ames, *State Docs. on Federal Relations*, No. 5, p. 14.

[4] *Ibid.*, 17, 19.

in remonstrance, but in "a firm and determined union of the people and the states of the south" against submission to interference. Already Georgia had placed herself in the attitude of resistance to the general government over the question of the Indians within the state. From the beginning of the nation, the Indians on the borders of the settled area of Georgia were a menace and an obstacle to her development. Indeed, they constituted a danger to the United States as well: their pretensions to independence and complete sovereignty over their territory were at various times utilized by adventurers from France, England, and Spain as a means of promoting the designs of these powers.[1] Jackson drove a wedge between the Indian confederacies of this region by his victories in the War of 1812 and the cessions which followed.[2] Although, in 1821, a large belt of territory between the Ocmulgee and Flint rivers was ceded by the Creeks to Georgia, the state saw with impatience some of the best lands still occupied by these Indians in the territory lying between the Flint and the Chattahoochee.

The spectacle of a stream of Georgia settlers crossing this rich Indian area of their own state to settle in the lands newly acquired in Alabama and Mississippi provoked Georgia's wrath, and numerous urgent calls were made upon the government to carry

[1] *Am. Hist. Rev.*, X., 249.
[2] Babcock, *Am. Nationality* (*Am. Nation*, XIII.), chaps. ii., xvii.

out the agreement made in 1802,[1] by completing the
acquisition of these Indian lands.  Responding to
this demand, a treaty was made at Indian Springs in
February, 1825, by which the Creeks ceded all of
their lands in Georgia; but when Adams came to the
presidency he was confronted with a serious situation arising from this treaty.  Shortly after it had
been ratified, McIntosh, a principal chief of the Lower
Creeks, who had signed the treaty, contrary to the
rule of the tribe and in spite of the decision to sell no
more land, was put to death; and the whole treaty
was repudiated by the great body of the Creeks, as
having been procured by fraud and made by a small
minority of their nation.  The difficulty arose from
the fact that the various villages of these Indians were divided into opposing parties: the Upper
Creeks, living chiefly along the forks of the Alabama,
on the Tallapoosa and the Coosa in Alabama, con-
stituting the more numerous branch, were determined to yield no more territory, while the principal
chiefs of the Lower Creeks, who dwelt in western
Georgia, along the Flint and Chattahoochee branches
of the Appalachicola, were not unfavorable to removal.

When Governor Troup, of Georgia, determined to
survey the ceded lands, he was notified that the
president expected Georgia to abandon the survey
until it could be done consistently with the provisions

[1] Phillips, " Georgia and State Rights," in Am. Hist. Assoc.,
*Report* 1901, II., 34.

CESSIONS OF
INDIAN LANDS
1816-1830

SCALE OF MILES

0   50  100      200      300      400

Ceded prior to 1816
Ceded 1816-1830
Unceded 1830
- - - - - Dotted Lines show earlier
cessions by tribes, where a later
cession by other tribes was required
to complete the possession.

BORMAY & CO., N. Y.

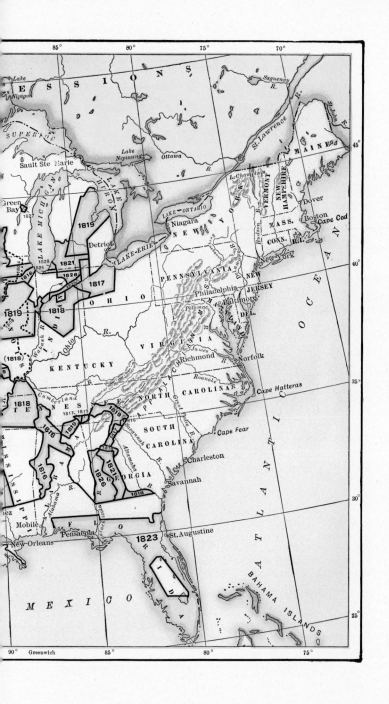

of the treaty.  Although the treaty had given the Creeks until September, 1826, to vacate, Governor Troup informed General Gaines, who had been sent to preserve peace, that, as there existed "two independent parties to the question, each is permitted to decide for itself," and he announced that the line would be run and the survey effected.  The defiant correspondence which now ensued between the governor and the war department doubtless reflected the personal hot-headedness of Troup himself, but Georgia supported her governor and made his defiances effective.  He plainly threatened civil war in case the United States used force to prevent the survey.[1]

On investigation, President Adams reached the conclusion that the treaty was wrongfully secured, and gave orders for a new negotiation.  This resulted in the treaty of Washington, in January, 1826, supplemented by that of March, 1826, by which the Creek Indians ceded all of their lands within the state except a narrow strip along the western border. This treaty abrogated the treaty of Indian Springs and it provided that the Indians should remain in possession of their lands until January 1, 1827. Throughout the whole of these proceedings Georgia was bitterly incensed.  Claiming that the treaty of Indian Springs became operative after its ratification,

[1] Ames, *State Docs. on Federal Relations*, No. 3, pp. 25–31; Phillips, "Georgia and State Rights," in Am. Hist. Assoc., *Report* 1901, II., 58–60; 40 (map).

and that the lands acquired by it were thereby incorporated with Georgia and were under her sovereignty, the state denied the right of the general government to reopen the question. "Georgia," said Troup, "is sovereign on her own soil," and he entered actively upon the survey of the tract without waiting for the date stipulated in the new treaty. When the surveyors entered the area not ceded by the later treaty, the Indians threatened to use force against them, and at the beginning of 1827 another heated controversy arose. The president warned the governor of Georgia that he should employ, if necessary, "all the means under his control to maintain the faith of the nation by carrying the treaty into effect." Having done this, he submitted the whole matter in a special message to Congress.[1]

"From the first decisive act of hostility," wrote Troup to the secretary of war, "you will be considered and treated as a public enemy"; and he announced his intention to resist any military attack on the part of the United States, "the unblushing allies of the savages."[2] He thereupon made preparations for liberating any surveyors who might be arrested by the United States, and for calling out the militia. In the House of Representatives, a committee recommended the purchase of the Indian title to all lands in Georgia, and, until such cession were procured, the maintenance of the treaty of Wash-

[1] February 5, 1827. Richardson, Messages and Papers, II., 370.
[2] Harden, Troup, 485.

ington by all necessary and constitutional means;
but the report of the Senate committee, submitted
by Benton, supported the idea that the ratification
of the treaty of Indian Springs vested the title
to the lands in Georgia, and reached the conclusion
that no preparations should be made to coerce the
state by military force. In November, 1827, the
Creeks consented to a treaty extinguishing the last
of their claims, and the issue was avoided.

In the mean time, the Cherokees in the northwestern portion of the state gave rise to a new problem by adopting a national constitution (July 26,
1827) and asserting that they constituted one of the
sovereign and independent nations of the earth, with
complete jurisdiction over their own territory to the
exclusion of the authority of any other state.[1]  This
bold challenge was met by Georgia in the same spirit
which guided her policy in regard to the Creek lands.
The legislature, by an act of December 20, 1828, subjected all white persons in the Cherokee territory to
the laws of Georgia, and provided that in 1830 the
Indians also should be subject to the laws of the
state. Thus Georgia completed her assertion of sovereignty over her soil both against the United States
and the Indians. But this phase of the controversy
was not settled during the presidency of Adams.

[1] Text in *Exec. Docs.*, 23 Cong., 2 Sess., III., No. 91 (Serial No.
273); Ames, *State Docs. on Federal Relations*, No. 3, p. 36; see
also *House Reports*, 19 Cong., 2 Sess. No. 98.

# CHAPTER XIX

## THE TARIFF OF ABOMINATIONS AND THE SOUTH CAROLINA EXPOSITION

### (1827–1828)

WHILE the slavery agitation was inflaming the minds of South Carolina and her sister states of the cotton region, and while Georgia, half a frontier state, was flinging defiance at the general government when it checked her efforts to complete the possession of her territory, the reopening of the tariff question brought the matter of state resistance to a climax.

The tariff of 1824 was unsatisfactory to the woollen interests. In the course of the decade there had been an astonishing increase of woollen factories in New England,[1] and the strength of the protective movement grew correspondingly in that section. By a law which took effect at the end of 1824, England reduced the duty on wool to a penny a pound, and thus had the advantage of a cheap raw material as well as low wages, so that the American mills found themselves placed at an increasing disadvantage. Under the system of ad valorem duties, the English

[1] See chap. ii., above.

exporters got their goods through the United States custom-house by such undervaluation as gravely diminished even the protection afforded by the tariff of 1824; and the unloading of large quantities of woollen goods by auction sales brought a cry of distress from New England. This led to an agitation to substitute specific duties in place of ad valorem, and to apply to woollens the minimum principle already applied to cottons. At the same time sheep-raisers were demanding increased protection.

Early in 1827, therefore, Mallory, of Vermont, a state which was especially interested in wool-growing, brought into the House of Representatives a report of the committee on manufactures, proposing a bill which provided three minimum points for woollen goods: with certain exceptions, those that cost less than 40 cents a square yard were to be rated as though they cost 40 cents in imposing the tariff; those which cost between 40 cents and $2.50 were reckoned at $2.50; and those which cost between $2.50 and $4, at $4. Upon unmanufactured wool, after 1828, a duty of forty per cent. was imposed, and all wool costing between 10 and 40 cents a pound was to be rated at 40 cents.[1]

The political situation exercised a dominant influence upon the tariff legislation at this time. As the campaign between Adams and Jackson was approaching its end, the managers of Jackson faced the problem of how to hold together the forces of the south,

[1] Stanwood, *Tariff Controversies*, I., 255.

which were almost to a man opposed to tariff legislation, and those of Pennsylvania and New York, where
protection was so popular. Jackson himself, as we
have seen, announced his belief in the home-market
idea, and, although with some reservations, committed himself to the support of the protective system.

While the forces of Jackson were not harmonious
on the tariff, neither was there consistency of interests between the friends of protection in New
England, the middle states, and the west. If New
England needed an increased tariff to sustain her
woollen factories, Pennsylvania, Ohio, and parts of
New York were equally interested in extending the
protection to wool, the raw material of the New
England mills. If the New England shipping interests demanded cheap cordage, on the other hand,
the Kentucky planters were ever ready to plead for
an increased duty upon the hemp which made the
ropes. If iron foundries were developing among
the towns of the New England coast, where ships
brought in the raw material from Sweden and from
England, the Pennsylvania forges found an opposite
interest in their desire for an increased duty on pig-
iron to protect the domestic product.

The history of the tariff has always been the history of the struggle to combine local and opposing
interests into a single bill. Such conditions furnished opportunity for the clever politicians who
guided Jackson's canvass to introduce discordant
ideas and jealousy between the middle states, the

west, and New England. The silence of the New England president upon the question of the tariff, the "selfishness of New England's policy," and the inducements offered to the middle region and the west to demand protection for their special interests were all successfully used to break the unity of the tariff forces. Even protectionist Pennsylvania, and Kentucky, home of the champion of the American system, gave a large share of their votes against the bill. Although it passed the House (February 10, 1827), the Senate laid it on the table by the casting-vote of Vice-President Calhoun, who was thus compelled to take the responsibility of defeating the measure,[1] and to range himself permanently with the anti-tariff sentiment of his section.

Hardly had the woollens bill met its fate when the rival forces began to reorganize for another struggle. From the south and from the shipping interests of New England came memorials in opposition to the tariff and in support of the theory of free-trade.[2] At a convention which met in Harrisburg, Pennsylvania, July 30, 1827, a hundred delegates from thirteen states met to promote the cause of protection. Finding it necessary to combine the various interests, the convention recommended increased duties both upon wool and woollen goods, and the establishment of the minimum system. This combination was

---

[1] See the account of Van Buren's tactics at this time, in Stanwood, *Tariff Controversies*, I., 258; and Calhoun, *Works*, III., 47.
[2] *Am. State Papers, Finance*, V. passim.

made possible by the proposal of effectively counter-balancing the prohibitory duties on wool by such use of the minimum device as would give a practical monopoly of the American market to the domestic manufacturers in the class of goods in which they were most interested. To conciliate other sections, the convention adopted the plan of an additional duty on hammered bar-iron, hemp and flax, and various other products.[1]

When the twentieth Congress met, in December, 1827, Stevenson, of Virginia, defeated the administration candidate, Taylor, of New York, for the speakership, and both branches of Congress and the important committees were put in the hands of the opposition to Adams. Rejecting the plan of the Harrisburg Convention, the House committee brought in a bill framed to satisfy the producers of raw material, wool, hemp, flax, and iron, and to deny the protection desired by New England.[2] Protection was afforded to raw material even where the producers did not seek it; and in some important cases high duties were imposed on raw material not produced in this country. The essential point of the provision respecting woollens favored by the Harrisburg Convention was the fixing of four minimum points, but the committee on manufactures inter-

---

[1] Stanwood, *Tariff Controversies*, I., 264; *Niles' Register*, XXXII., 369, 386, XXXIII., 187; Elliott, *Tariff Controversy*, 239.

[2] Taussig, *Tariff Hist.*, 89–92; Dewey, *Financial Hist. of the U. S.*, 178–181.

posed between the minimum of 50 cents and that of
$2.50 a minimum of $1, which effectively withdrew
protection from the woollen goods most largely manufactured in New England. Moreover, the committee refused to establish the increasing rate of
duty asked for at Harrisburg.

Calhoun afterwards explained the attitude of the
southern representatives as follows:[1] Having before
them the option of joining New England in securing
amendments satisfactory to the section, or, by resisting all amendment, to force New England to
join with the south in rejecting the bill, which would
involve Adams in the responsibility for its defeat,
they chose the latter alternative. Assurances were
given them by Jackson men that the two tariff interests would not be united by mutual concession in the
last stages of the discussion to insure the passage of
the bill; and so the south consistently threw its
weight against the passage of amendments modify-
ing this designedly high tariff. "We determined,"
said McDuffie later, "to put such ingredients in the
chalice as would poison the monster, and commend
it to his own lips." At the same time the Jackson
men in Pennsylvania, New York, and the west shifted their votes so as to deprive New England of her
share in the protective system. When an amendment was proposed, striking out the duty on molas-

[1] Calhoun, *Works*, III., 49; cf. Houston, *Nullification in S. C.*,
34, for similar explanations by Mitchell and McDuffie; Clay,
*Works* (Colton's ed.), II., 13; Jenkins, *Wright*, 53.

ses—an article essential to the rum distilleries of New England, but obnoxious to the distillers of whiskey in Pennsylvania and the west—Pennsylvania and a large share of the delegation from Ohio, New York, Indiana, and Kentucky voted with most of the south against the amendment. On the motion to substitute the proposals of the Harrisburg Convention with respect to wool and woollens, almost all of the delegation of Pennsylvania, and a large portion of that of New York and Kentucky, as well as the members from Indiana and Missouri and the south, opposed the proposition. Thus the interests of the seaboard protectionists were overcome by the alliance between the middle states and the south, while the west was divided.

Bitter as was the pill, it was swallowed by enough of the eastern protectionists to carry the act. The vote, 105 to 94, by which the measure passed in the House [1] (April 22, 1828) showed all of the south in opposition, with the exception of certain districts in Maryland and the western districts of Virginia, while the great area of the states of the Ohio Valley and the middle region was almost a unit in favor. The lower counties of New York along the Hudson revealed their identity with the commercial interests by opposing the bill. New England broke in two; Vermont, New Hampshire, and Connecticut voted almost unanimously in favor of the proposition; while Maine cast a unanimous vote in opposition.

[1] See map.

Rhode Island was divided, and in Massachusetts only two districts—that of the Berkshire wool-growing region and the Essex county area—supported the bill.

In the Senate, an amendment was passed making the duty on woollens an ad valorem rate of forty-five per cent., but retaining the minima. Various considerations induced some New England friends of Adams to support the measure. Webster defended his action in voting for the bill by declaring that New England had accepted the protective system as the established policy of the government, and after 1824 had built up her manufacturing enterprises on that basis. Nevertheless, in the final vote in the Senate, the five northern members who opposed were all from New England.

Thus the "tariff of abominations," shaped by the south for defeat, satisfactory to but a fraction of the protectionists, was passed by a vote of 26 to 21 in the Senate, May 13, 1828, and was concurred in by the House. John Randolph did not greatly overstate the case when he declared that "the bill referred to manufactures of no sort or kind, but the manufacture of a President of the United States"; for, on the whole, the friends of Jackson had, on this issue, taken sides against the friends of Adams, and in the effort to make the latter unpopular had produced a tariff which better illustrated sectional jealousies and political intrigues than the economic policy of the nation.[1]

[1] *Register of Debates*, 20 Cong., 1 Sess., IV., pt. ii., 2472; *Niles' Register*, XXV., 55–57, analyzes the votes to show the political groupings; cf. Taussig, *Tariff History*, 101, 102.

The tariff agitation of 1827 and the passage of the act of 1828 inflamed the south to the point of conflagration. John Randolph's elevation of the standard of revolt in 1824 now brought him credit as the prophet of the gospel of resistance. "Here is a district of country," he had proclaimed, in his speech on the tariff in that year, "extending from the Patapsco to the Gulf of Mexico, from the Alleghany to the Atlantic; a district . . . which *raises five-sixths* of all the exports of this country that are *of home growth.* . . . I bless God that in this insulted, oppressed and outraged region, we are as to our counsels in regard to this measure, but as one man. We are proscribed and put to the ban; and if we do not feel, and feeling, do not act, we are bastards to those fathers who achieved the Revolution." [1]

It was South Carolina, rather than Virginia, however, that led in violent proposals.[2] Dr. Cooper, an Englishman, president of South Carolina College, had long been engaged in propagating the Manchester doctrines of *laissez-faire* and free-trade, and he was greeted with applause when he declared that the time had come to calculate the value of the Union.[3] Agricultural societies met to protest and to threaten. Turnbull, an aggressive and violent writer, in a stirring series of papers published in 1827, under the title of *The Crisis*, over the signature of Brutus,

---

[1] *Annals of Cong.*, 18 Cong., 1 Sess., II., 2360.
[2] Houston, *Nullification in S. C.*
[3] *Niles' Register*, XXXIII., 59.

sounded the tocsin of resistance. He repudiated the
moderation and nationalism of "Messrs. Monroe and
Calhoun," and stood squarely on the doctrine that
the only safety for the south was in the cultivation
of sectionalism. "In the Northern, Eastern, Middle,
and Western States," said he, "the people have no
fears whatever from the exercise of the implied
powers of Congress on any subject; but it is in the
*South* alone where uneasiness begins to manifest itself, and a sensitiveness prevails on the subject of
consolidation." "The more *National* and the less
*Federal* the government becomes, the more certainly
will the interest of the great majority of the States
be promoted, but with the same certainty, will
the interests of the *South* be depressed and destroyed."

On their return from the session of 1828, the
South Carolina delegation added fuel to the fire. In
a caucus of the members, held shortly after the passage of the tariff, proposals were even made for the
delegation to vacate their seats in Congress as a protest, and in this temper they returned to their state.[1]
McDuffie told his constituents that there was no hope
of a change of the system in Congress; that the
southern states, by the law of self-preservation, were
free to save themselves from utter ruin; and that the
government formed for their protection and benefit
was determined to push every matter to their annihi-
lation. He recommended that the state should levy

[1] *Niles' Register*, XXXV., 184, 202.

a tax on the consumption of northern manufactured goods, boycott the live-stock of Kentucky, and wear homespun; and he closed by drawing a comparison between the wrongs suffered by the colonists when they revolted from Great Britain and that by which the south was now oppressed.[1]

Although South Carolina and all of the staple-producing section except Louisiana and Kentucky were in substantial agreement upon the iniquity of the tariff, yet, in respect to the remedy, they were widely at variance. Protest had proven ineffective; proposals of resistance by force, plans for a southern convention, and threats of disunion were rife.[2]

Such was the situation which confronted Calhoun when he returned from Washington and found that his section had passed beyond him. The same considerations that had aroused this storm of opposition also had their effect upon him. But he was still hopeful that, by the election of Jackson, a cotton-planter, the current of northern power might be checked; and he looked forward also to the prospect that he himself might eventually reach the presidential chair. Before him lay the double task of uniting himself to his friends in South Carolina, lest he lose touch with the forces of his own section, and of framing a platform of opposition that should be consistent, logical, and defensible; and, at the same time, of providing some mode of avoiding the

[1] *Niles' Register*, XXXIII., 339; cf. *ibid.*, XXXV., 82, 131.
[2] Houston, *Nullification in S. C.*, 49–52, 73–75.

forcible revolution that the hotheads of his section threatened as an immediate programme.

It was by the very processes of western growth that the seaboard south now found itself a minority section and the home of discontent. As the rich virgin soil of the Gulf plains opened to cotton culture, the output leaped up by bounds. In 1811 the total product was eighty million pounds; in 1821 it was one hundred and seventy-seven millions; in 1826 it was three hundred and thirty millions. Prices fell as production increased. In 1816 the average price of middling uplands in New York was nearly thirty cents, and South Carolina's leaders favored the tariff; in 1820 it was seventeen cents, and the south saw in the protective system a grievance; in 1824 it was fourteen and three-quarters cents, and the South-Carolinians denounced the tariff as unconstitutional. When the woollens bill was agitated in 1827, cotton had fallen to but little more than nine cents, and the radicals of the section threatened civil war.

Moreover, the price of slaves was increased by the demands of the new cotton-fields of Alabama, Mississippi, and the rest of the southwest, so that the Carolina planter had to apply a larger capital to his operations, while, at the same time, the cheap and unexhausted soil of these new states tended still further to hamper the older cotton areas in their competition, and the means of transportation from the western cotton-fields were better than from those of South Carolina. By devoting almost exclusive

attention to her great staple, South Carolina had
made herself dependent on the grain and live-stock
of the west and the manufactures of the north or of
England; and, when the one crop from which she
derived her means of purchasing declined in value,
the state was plunged in unrelieved distress. Nevertheless, the planters of the old south saw clearly but
two of the causes of their distress: the tariff, which
seemed to them to steal the profits of their crops;
and internal improvements, by which the proceeds
of their indirect taxes were expended in the west
and north. Their indignation was also fanned to a
fiercer flame by apprehensions over the attitude of
the north towards slavery.

In the summer of 1828, Calhoun addressed himself to the statement of these grievances and to the
formulation of a remedy. After consultation with
leading men in his home at Fort Hill, he was ready
to shape a document which, nominally a report of a
legislative committee (since it was not expedient for
the vice-president to appear in the matter), put in
its first systematic form the doctrine of nullification.
This so-called Exposition,[1] beginning with the un-
constitutionality and injustice of protection, developed the argument that the tax on imports, amounting to about twenty-three million dollars, fell, in
effect, solely on the south, because the northern
sections recompensed themselves by the increased
profits afforded to their productions by protection;

[1] Calhoun, *Works*, VI., 1–59.

while the south, seeking in the markets of the world customers for its staples, and obliged to purchase manufactures and supplies in return, was forced to pay tribute on this exchange for the benefit of the north. "To the growers of cotton, rice, and tobacco, it is the same whether the Government takes one-third of what they raise, for the liberty of sending the other two-thirds abroad, or one-third of the iron, salt, sugar, coffee, cloth and other articles they may need in exchange for the liberty of bringing them home."

Estimating the annual average export of domestic produce at fifty-three million dollars, the Exposition attributed to the planting section at least thirty-seven million dollars—over two-thirds of the total exports; the voting power of this section in the House of Representatives was but seventy-six, while the rest of the Union had one hundred and thirty-seven members. Thus, one-third of the political Union exported more than two-thirds of the domestic products. Assuming imports to equal exports, and the tariff of 1828 to average forty-five per cent., the south would pay sixteen million six hundred and fifty thousand dollars as its share of contributions to the national treasury. Calhoun then presented the ominous suggestion that, if the staple section had a separate custom-house, it would have for its own use a revenue of sixteen million six hundred and fifty thousand dollars from foreign trade alone, not counting the imports from the north, which would bring in millions more.

"We are mere consumers," he declared, "the serfs of the system—out of whose labor is raised, not only the money paid into the Treasury, but the funds out of which are drawn the rich rewards of the manufacturer and his associates in interest."

Taking for granted that the price at which the south could afford to cultivate cotton was determined by the price at which it received its supplies, he argued that, if the crop could be produced at ten cents a pound, the removal of the duty would enable the planter to produce it at five and one-half cents, and thus to drive out competition and to add three or four hundred thousand bales annually to the production, with a corresponding increase of profit. The complaints of the south were not yet exhausted, for the Exposition went on to point out that, in the commercial warfare with Europe which protection might be expected to engender, the south would be deprived of its market and might be forced to change its industrial life and compete with the northern states in manufactures. The advantages of the north would probably insure it an easy victory; but if not, then an attack might be expected on the labor system of the south, in behalf of the white workmen of the north.

What, then, was the remedy? Calhoun found this, although in fragmentary form, ready to his hand. The reserved rights of the sovereign states had long been the theoretical basis of southern resistance. In the argumentation of such writers as

Taylor, Turnbull, and Judge Roane, not to mention
Madison and Jefferson in the Virginia and Kentucky
resolutions, there was material for the system; but
as yet no one had stated with entire clearness the
two features which Calhoun made prominent in his
Exposition.  First, he made use of reasoning in
sharp contrast to that of the statesmen of the days
of the American Revolution, by rejecting the doctrine of the division of sovereignty between the
states and the general government.[1]  Clearly differ-
entiating government from sovereignty, he limited
the application of the division to the powers of government, and attributed the sovereignty solely to
the people of the several states.  This conception of
the unity of sovereignty was combined with the
designation of the Constitution as articles of compact between sovereign states, each entitled to determine whether or not the general government had
usurped powers not granted by the Constitution, and
each entitled peacefully to prevent the operation of
the disputed law within its own limits, pending a
decision by the same power that could amend the
Constitution—namely, three-fourths of the states.

These doctrines were brought out with definiteness
and with the deliberate intention of creating from
them a practical governmental machinery to be
peacefully applied for the preservation of the rights
of the states.  In effect, therefore, Calhoun, the logi-
cian of nationalism in the legislation that followed

[1] McLaughlin, in *Am. Hist. Rev.*, V., 482, 484.

the War of 1812, became the real architect of the
system of nullification as a plan of action rather than
a protest. As it left his hands, the system was essentially a new creation. In the Exposition, the doctrine was sketched only in its larger lines, for it was
in later documents that he refined and elaborated it.
It was intended as a substitute for revolution and
disunion—but it proved to be the basis on which
was afterwards developed the theory of peaceable
secession. Calhoun did not publicly avow his authorship or his adhesion to nullification until three
years later.

The rallying of the party of the Union in South
Carolina against this doctrine, the refusal of Georgia,
Virginia, and other southern states to accept it as
the true exposition of the Virginia and Kentucky
resolutions, the repudiation of it by the planting
states of the southwest, all belong to the next volume
of this series.

Yet the Exposition marks the culmination of the
process of transformation with which this volume
has dealt. Beginning with nationalism, the period
ends with sectionalism. Beginning with unity of
party and with the almost complete ascendency of
republicanism of the type of Monroe, it ends with
sharply distinguished rival parties, as yet unnamed,
but fully organized, and tending to differ fundamentally on the question of national powers. From the
days when South-Carolinians led in legislation for
tariff and internal improvements, when Virginians

promoted the Colonization Society, and Georgians advocated the policy of mitigating the evils of slavery by scattering the slaves, we have reached the period when a united south protests against "the American system," and the lower south asserts that slavery must not be touched—not even discussed.

In various southern states the minority counties of the coast, raising staples by slave labor, had protected their property interests against the free majority of farmers in the interior counties by so apportioning the legislature as to prevent action by the majority. Now the same conditions existed for the nation. The free majority embraced a great zone of states in the north and west; the south, a minority section, was now seeking protection against the majority of the Union by the device of state sovereignty; and Calhoun made himself the political philosopher of the rights of this minority section, applying to the nation the experience of South Carolina.[1]

Still the great currents of national growth ran on. New England was achieving unity and national feeling as a manufacturing region, and Webster was developing those powers which were to make him the orator of consolidation. While the leaders of the middle states played the game of personal politics, their people and those of the growing west were rallying around the man who personified their passion for democracy and nationalism—the fiery

[1] Calhoun, *Works*, I., 400-405

Jackson, who confused sectional opposition to the government with personal hostility to himself. This frontiersman was little likely to allow political metaphysics, or even sectional suffering, to check his will. And on the frontier of the northwest, the young Lincoln sank his axe deep in the opposing forest.

# CHAPTER XX

## CRITICAL ESSAY ON AUTHORITIES

### BIBLIOGRAPHICAL AIDS

THE authorities characterized in the Critical Essays of
Babcock's *Rise of American Nationality*, MacDonald's
*Jacksonian Democracy*, and Hart's *Slavery and Abolition*
(*American Nation*, XIII., XV., XVI.), include most of the
general authorities, and need not be repeated here in detail.
In addition, account should be taken of several indexes to
government documents: L. C. Ferrell, *Tables . . . and Annotated Index* (1902); two by J. G. Ames: *Finding List*
(1893) and *Check List* (1895); J. M. Baker, *Finding List*
(1900–1901); the *Index to the Reports of . . . Committees of
the House* (1887); and *Index to Reports of . . . Committees
of the Senate* (1887); Ben Perley Poore, *Descriptive Catalogue of Government Publications* (1885); L. P. Lane, *Aids
in the Use of Government Publications* (American Statistical
Association, *Publications*, VII. (1900), 40–57; L. C. Ferrell,
"Public Documents of the United States" (*Library Journal*,
XXVI., 671); Van Tyne and Leland, *Guide to the Archives
of the Government of the United States in Washington* (Car-
negie Institution, *Publications*, No. 14, 1904). For bibliography of state official issues, see R. R. Bowker [editor],
*State Publications: a Provisional List of the Official Publica-
tions of the Several States of the United States from their
Organization* (3 vols., issued 1899–1905); see also J. N.
Larned, *Literature of American History* (1902), 7–13; and
I. S. Bradley, in American Historical Association, *Report*,
1896, I., 296–319, a bibliography of documentary and newspaper material for the Old Northwest.

## GENERAL SECONDARY WORKS

The general histories of the period 1819–1829 almost
without exception extend over earlier or later fields, and
are described in earlier or later volumes of this series.  To
the usual list, James Schouler, J. B. McMaster, George
Tucker, H. E. Von Holst, J. P. Gordy, may be added: S.
Perkins, *Historical Sketches of the United States, from the
Peace of 1815 to 1830* (1830), the work of a careful contemporary.

## BIOGRAPHIES

The most serviceable biographies in this period can be
found through the lists in Channing and Hart, *Guide to the
Study of American History* (1896), § 25.  The volumes of
the *American Statesmen* series are accurate and well written,
especially Morse's *John Quincy Adams*, Schurz's *Henry Clay*,
Adams's *John Randolph*, Roosevelt's *Thomas H. Benton*,
McLaughlin's *Lewis Cass*, Shepard's *Van Buren*.

## SECTIONAL HISTORY

Among the bibliographies useful for attacking the mass
of local and state histories for this period are the following:
R. R. Bowker, *State Publications* (New York, 1899, 1902,
1905); A. P. C. Griffin, *Bibliography of Historical Societies
of the United States* (American Historical Association, *Reports*, 1890, 1892, 1893).

NEW ENGLAND.—The history of this section, since the
Revolution, has been neglected, but indications of its importance appear in Justin Winsor, *Memorial History of Boston* (4 vols., 1880–1882), III., IV., and I. B. Richman, *Rhode
Island: a Study in Separatism* (1905).  M. Louise Greene,
*The Development of Religious Liberty in Connecticut* (1905),
deals with the toleration movement.  The various historical societies print documentary material; but, for the most
part, New England's activity in this decade must be sought
in original material, biographies, travels, scattered monographs, and, in fragments, in state histories.

MIDDLE STATES.—The state and local histories of the middle region are more satisfactory on this period, but the political life must be sought chiefly in biographies; and the economic and social conditions in the scattered material elsewhere cited in this bibliography. J. G. Wilson, *Memorial History of the City of New York* (4 vols., 1891–1893); and Scharf and Westcott, *History of Philadelphia* (3 vols., 1884), are serviceable accounts of the development of the great cities of the section.

THE SOUTH.—Virginia has been neglected in this period, but the travellers afford interesting material; and a good view of plantation life is T. C. Johnson, *Life and Letters of Robert Lewis Dabney* (1903). For North Carolina, the literature is cited in S. B. Weeks, *Bibliography of the Historical Literature of North Carolina* (1895). Two monographs by J. S. Bassett, *Anti-Slavery Leaders of North Carolina* (*Johns Hopkins University Studies*, XVI., No. 6), and *History of Slavery in North Carolina* (*ibid.*, XVII., Nos. 7, 8), are especially important for the up-country. W. E. Dodd, *Life of Nathaniel Macon* (1903), is useful on this period. South Carolina conditions are shown in R. Mills, *Statistics of South Carolina* (1826); and W. A. Schaper, *Sectionalism and Representation in South Carolina* (American Historical Association, *Report*, 1900, I.). Georgia is depicted in U. B. Phillips, *Georgia and State Rights* (*ibid.*, 1901, II.); [G. R. Gilmer], *Sketches of Some of the First Settlers of Upper Georgia* (1855); and [A. B. Longstreet], *Georgia Scenes* (last edition, 1897), the latter made up of rollicking character-sketches. Among the many travellers useful (after criticism) for the South and Southwest may be mentioned, the Duke of Saxe-Weimar, Murat, Paulding, Hodgson, and Mrs. Royall. Correspondence illustrating Mississippi conditions is printed in J. F. H. Claiborne, *Life and Correspondence of John A. Quitman* (2 vols., 1860). Two lists by T. M. Owen, *Bibliography of Alabama* (American Historical Association, *Report*, 1897); and *Bibliography of Mississippi* (*ibid.*, 1889, I.), open a wealth of southwestern material. For Louisiana, there are various popular histories of New

Orleans; and A. Fortier, *History of Louisiana* (1904), III.; S. D. Smedes, *Memorials of a Southern Planter* [Thomas Dabney], (1887, also 1890), is highly valuable in the developed opening of the Gulf area. One of the best pictures of southwestern conditions is Lincecum's "Autobiography" (so called), in the Mississippi Historical Society, *Publications*, VIII. W. G. Brown, *Lower South in American History* (1902), is illuminative.

THE WEST.—The material for the West is scattered, the general histories of the Mississippi Valley failing to deal extensively with settlement. John B. McMaster, *History of the People of the United States* (1883–1900), IV., chap. xxxiii., and V., chap. xlv., give good accounts of the westward movement. B. A. Hinsdale, *Old Northwest* (2 vols., 1888, 1899), is scholarly, but brief on this period. W. H. Venable, *Beginnings of Literary Culture in the Ohio Valley* (1891), is important. Of especial value are the travellers, gazetteers, etc., among which the following are exceptionally useful: Timothy Flint, *Recollections of the Last Ten Years* (1826); Timothy Flint, *History and Geography of the Mississippi Valley* (2 vols., 2d edition, 1832); four books by J. Hall, viz.: *Letters from the West* (1828), *Legends of the West* (1833 and 1869), *Notes on the Western States* (1838), *Statistics of the West* (1836); *Ohio Navigator* (1821 and many other editions); J. M. Peck, *Guide for Emigrants* (1831); H. S. Tanner, *View of the Valley of the Mississippi* (1834). All of these, of course, must be used critically.

Among the contemporaneous state histories, T. Ford, *History of Illinois* (1854); J. Reynolds, *My Own Times* (1854–1855, also 1879), though unreliable in detail, have a value as material on pioneer conditions. The historical societies of the western states abound in old settlers' accounts. W. C. Howells, *Recollections of Life in Ohio* (1895), is a gem. P. G. Thomson, *Bibliography of Ohio* (1880), is the key to an extensive literature. There is no good history of Kentucky in this period; but J. Phelan, *History of Tennessee* (1888), is excellent. Lives of Clay, Jackson, and Benton all aid in understanding the region.

THE FAR WEST.—H. M. Chittenden, *The American Fur Trade of the Far West* (3 vols., 1902), is excellent. The larger histories of the Pacific states, viz.: H. H. Bancroft, *Works;* Hittell, *California;* and Lyman, *Oregon*, are characterized by Garrison, *Westward Expansion* (*American Nation*, XVII.). The publications of the Oregon Historical Society and the *Quarterly* of the Texas Historical Society are extremely useful. D. G. Wooten [editor], *Comprehensive History of Texas* (2 vols., 1899), has material on settlement in this period. G. P. Garrison, *Texas* (1903), is an excellent little book. Brief accounts of exploration in this period are in E. C. Semple, *American History and Its Geographic Conditions* (1903); and R. G. Thwaites, *Rocky Mountain Exploration* (1904). J. Schafer, *History of the Pacific Northwest* (1905), and G. W. James, *In and about the Old Missions of California* (1905), are useful brief presentations of conditions on the coast. For all this field the H. H. Bancroft library, now the property of the University of California, is the great collection of documentary material. Illustrative books by contemporaries are: R. H. Dana, *Two Years before the Mast* (1849 and other editions), giving California life; W. Irving, *Adventures of Captain Bonneville* (1849), giving Rocky Mountain life; and J. Gregg, *Commerce of the Prairies; or, the Journal of a Santa Fé Trader* (2 vols., 1844, also in Thwaites, *Early Western Travels*, XIX., XX.).

### HISTORIES OF PARTIES AND POLITICAL INSTITUTIONS

Charles McCarthy, *The Antimasonic Party* (American Historical Association, *Report*, 1902, I.), sets a high standard as a monographic party history; C. H. Rammelkamp gives a detailed study of the *Campaign of 1824 in New York* (in *ibid.*, 1904, pp. 175–202); all of the biographies of the contemporary statesmen deal with the parties of this period; and J. D. Hammond, *History of Political Parties in the State of New York* (2 vols., 1852), is a good history by a contemporary. U. B. Phillips, *Georgia and State Rights*

(American Historical Association, *Report*, 1901, II.), gives a modern treatment of state politics.

On political institutions the following are particularly useful: Edward Stanwood, *History of the Presidency* (1898); M. P. Follett, *The Speaker of the House of Representatives* (1896); L. G. McConachie, *Congressional Committees* (1898); C. R. Fish, *The Civil Service and the Patronage* (*Harvard Historical Studies*, XI., 1905); F. W. Dallinger, *Nominations for Elective Office in the United States* (*ibid.*, IV., 1897); J. B. McMaster, *Acquisition of Political, Social, and Industrial Rights of Man in America* (1903).

### PUBLIC DOCUMENTS

For a list of records of debates, legislative journals, documents, statutes, judicial decisions, treaties, and the like, see the "Critical Essays" in the neighboring volumes, and in Channing and Hart, *Guide*, § 30.

### WORKS OF AMERICAN STATESMEN

To the various editions of the works of James Monroe, Henry Clay, Daniel Webster, John C. Calhoun, Thomas Jefferson, James Madison, Rufus King, described in other volumes of this series, may be added John Quincy Adams, *Memoirs: Comprising Portions of His Diary from 1795 to 1848* (edited by Charles Francis Adams, 12 vols., 1874–1877). The diary is unusually full, and abounds in valuable material for understanding the politics of the period and the character of Adams. He was biased and harsh in his judgment of contemporaries, but conscientious in his record. The Adams papers are now in the private archives of the family at Quincy.

For statesmen of lesser distinction, see W. W. Story, *Life and Letters of Joseph Story* (2 vols., 1851); L. G. Tyler, *Letters and Times of the Tylers* (3 vols., 1884, also 1896). A collection of De Witt Clinton's letters was published in *Harper's Magazine*, L., 409, 563, and other letters and papers are in the following: David Hosack, *Memoir of De Witt Clinton* (1829); W. C. Campbell, *Life and Writings of De Witt Clinton* (1849); James Renwick, *Life of De Witt Clinton* (1854). There is no collection of Crawford's works; he is said to have destroyed his papers; a few letters remain, some of them in the possession of Dr. U. B. Phillips (University of Wisconsin). In E. B. Washburne [editor], *Edwards Papers* (1884), and N. W. Edwards, *History of Illinois and Life and Times of Ninian Edwards* (1870), are important letters illustrating national as well as western politics; see also the letters of Senator Mills of Massachusetts, in Massachusetts Historical Society, *Proceedings*, 1st series, XIX., 12–53; and those of Marshall, Kent, Story, and Webster, in *ibid.*, 2d series, XIV., 320 et seq., 398, 412 et seq. A collection of Macon's letters in this decade is in North Carolina University, *James Sprunt Historical Monographs*, No. 2.

Literary men and journalists are described by Herbert B. Adams, *Life and Writings of Jared Sparks* (2 vols., 1893); John Binns, *Recollections of His Life, Written by Himself* (1854); Amos Kendall, *Autobiography* (edited by W. Stickney, 1872), valuable for Dartmouth College life and for Kentucky in this period; Thurlow Weed, *Autobiography* (1883), useful also for western New York; E. S. Thomas, *Reminiscences of the Last Sixty-five Years* (2 vols., 1840), editor in Charleston, South Carolina, and in Cincinnati; *William Winston Seaton of the National Intelligencer: a Biographical Sketch* (1871), contains useful letters by various persons from Washington; *The John P. Branch Historical Papers* of Randolph - Macon College, Nos. 2 and 3 (1902, 1903), contain some letters and a biography of Thomas Ritchie, editor of the *Richmond Enquirer*.

## AUTOBIOGRAPHIES

In the group of autobiographies, reminiscences, etc., Thomas H. Benton, *Thirty Years' View; or, A History of the Working of the American Government, 1820 – 1850* (2 vols., 1854), is the most important: as a member of the

Senate, Benton was active and influential, and, despite
his positive character, he aims at fairness; Nathan Sargent,
*Public Men and Events* [1817–1853], (2 vols., 1875), is made
up of chatty sketches, with an anti-Jackson bias; Josiah
Quincy, *Figures of the Past* (1901), pen-pictures of men
of the period; B. F. Perry, *Reminiscences of Public Men*
(two series: 1st, 1883; 2d, 1889), anecdotal views of South
Carolinians; S. G. Goodrich, *Recollections of a Lifetime; or,
Men and Things I Have Seen* (2 vols., 1886).

## MANUSCRIPT COLLECTIONS

Manuscript collections are located in the reports of the
Historical Manuscripts Commission, published by the American Historical Association in its annual *Reports;* and in
Justin Winsor, *Narrative and Critical History of America*,
VIII. (1889). The Library of Congress contains important
manuscripts of Madison (calendared in Bureau of Rolls and
Library, Department of State, *Bulletin*, IV.); of Jefferson
(*ibid.*, VI., VIII., X.); Monroe (indexed in *ibid.*, II.), and in
W. C. Ford [editor], *Papers of James Monroe* (1904); in-
dexes of the manuscripts of Jackson and Van Buren are in
progress. In the New York Public Library are collections
of correspondence of various statesmen of the period (New
York Public Library, *Bulletin*, V., 306 et seq.), including
Monroe (calendared in *ibid.*, V., 316, VII., 210, 247–257);
Jackson (*ibid.*, IV., 154–162, 188–198, 292–320, V., 316);
Calhoun (*ibid.*, III., 324–333); James Barbour (*ibid.*, V.,
316, VI., 22–34). The Clinton Papers are in the State
Library at Albany, N. Y. (American Historical Associa-
tion, *Report*, 1898, p. 578). The papers of Senator Mahlon
Dickerson, of New Jersey, including letters from impor-
tant statesmen of the period, are in the possession of Will-
iam Nelson, corresponding secretary of the New Jersey
Historical Society. The correspondence of Senator W. P.
Mangum, of North Carolina, including letters from Clay,
Webster, etc., is in the possession of Dr. S. B. Weeks, San
Carlos, Arizona. The papers of Vice-President Tompkins

in the State Library at Albany are described in *Albany
Institute, Transactions*, XI., 223-240. The Plumer papers
are in the New Hampshire Historical Society.

The newspapers and periodicals constitute indispensable
sources. For the former the following catalogues are useful: *Check List of American Newspapers in the Library of
Congress* (1901); Wisconsin Historical Society, *Annotated
Catalogue of Newspaper Files* (1899); W. F. Poole [editor],
*Index to Periodical Literature* (1853 and later editions),
renders the magazines of the period accessible; and W. B.
Cairns, *Development of American Literature from 1815 to
1833, with especial Reference to Periodicals*, in University of
Wisconsin, *Bulletin* (*Literature Series*, I., 1898), enumerates
a list of periodicals not indexed in Poole. Easily first in
importance among the periodicals useful on the period from
1819 to 1829 is *Niles' Weekly Register*, edited by Hezekiah
Niles (76 vols., 1811-1849), which abounds in material, political, social, and economic; although Niles was a strong protectionist, he was also fair-minded and conscientious in collecting information. *The North American Review* (Boston,
begun in 1815 and still continues); *The American Quarterly
Review* (Philadelphia, 1827-1837); *The Southern Review*
(Charleston, 1828-1832); *The American Annual Register*
(New York, 1825-1833). *The Quarterly Register and Journal of the American Education Society* (1829-1843); *The
Methodist Magazine* (1818-1840); *The Christian Examiner*
(Boston, 1824-1869); and *Christian Monthly Spectator*
(1819-1828), are examples of religious and educational publications. Among periodicals which contain articles dealing with the decade, although published later, are *The
Democratic Review*, of which the first number appeared in
1837; *Hunt's Merchants' Magazine and Commercial Review*
(first volume, 1839); and *D. B. De Bow's Commercial Review of the South and West* (first volume, 1846). Among
the short-lived magazines of the West are: *The Western*

*Review* (Lexington, 1820–1821); *The Western Monthly Review* (edited by Timothy Flint, Cincinnati, 1827–1830); *The Illinois Monthly Magazine* (edited by James Hall, 1830–1831); *The Western Monthly Magazine* (continuation of the former, Cincinnati, 1833–1837).

## GAZETTEERS AND GUIDES

Among the important sources for understanding the growth of the country are various descriptions, gazetters, etc. Of the many books of this class may be mentioned the following: *Emigrants' Guide; or, Pocket Geography of the Western States and Territories* (Cincinnati, 1818); William Amphlett, *Emigrants' Directory of the Western States of North America* (London, 1819); D. Blowe, *Geographical, Commercial, and Agricultural View of the United States* (Liverpool, about 1820); John Bristed, *Resources of the United States of America* (New York, 1818); S. R. Brown, *The Western Gazetteer* (Auburn, N. Y., 1817); J. S. Buckingham, *America, Historical, Statistical, and Descriptive* (New York and London, 1841); J. S. Buckingham, *Eastern and Western States* (London, 1842); J. S. Buckingham, *Slave States* (London, 1842); William Cobbett, *The Emigrant's Guide* (London, 1830); S. H. Collins, *The Emigrant's Guide to and Description of the United States of America* (Hull, 1830); Samuel Cumings, *Western Pilot* (Cincinnati, 1840); E. Dana, *Geographical Sketches on the Western Country* (Cincinnati, 1819); William Darby, *Emigrants' Guide to Western and Southwestern States and Territories* (New York, 1818); William Darby, *Geographical Description of the State of Louisiana, the Southern Part of the State of Mississippi, and Territory of Alabama* (New York, 1817); Timothy Flint, *Condensed Geography and History of the Western States* (2 vols., Cincinnati, 1828); Timothy Flint, *History and Geography of the Mississippi Valley* (2 vols., Cincinnati, 1833); F. Hayward, *The New England Gazetteer* (3d edition, Boston, 1839); D. Hewett, *The American Traveller* (Washington, 1825); Isaac Holmes, *An Account of the United States of America* (London, 1823); *Indiana Gazetteer* (2d edition, Indianapolis, 1833); John Kilbourne, *Ohio Gazetteer* (Columbus, 1819, 1833); Wm. Kingdom, Jr., *America and the British Colonies* (London, 1820); W. Lindsay, *View of America* (Hawick, 1824); E. Mackenzie, *Historical, Topographical, and Descriptive View of the United States* (Newcastle-upon-Tyne, 1819); Joseph Martin, *New and Comprehensive Gazetteer of Virginia* (Charlottesville, 1835); John Melish, *A Geographical Description of the United States* (Philadelphia, 1816, 1822, 1826); John Melish, *Information and Advice to Emigrants to the United States* (Philadelphia, 1819); John Melish, *The Travellers' Directory through the United States* (Philadelphia, 1815, 1819, 1822, New York, 1825); Robert Mills, *Statistics of South Carolina* (Charleston, 1826); J. M. Peck, *A Guide for Emigrants* (Boston, 1831, 1837); J. M. Peck, *New Guide to the West* (Cincinnati, 1848); J. M. Peck, *Gazetteer of Illinois* (Jacksonville, 1834; Philadelphia, 1837); Abiel Sherwood, *Gazetteer of the State of Georgia* (3d edition, Washington, 1837); T. Spofford, *Gazetteer of the State of New York* (New York, 1824); [H. S. Tanner, publisher], *View of the Valley of the Mississippi* (Philadelphia, 1834); [H. S. Tanner, publisher], *Geographical, Historical, and Statistical View of the Central or Middle United States* (Philadelphia, 1841); D. B. Warden, *Statistical, Political, and Historical Account of the United States of North America* (3 vols., Edinburgh, 1819.)

## TRAVELS

The life of this period is illustrated by the reports of travellers; but the reader must remember that the traveller carries his prejudices, is prone to find in striking exceptions the characteristics of a region, and is exposed to misinformation by the natives; many of these travellers are, nevertheless, keen observers, well worth attention, and, when checked by comparison with others, they are a useful source. A full list of the travels bearing on the West and South from 1819 to 1829 would take more space than can be allotted here.    Bibliographies of travels in the United States may be found in Justin Winsor, *Narrative and Critical History of America* (1884–1889), VIII., 493; Channing and Hart, *Guide to American History* (1896), § 24; W. B. Bryan, *Bibliography of the District of Columbia* (1900), Article "America" (*Senate Document*, 56 Cong., 1 Sess., No. 61); P. G. Thomson, *Bibliography of Ohio* (1880); R. G. Thwaites, *On the Storied Ohio* (1897), App.; H. T. Tuckerman, *America and Her Commentators* (1864); B. C. Steiner, *Descriptions of Maryland* (*Johns Hopkins University Studies*, XXII., No. 6.), 608–647.    The most important collection of travels is R. G. Thwaites [editor], *Early Western Travels* (1748–1846), to be completed in thirty volumes and an analytical index.    For an estimate of English travellers, see J. B. McMaster, *United States*, V., chap. xlviii.    A list of travels in the period 1820–1860 will be found in Albert Bushnell Hart, *Slavery and Abolition* (*American Nation*, XVI.), chap. xxii.

### SLAVERY, COTTON, AND THE MISSOURI COMPROMISE

For works on slavery, see Hart, *Slavery and Abolition* (*American Nation*, XVI.), chap. xxii.    The general histories, such as W. H. Smith, *Political History of Slavery* (1903), and G. W. Williams, *History of the Negro Race in America* (2 vols., 1883), leave much to be desired.    Among the most important references are the *Reports* of the American Colonization Society;   J. H. T. McPherson, *History of Liberia* (*Johns Hopkins University Studies*, IX., No. 10.); John S. Bassett, *Anti-Slavery Leaders of North Carolina* (*ibid.*, XVI., No. 6); and *Slavery in the State of North Carolina* (*ibid.*, XVII., Nos. 7, 8); H. S. Cooley, *Study of Slavery in New Jersey* (*ibid.*, XIV., Nos. 9, 10); S. B. Weeks, *Anti-Slavery Sentiment in the South* (Southern History Association, *Publications*, II., No. 2); S. B. Weeks, *Southern Quakers and Slavery* (1896); William Birney, *James G. Birney and His Times* (1890); W. H. Collins, *Domestic Slave-Trade* (1904); W. E. B. Du Bois, *The Suppression of*

*the African Slave-Trade to the United States of America*
(*Harvard Historical Studies*, I., 1896); Mary S. Locke,
*Anti-Slavery in America . . . 1619–1808* (*Radcliffe College
Monographs*, No. 11, 1901); J. P. Dunn, *Indiana, a Re-
demption from Slavery* (1888); N. D. Harris, *The History
of Negro Servitude in Illinois* (1904); E. B. Washburne,
*Sketch of Edward Coles, Second Governor of Illinois, and of
the Slavery Struggle of 1823–4* (1882). The economic his-
tory of slavery can be written only after much mono-
graphic work; compare U. B. Phillips, "Economic Cost of
Slave - Holding in the Cotton Belt," in *Political Science
Quarterly*, XX., 267.

On the history of cotton, see M. B. Hammond, *Cotton
Industry*, in American Economic Association, *Publications*,
new series, No. 1 (1897); E. Von Halle, *Baumwollproduktion*
(in Schmoller, *Staats und Social-wissenschaftliche Forschungen*, XV.); E. G. Donnell, *History of Cotton* (1872); J. L.
Watkins, *Production and Price of Cotton for One Hundred
Years* (U. S. Department of Agriculture, Division of Statistics, *Miscellaneous Series, Bulletin*, No. 9, 1895).

The best sketch of the Missouri Compromise is J. A.
Woodburn, *The Historical Significance of the Missouri Compromise* (American Historical Association, *Report*, 1893, pp.
249–298). Source material is in the *Annals of Congress;* the
works of King, Jefferson, Benton, and J. Q. Adams, above-
mentioned; and also *Congressional Globe*, 30 Cong., 2 Sess.,
App.; *William and Mary College Quarterly*, X.

## STATE SOVEREIGNTY

On the reaction towards state sovereignty, documentary
material so well selected as to have the effect of a mono-
graph is in H. V. Ames, *State Documents on Federal Relations* (1900–1905), Nos. 3–5. The works of John Taylor
of Caroline are essential, especially *Construction Construed*
(1820), *Tyranny Unmasked* (1822), and *New Views of the
Constitution of the United States* (1823); Brutus [R. Turn-
bull], *The Crisis; or, Essays on the Usurpations of the Federal*

*Government* (1827), is equally important. *Defence of a Liberal Construction of the Powers of Congress as regards Internal Improvements, etc., with a Complete Refutation of the Ultra Doctrines Respecting Consolidation and State Sovereignty, Written by George M'Duffie, Esq., in the Year 1821 over the Signature "One of the People"* (1831), is an important pamphlet to mark the extent of the changing views of southern leaders. Judge Spencer Roane's antagonism to Marshall's nationalizing decisions is brought out in his articles in Randolph - Macon College, *John P. Branch Historical Papers*, No. 2; see also Jefferson, *Writings* (Ford's edition), X.; Massachusetts Historical Society, *Proceedings*, 2d series, XIV., 327 (Marshall's strictures on Roane); and the case of Cohens *vs.* Virginia, in 6 Wheaton, 264. Calhoun's "Exposition of 1828" is in his *Works*, VI., 1–59. Governor Troup's defiance of the United States is best given in E. J. Harden, *Life of George M. Troup* (1859), containing many of his letters. T. Cooper, *Consolidation, an Account of Parties* (2d edition, 1830, and in *Examiner*, II., 86, 100), is a South Carolina view. The best monographs in this field are David F. Houston, *A Critical Study of Nullification in South Carolina* (*Harvard Historical Studies*, III., 1893), and U. B. Phillips, *Georgia and State Rights* (American Historical Association, *Report*, 1901, II.).

#### ECONOMIC AND SOCIAL TOPICS

COMMERCE AND TRADE.—For this period, the best commercial authorities, aside from government documents, are Timothy Pitkin, *A Statistical View of the Commerce of the United States of America* (1835), and W. P. Sterns, *Foreign Trade of the United States, 1820–1840*, in *Journal of Political Economy*, VIII., 34, 452. See also *Hazard's United States Commercial and Statistical Register* (6 vols., 1840–1842); *Register of Pennsylvania* (16 vols., 1828–1835); J. R. M'Culloch, *A Dictionary, Practical, Theoretical, and Historical, of Commerce and Commercial Navigation* (edited by Henry Vethake; 2 vols., 1852); John MacGregor, *Com-*

*mercial Statistics of America: a Digest of Her Productive Resources, Commercial Legislation, Customs, Tariffs, Shipping, Imports and Exports, Monies, Weights, and Measures* (London, no date). On internal trade, see W. F. Switzler. *Report on Internal Commerce of the United States*, Treasury Department, Bureau of Statistics, submitted January 30, 1888, pt. ii., Document No. 1039b; Timothy Flint, *History and Geography of the Mississippi Valley;* and H. S. Tanner [publisher], *View of the Valley of the Mississippi*, both cited above.

NAVIGATION AND SHIPPING.—See the above and the following: W. H. Bates, *American Navigation: the Political History of Its Rise and Ruin, and the Proper Means for Its Encouragement* (1902); W. L. Marvin, *The American Merchant Marine : Its History and Romance from 1620 to 1902* (1902); D. A. Wells, *Our Merchant Marine : How It Rose, Increased, Became Great, Declined, and Decayed* (1882). In these works there is a tendency to controversy.

FINANCE.—The best manual on the financial history of the period is Davis R. Dewey, *Financial History of the United States* (1903), clear and judicious, with full bibliography. The best accounts of banking are: R. C. H. Catterall, *The Second Bank of the United States* (University of Chicago, *Decennial Publications*, 2d series, II., 1903); W. G. Sumner, *A History of Banking in the United States* (in *A History of Banking in All the Leading Nations*, I.), 1896.

MANUFACTURES.—On the development of manufactures, see C. D. Wright, *Industrial Evolution of the United States* (1905); William Bagnall, *Textile Industries of the United States* (1893); J. L. Bishop, *A History of American Manufactures from 1608 to 1860* (3d edition, 3 vols., 1868); S. N. D. North, *A Century of Wool Manufacture* (Association of Wool Manufacturers, *Bulletin*, 1894); J. M. Swank, *History of the Manufacture of Iron* (1884, revised 1892); Eleventh Census of the United States, *Report on Manufacturing Industries* (1890). *American State Papers, Finance*, IV.; Secretary of the Treasury, *Report*, 1854–1855 (*Executive Documents*, 34 Cong., 1 Sess., No. 10). 86–92, valuable statistics.

THE TARIFF.—For the history of the tariff in the decade, the following are useful: O. L. Elliott, *The Tariff Controversy in the United States, 1789–1833* (Leland Stanford, Jr., University, *Monographs, History and Economics*, No. 1, 1892); Edward Stanwood, *American Tariff Controversies in the Nineteenth Century* (2 vols., 1903); F. W. Taussig, *Tariff History of the United States* (1888); *American State Papers, Finance*, III.-V., memorials up to 1828; Edward Young, *Special Report on the Customs-Tariff of the United States* (1872); Committee on Finance, U. S. Senate, *The Existing Tariff on Imports into the United States, etc., and the Free List, together with Comparative Tables of Present and Past Tariffs, and Other Statistics Relating Thereto* (*Senate Reports*, 48 Cong., 1 Sess., No. 12), cited as *Tariff Compilation of 1884*.

LABOR.—The labor movement in the period is as yet insufficiently studied; but see John B. McMaster, *History of the People of the United States*, V.; and R. T. Ely, *The Labor Movement in America* (1886; 3d edition, 1890); G. E. McNeill, *The Labor Movement, the Problem of To-Day* (1887); John B. McMaster, *Acquisition of the Rights of Man in America*, above mentioned; C. D. Wright, *The Industrial Evolution of the United States* (1895).

LAND.—On the land question, the *American State Papers, Public Lands*, are the main reliance. See also Thomas Donaldson, *The Public Domain: Its History, with Statistics* (Washington, 1884; also in *House Miscellaneous Documents*, 47 Cong., 2 Sess., XIX., 1882–1883); Emerick, *The Credit System and the Public Domain* (Vanderbilt Southern History Society, *Publications*, No. 3, 1899). The actual operation of the land system may be studied in the emigrant guides and works of travellers previously cited.

### INTERNAL IMPROVEMENTS

GENERAL VIEWS.—Upon the internal improvements of the United States note the following: [G. Armroyd], *Connected View of the Whole Internal Navigation of the United States* (Philadelphia, 1826; 2d edition, 1830); G. T.

Poussin, *Travaux d'améliorations interieurs des États-Unis de 1824 à 1831* (Paris, 1836); S. A. Mitchell, *Compendium of the Internal Improvements of the United States* (Philadelphia, 1835); Michel Chevalier, *Society, Manners, and Politics in the United States* (Boston, 1839); D. Hewett, *The American Traveller; or, National Directory Containing an Account of all the Great Post-Roads and Most Important Cross-Roads in the United States* (Washington, 1825). The best estimate of the significance of internal improvements in this period is G. S. Callender, "Early Transportation and Banking Enterprises of the States in Relation to the Growth of Corporations," in *Quarterly Journal of Economics*, XVII., 3–54. A useful history of federal internal improvement legislation is H. G. Wheeler, *History of Congress* (1848), II., 109–513. J. L. Ringwalt, *Development of Transportation Systems in the United States* (1888), a summary but valuable account; H. V. Poor, *Sketch of the Rise and Progress of Internal Improvements*, in his *Manual of the Railroads of the United States* for 1881.

OFFICIAL PUBLICATIONS. — Especially significant are: *Niles' Register*, XXXVI., 168, a statement of the amount of money expended in each state and territory upon works of internal improvement to October 1, 1828; J. C. Calhoun's report on carrying out the general survey act of 1824, in his *Works*, V., 137–147; the historical survey of the canals of the United States, *Census of the United States*, 1880, IV. In the *American State Papers, Post-Office*, 120, is the Report of the Postmaster - General, January, 1825, giving post routes, frequency of mails, and cost of transportation. See, for statistical data on internal improvements, *River and Harbor Legislation from 1790 to 1887* (*Senate Miscellaneous Documents*, 49 Cong., 2 Sess., No. 91); and Secretary of the Interior, *Statement Showing Land Grants Made by Congress to Aid in the Construction of Railroads, Wagon Roads, Canals, and Internal Improvements, . . . from Records of the General Land Office* (1888).

CONSTITUTIONAL ASPECTS.—For this side of the question, see Joseph Story, *Commentaries on the Constitution of the*

*United States* (2 vols., 5th edition, 1891); James Monroe, *View of the Conduct of the Executive in Foreign Affairs of United States*, in his *Writings*, VI., 216–284, and in J. D. Richardson, *Messages and Public Papers of the Presidents*, II., 144–183 (1899); E. C. Nelson, "Presidential Influence on the Policy of Internal Improvements," in *Iowa Journal of History and Politics*, IV., 3–69.

SPECIAL MONOGRAPHS.—Among the more useful are R. Mills, *Treatise on Inland Navigation* (1820); G. W. Ward, *The Early Development of the Chesapeake and Ohio Canal Project* (*Johns Hopkins University Studies*, XVII., 431, 1899); C. C. Weaver, *History of Internal Improvements in North Carolina Previous to 1860* (*ibid.*, XXI., 1903); E. J. Benton, *The Wabash Trade Route, in the Development of the Old Northwest* (*ibid.*, XXI., 1903); J. S. Young, *Political and Constitutional Study of the Cumberland Road* (University of Chicago Press, 1904), is badly arranged, but useful; T. B. Searight, *Old Pike* (Uniontown, Pa., 1894), entertaining; T. K. Worthington, *Historical Sketch of Finances of Pennsylvania*, in American Economic Association, *Publications*, II., 126, gives a good sketch of the internal improvements of that state; C. McCarthy, *Antimasonic Party*, in American Historical Association, *Report*, 1902, chaps. viii.–x., shows the political influence of canal schemes in Pennsylvania. For Ohio internal improvements, see C. N. Morris, *Internal Improvements in Ohio*, in American Historical Association, *Papers*, III., 107 (1889); G. W. Dial, in Ohio Archæological and Historical Society, *Publications*, XIII., 479; C. P. McClelland and C. C. Huntington, *History of the Ohio Canals*; A. B. Hulbert, *Historic Highways of America* (16 vols., 1902–1905), including IX., *Waterways of Westward Expansion;* X., *The Ohio River and Its Tributaries;* XI., *The Cumberland Road;* XII., *Pioneer Roads and Experiences of Travellers;* XIII., XIV., *Great American Canals* [Chesapeake and Ohio, Pennsylvania, and Erie], useful, but not well digested.

The best sources for the Erie Canal are *Laws of the State of New York, in Relation to the Erie and Champlain Canals, together with the Annual Reports of the Canal Commissioners* (Albany, 1825), and the succeeding *Reports of the Canal Commissioners; View of the Grand Canal* (pamphlet, Albany, 1825); and the biographies of Clinton by Hosack and Renwick above mentioned.

### FOREIGN RELATIONS

On foreign relations, especially the Monroe Doctrine, see C. Seignobos, *Political History of Europe since 1814* (1899), 762, for bibliography of the Holy Alliance. The following serve to elucidate British policy: H. W. V. Temperley, *Life of Canning* (1905); A. G. Stapleton, *Political Life of the Right-Honourable George Canning* (3 vols., 1831); E. J. Stapleton, *Some Official Correspondence of George Canning* (2 vols., 1887); Festing, *J. H. Frere and His Friends; Memoirs and Correspondence of Viscount Castlereagh* (8 vols., 1848–1851), VII.; and Richard Rush, *Memoranda of a Residence at the Court of London* [1817–1819], (2d edition, 1833), and *Memoranda of a Residence at the Court of London . . . from 1819 to 1825* (1845). For Spanish America, see F. L. Paxson, *Independence of the South American Republics* (1903), an excellent sketch, with bibliography; J. H. Latané, *Diplomatic Relations of the United States and Spanish America* (1900); J. M. Callahan, *Cuba and International Relations* (1899). On the genesis of Monroe's message announcing the Doctrine, the best survey is in the two articles by Worthington C. Ford, *John Quincy Adams: His Connection with the Monroe Doctrine*, in Massachusetts Historical Society, *Proceedings*, 2d series, XV. (1902), 373–436, and in *American Historical Review*, VII., 676–696, and VIII., 28–52. W. F. Reddaway, *The Monroe Doctrine* (1898; 2d edition, 1906), is a particularly lucid and valuable study. Albert Bushnell Hart, *Foundations of American Foreign Policy* (1901), chap. vii.; John B. Moore, in *Harper's Magazine*, CIX., 857; G. Tucker, *Monroe Doctrine* (Boston, 1885); and D. C. Gilman, *James Monroe* (Boston, 1883), are other useful brief accounts.

See also Frances Wharton [editor], *Digest of the International Law of the United States* (3 vols., 1887), I., superseded by John B. Moore, *Digest* (5 vols., 1906).

On the Panama Congress, considerable material is collected in *The Congress of 1826 at Panama* (*International American Conference*, IV., Historical Appendix ,1890).

# INDEX